GOOD TO GREAT
TO INNOVATE

GOOD TO GREAT TO INNOVATE

RECALCULATING THE ROUTE TO CAREER READINESS, K–12+

Lyn Sharratt—Gale Harild

Foreword by Michael Fullan

A Joint Publication With

FOR INFORMATION:

Corwin

A SAGE Company

2455 Teller Road

Thousand Oaks, California 91320

(800) 233-9936

www.corwin.com

SAGE Publications Ltd.

1 Oliver's Yard

55 City Road

London EC1Y 1SP

United Kingdom

SAGE Publications India Pvt. Ltd.

B 1/I 1 Mohan Cooperative Industrial Area

Mathura Road, New Delhi 110 044

India

SAGE Publications Asia-Pacific Pte. Ltd.

3 Church Street

#10-04 Samsung Hub

Singapore 049483

Executive Editor: Arnis Burvikovs

Associate Editor: Ariel Price

Editorial Assistant: Andrew Olson

Production Editor: Amy Schroller

Copy Editor: Melinda Masson

Typesetter: C&M Digitals (P) Ltd.

Proofreader: Dennis W. Webb

Indexer: Judy Hunt

Cover Designer: Janet Kiesel

Marketing Manager: Lisa Lysne

Copyright © 2015 by Corwin

Printed in the United States of America

A catalog record of this book is available from the Library of Congress.

ISBN 978-1-4833-3186-7

This book is printed on acid-free paper.

Certified Chain of Custody
Promoting Sustainable Forestry
www.sfiprogram.org
SFI-01268

SFI label applies to text stock

14 15 16 17 18 10 9 8 7 6 5 4 3 2 1

CONTENTS

LIST OF FIGURES AND TABLES

FOREWORD

Professor Emeritus Michael Fullan

Lyn Sharratt and Gale Harild have written a gold mine of a book covering virtually everything that matters in instructional improvement and whole-system success. The book is crystal clear on charting the course, showing how leadership matters, bringing *all* children into the picture, closing the gap of learning, positioning choice of pathways, and being explicit that skilled teachers matter a great deal.

Every chapter is a treasure trove of ideas, tools for action and assessment, and strategies and tactics rendered with magnificent clarity through graphics, charts, checklists, and guides to moving from good to great through continuous action.

Here is a book that has more features and aids to thinking and action than I have ever seen in one location. Each of the six chapters manages variety, comprehensiveness, coherence, and specificity. We find clear narratives, conceptual frames, step-by-step guidelines, powerful graphics, summary tables and figures, and clear data and evidence. We have story vignettes of what "good to great to innovate" looks like in practice as told by direct implementers. And a special treat: Each chapter is capped by commentary from leading researcher/practitioners who are specialists on the topic: Avis Glaze reflects on "charting the course," Ken Leithwood on "leadership matters," Alma Harris on "all faces matter," Louise Stoll on "closing the gap," Yong

Zhao on "choice matters," and Suzie Boss on "skilled teachers matter"; and Andy Hargreaves provides a thought-provoking epilogue.

Good to Great to Innovate is at once complete in its coverage but seems compact. I think Lyn and Gale are able to do this because they have lived this journey with their own local action and depth, but have also refined and extended their savvy by so much work and application around the world. The authors have distilled their wide range of knowledge in a manner that is clear while having depth. They make it inevitable for the reader to see both the forest and the trees.

There is a great deal of reform going on in the education world, but much of it misses the point, or approaches it superficially—what I have called "the wrong drivers for whole-system reform." There is a huge emphasis these days on teacher appraisal and instructional leadership for principals, again missing the mark as I have recently described in *The Principal* (Jossey-Bass, 2014). We should all pause and absorb the depth of *Good to Great to Innovate* and implement the steps to *all* students' success. You will think differently, be able to challenge the "status quo," and have greater impact by using this high-yield treat of a book.

About Professor Emeritus Michael Fullan

Michael Fullan, OC (Order of Canada), is professor emeritus at the Ontario Institute for Studies in Education of the University of Toronto. He was awarded the prestigious Order of Canada in December 2012. Recognized as a worldwide authority on educational reform, Michael is engaged in advising policymakers and local leaders around the world in helping to achieve the moral purpose of all children learning. His books have been published in many languages.

Fullan has served as a special advisor to the premier and minister of education in Ontario from 2003 to the present. He holds honorary doctorates from the University of Edinburgh, Scotland; Nipissing University in Canada; the University of Leicester in England; and Duquesne University in the United States.

His book *Leading in a Culture of Change* was named the 2002 Book of the Year by Learning Forward, *Breakthrough* (with Peter Hill and Carmel Crévola) won the 2006 Outstanding Book Award from the American Association of Colleges for Teacher Education, *Turnaround Leadership in Higher Education* (with Geoff Scott) won the Bellwether Book Award in 2009, *Change Wars* (with Andy Hargreaves) was named the 2009 Book of the Year by Learning Forward, and *Putting FACES on the Data* (with Lyn Sharratt) was named the 2012 Book of the Year by Corwin. A list of his books, articles, and other resources can be found at www .michaelfullan.ca.

PREFACE

"How can you get very far,
If you don't know who you are?
How can you do what you ought,
If you don't know what you've got?
And if you don't know which to do
Of all the things in front of you,
Then what you'll have when you are through
Is just a mess without a clue
Of all the best that can come true
If you know What and Which and Who."

—*The Tao of Pooh (Hoff, 1983, p. 58)*

We have an opportunity to shape education for our students' prosperity and our educators' professional success in the future. In this book, we discuss the components of doing just that. We know it is time for education policy and programming to be linked to economic development at every level in order to close the gap between perceived student needs by educators and what employers actually expect and want. We address the importance of developing students who are critical thinkers, problem solvers, and innovators as well-prepared literate graduates of the 21st century and beyond. By providing learners with feedback to understand their strengths and abilities, by offering a rigorous curriculum, and by giving learners the opportunity to apply their knowledge through Collaborative Inquiry and Experiential Learning, K–12+, we will Recalculate the Route to *Career Readiness*. Our aim is to develop students who are lifelong contributors (C. Bereiter, personal communication, December 2013) so that they have the requisite skills to meet future global demands.

In writing *Good to Great to Innovate*, "align—focus—feedback" has been our mantra. We know that in doing this hard work with high-performing systems, schools, and classrooms, leaders must move along the learning continuum from good to great to innovate, which demands attracting multiple community partners to work alongside them and collaboratively resolving their likely differences to produce powerful, sustainable relationships and lasting, continuously improving programs.

Innovation is defined as something new that can be applied in a useful way. Unlike inventions that refer more directly to the creation of an idea or method, innovation refers to the use of the better idea or method. It builds on the notion of doing something different rather than just doing the same things better as we might consider in improvement planning.

We examined three research questions in reaching out to participants in four countries: Canada, Australia, the United States, and the United Kingdom. Over 40 jurisdictions responded to our questions: (1) Describe a program or strategy that has worked well within your school or district to improve student achievement; (2) How do you know it is making a difference; and (3) Under what conditions does this work? We took many of the stories that we heard in collecting our data and inserted them throughout the text as examples of best practices to engage all students and teachers in this work. They responded with valuable insights into how they offer students multiple *Pathways* to reach the top of their game to become contributing members of society.

This book examines **What Matters Most** for all students in realizing their potential and having personal choice and a voice in their

Pathway to becoming *The Literate Graduates* that they have a right to become. Using the analogy of a journey, we look at "Charting the Course" in Chapter 1. Chapter 2, "Leadership Matters," examines the leadership needed to move from good to great to innovate. In Chapter 3, we invest in the fact that "All FACES Matter"—all of our students must be "on route." In Chapter 4, we take a serious look at "Closing the Gap to Raise the Bar" in all districts with all students. Chapter 5, "Choice Matters," considers the choices that students must be offered. We close in Chapter 6 with our already-known route masters to success: "Skilled Teachers Matter!"

Our journey would not be complete if we didn't have external reflectors who considered and added to our thinking and writing through their effective descriptive feedback. These giants in the educational research world—our colleagues, mentors, and friends—complete our thoughts and play a large role in finalizing this book: Michael Fullan writes our Foreword to set the tone; Avis Glaze reflects on Chapter 1, Ken Leithwood on Chapter 2, Alma Harris on Chapter 3, Louise Stoll on Chapter 4, Yong Zhao on Chapter 5, and Suzie Boss on Chapter 6; and Andy Hargreaves brings our book to a close by writing the Epilogue. How fortunate we are to hear and read their thinking on the state of K–12+ education (the + indicates "and beyond") and what it takes to be great.

Ensuring that all students know "What and Which and Who" as Pooh began is our focus, as students must be able to reflect independently and collectively on their multiple *Pathways* to opportunity and success. Please join us on the journey—what is your *TrueNorth*?

ACKNOWLEDGMENTS

Many people helped to shape and inform this book. The book itself represents a learning journey that has spanned many years with course corrections provided by so many voices. While it is not possible, within the scope of this text, to acknowledge everyone, there are some who deserve special recognition given their navigational skills.

We are most appreciative of **Jim Coutts** and **John Harild** who not only served as sounding boards for author angst but also edited and reviewed content using a community partner lens. Jim, your positive thoughts that never fail and your detail in writing and editing tasks made the journey so much smoother! John and Jim, your continuing encouragement and wry humor helped to keep us grounded.

Thank you to **Regina Hui**, who patiently formatted and edited our drafts, redrafts, and final chapters. Your eye for detail and consistency of format was most appreciated, Regina.

A special thank-you to our contributing authors, **Michael Fullan, Andy Hargreaves, Avis Glaze, Ken Leithwood, Alma Harris, Louise Stoll, Yong Zhao,** and **Suzie Boss,** for completing our thoughts and adding your own navigational markers to our learning journey.

A number of busy educators made time to respond to our survey, sharing practices and strategies that make a difference. Special thanks to **Andy Scott**, coordinator of International School Leadership for the Ontario Principals' Council; **Bill Garland**, director of education for the Catholic District School Board of Eastern Ontario; and **Dave Chaplin**, principal of Notre Dame Catholic High School in Carleton Place, Ontario; all of whom exemplify innovation leadership in Ontario. Thank you, **Steve Blake,** superintendent of education from Simcoe County District School Board, for sharing the innovative approaches being initiated in your district by **Tracy McPhail.**

Thank you to **Michelle Sharratt**, preservice coordinator for the Ontario Institute for Studies in Education at the University of Toronto, and **Jenna Harild**, master's candidate and co-op teacher at Bill Crothers Secondary School, for ensuring our journey was grounded in the current realities of teaching and learning.

Thank you to **Melanie Greenan** and **Scott Woolford** for your masterful editing and valuable contributions, which come from the insightful work you do across the province of Ontario. Thank you, **Kim Newlove**, educational consultant from Saskatchewan, for your very insightful comments that strengthened the text, and **Beate Planche**, educational consultant from Ontario, for sharing your research and your thinking about promising practices. Thank you, **Dan Compagnon**, principal of St. Thomas Aquinas Secondary School, and **Max Vecchiarino**, superintendent of schools for the Dufferin-Peel Catholic District School Board, for contributing a thought-provoking example of Collaborative Inquiry to support the strong work being done in this district.

To the voices of the many teachers and students who informed our work, we are indebted. You remind us every day how important it is for us to get this journey right. As captured by Albert Einstein, "The significant problems we face cannot be solved at the same level of thinking we were at when we created them" (Albert Einstein Site Online, 2012, "General" section). Your stories push our thinking as your innovative mind-sets lead us into uncharted waters.

To our friends at Corwin, thank you for providing us with a platform for sharing this learning journey as we continue to grow our ideas together. Our sincere thanks to Arnis Burvikovs, executive editor at Corwin, who gave us a voice and supported our thinking. And thank you to Ariel Price, Amy Schroller, Cassandra Seibel, Lisa Shaw, Melinda Masson, Janet Kiesel and the rest of the Corwin family—you are all awesome in the pride that you take in the beautiful books that you produce.

ABOUT THE AUTHORS

 **Gale Harild** is an educational practitioner and Pathways consultant. As an instructional leader, she supports the Faculty of Education: Professional Development program at York University. Gale served as curriculum administrator for the York Region District School Board in Ontario where over the past 12 years she provided regional leadership and program/resource development for experiential learning models including, but not limited to, cooperative education programming, international programming, service learning, and apprenticeship programs. Working with her Pathways team, Gale initiated and supported the successful start-up of 60 Specialist High Skills Major (SHSM) programs across the district. SHSM performance measures for the district met and in some cases exceeded ministry targets, with program completion rates and credit attainment rates higher than provincial averages. Gale has served on advisory and curriculum writing teams with the ministry over the course of her career. Prior to her role as a curriculum administrator, Gale was a high school teacher for 22 years. Her position as department head for cooperative education took her work into elementary schools and postsecondary destinations. Collaborating with community and industry sector partners, as well as postsecondary institutions, she has helped build and support *Pathways* for all students by deepening the understanding of the interconnectedness between the curriculum and the work habits/essential skills that

make up the profile of *The Literate Graduate* for the 21st century. Gale is committed to ensuring quality instruction so that every *Pathway* leads to an opportunity. Visit Gale at LinkedIn.

 **Lyn Sharratt** coordinates the doctoral internship program for the Educational Administration Department at the Ontario Institute for Studies in Education at the University of Toronto. Lyn is the former superintendent of curriculum and instruction services in the York Region District School Board, a large Canadian school district, where she and her curriculum team analyzed assessment data and developed a comprehensive literacy improvement program, which they launched with the cooperation of senior leadership, principals, and over 8,800 teachers. The continuously improving 14-parameter program resulted in increased achievement for a diverse, multicultural, and multilingual population of over 115,000 students, and the district became the top-performing district in Ontario. Lyn has been a curriculum consultant and administrator, and she has also taught all elementary grades and secondary-age students in inner-city and rural settings. Lyn has analyzed and commented on public policy for a provincial trustee organization, the Ontario Public School Boards' Association; taught preservice education at York University; and led in-service professional learning in a provincial teachers' union head office. She is lead author, with Michael Fullan, of *Realization: The Change Imperative for Increasing District-Wide Reform* (Corwin, 2009) and *Putting FACES on the Data: What Great Leaders Do!* (Corwin, 2012). Currently, Lyn is an advisor to the International School Leadership Program for the Ontario Principals' Council, is an author consultant for Corwin, and consults internationally, working with states, districts, administrators, curriculum consultants, and teachers in Chile, Australia, the United States, the United Kingdom, and Canada to systematically increase all students' achievement by putting FACES on the data and taking intentional action. Visit her website at www .lynsharratt.com.

To my parents, Rayma and Charles, for giving me "choice," and loved ones John, Laura, Jeff, Nathan, Jenna, D. J., Beth, and Alexander, for giving me my "voice."

—Gale

To Jim, Robert, Sarah, Robbie, Madeleine, Michelle, Bob, Jackson, Ryan, Stephanie, Chris, Aeson, Taylor, and Karen, with love.

—Lyn

CHARTING THE COURSE

Understanding Current Structures

U nprecedented parallel realities have forced Education to rethink itself. On one hand, global economic changes, predominantly fueled by rapidly evolving technologies and competitive international manufacturing pricing, have pressured decision makers. On the other hand, growing student dropout rates, lack of student intellectual engagement, and devaluation of the teacher's role, as well as growing disconnection among the high school experience (students aged 14 to 18+), postsecondary opportunities, and ultimately the workplace, have begun to push education toward a period of dramatic change. Many countries and states have responded to the competitive future with standardized assessments where performance is measured and compared by standard scores and displayed in league tables. These directions may be politically and/or education/bureaucracy–inspired responses to what may be seen as the current state of curriculum, assessment, and instruction. We *will not argue* the positives or negatives of these

QUESTIONS THAT MATTER MOST

1. Do you have an **equitable learning community** within your classrooms, schools, and systems?

2. What approaches are you taking to ensure equitable access to opportunities for all students, regardless of their postsecondary destination?

3. How are your shared beliefs and understandings constructed, shared, and acted upon in *a structured, collaboratively planned approach*?

4. Is there **a robust and relevant K–12+ curriculum**?

5. Whom do you consider part of your school community?

6. Do you have a culture of **innovative leadership** to support your work?

7. Do your lessons, schools, and systems value all postsecondary destinations?

8. What is your school, system, and state understanding of *Pathways*?

9. What strategies are you using in your classrooms, schools, and systems to ensure that your graduates are prepared for their postsecondary transition and ultimately the workplace?

10. In what ways do your schools, classrooms, and office spaces reflect all postsecondary destinations?

strategies or their execution. Growth in national and state student achievement now and in future years will make the decision makers' points powerfully. We *do argue* that it is time to chart new *Pathways to Career Readiness* for our high school students beginning with accelerated preparedness for that process in elementary schools.

Many believe educators cannot do this by themselves. We, however, believe that, while the issue is massive and divisive, it is time for educators to solve the problems of the new realities and to identify the new learning required to provide for future citizen success—as only teachers can. We believe it is time for education leaders and teachers to reclaim their leadership role in this dynamic change process and to Recalculate the Route.

Moral Purpose and Social Drivers—It's More Than We Know!

If there are to be profound or tertiary changes through either instructional approaches or the structures within our institutions, research tells us that this is best accomplished when there is a strong sense of moral purpose. Andy Hargreaves and Dennis Shirley in their book *The Global Fourth Way* (2012) outline the importance of the right kind of purpose: "To be high achieving, educators in school systems need the right kind of purpose that inspires them, a strengthened professionalism that propels them forward, and a cultural and structural coherence that holds them together" (p. xi).

Good teachers have always had the right kind of moral purpose—to do what's best for their students—but current empirical evidence of disconnections between education and the rapidly changing global economy have introduced social drivers that now need to be considered. The devaluation of the teaching profession, the changing realities of the workplaces and careers, technological advancements, and the economic downturn all serve as examples of the social drivers to which we refer. How will teachers and their leaders, policymakers, and union leaders fulfill their moral purpose—to do what's best for the student—in meeting and responding to the demands imposed by these social drivers?

Taking a Closer Look at the Disconnections

National labor statistics, newspaper/magazine articles, business sector reports, and international organizations such as the Organisation for Economic Co-operation and Development (OECD, 2010, 2012) are among a sampling of sources that forewarn of social drivers driven by economic and social disconnections.

The big picture reported by OECD is that one in eight of all 15- to 24-year-olds in OECD countries is not engaged in employment, education, or training (Mourshed, Farrell, & Barton, 2012, p. 11). Closer to home, the statistics are reflected in the reality of parents and families who know only too well the impact of disconnection as their children struggle to find that first job and achieve financial independence under the weight of costly tuition fees and limited job markets. A report by the McKinsey Center for Government (Mourshed et al., 2012) cites that in 2011, the unemployment rate for young people (aged 15 to 29) was 15% across more than 100 countries, three times the unemployment rate of those over 30 (p. 40). "According to the International Labour Organization, nearly 75 million young people are unemployed around the world, an increase of more than 4 million since 2007. Youth unemployment is projected to remain at this level until 2016" (Hannon, Gillinson, & Shanks, 2013, p. 21). Instability is becoming the new normal as we move away from the notion of "jobs for life." This has long-term consequences for the growth of the economy as well as the future opportunities that might be afforded our youth.

It is important to understand that globalization has been increasing the connectivity between world economies. That relationship is intensified by the stresses experienced in the global environment in which we all share. Jeremy Rifkin speaks of the "Third Industrial Revolution" driven by the combined forces of energy and communication revolutions (personal communication, November 15, 2012).

What does this mean for education? For future employment opportunities? For the way we live our lives as global citizens? We have already seen fracturing of large-scale manufacturing and outsourcing of jobs to lower-cost production countries. We have seen changes in the profile of the workforce to include more women and to exclude those who are not well educated. We have seen early signs of recognition that entrepreneurism is becoming an important topic at business schools and in high school education preparation for transition to the workplace. It means the problem-solving, Collaborative Inquiry approaches to teaching and learning—using technologies for student information gathering, analyzing, and critical thinking—will be a right direction to follow (Rifkin, 2012).

These energy and communication revolutions, creating changes in the economic paradigm, in turn, are calling upon the need for a new educational model. As Rifkin says, "I believe the 21st century is going to be the defining moment for the future of our civilization and for our species on this planet. This is going to require that we rethink the entire way we educate the present and future generations" (personal communication, November 15, 2012).

This "perfect storm" is resulting in a sense of urgency for our schools, to "get it right" in developing expert knowledge workers, as we refer to *The Literate Graduate*. "The need for knowledge workers to create and innovate new products and services that solve real problems and meet the needs of real customers is a major driving force for economic growth and work in the 21st Century" (Trilling & Fadel, 2009, p. 24).

Add to the mix high rates of youth unemployment as well as youth underemployment, and you now have, for the first time, a strong economic driver pushing educational reform, creating a social responsibility for our educational system and the teachers who serve it. In a nutshell, it is becoming *essential* for national economic policies to be aligned with national educational policies of any given nation. Economic priorities now need to include and support high-yield impactful educational strategies to ensure that the current and future labor force moves out of instability into a more secure and sustainable growth pattern, thereby reducing the differential between "jobs without people" and "people without jobs."

> "The fact of the matter is that unless we adopt proactive policies now, we will face a world in which there will be a lot of people without jobs and simultaneously an even larger number of jobs without people. This is surely not a world anyone can, or should, look forward to" (Miner, 2010, p. 18)..

All these shifts have resulted in teachers finding that their moral purpose has now also become part of a larger urgent social driver. The paradox of reported, critical skills shortages and underemployed youth statistics raises important questions concerning the effectiveness of youth's educational preparedness for transitions to the workplace. Faced with disengaged students, who might already be possible victims of an irrelevant curriculum, holding onto a perception that there is no *real* interest in them as people is an anathema to most caring educators and raises more questions.

1. What is the learning (skills, abilities, knowledge, and opportunities) students require for successful transition from schooling into successful postsecondary training or education (be that the workplace, college, an apprenticeship, or university)?

2. What are the most impactful ways to provide this level of learning on a large system scale?

3. How do we ensure that the requisite skills and knowledge are continually assessed, evaluated, and modified as to their appropriateness?

4. Do we alone, as educators, have the skills and knowledge to determine what our students require for their future? Can we, alone, Recalculate the Route?

5. Whom would we, as educators, trust as partners to work with us?

6. How do we Recalculate Our Own Route, as teacher-educators, to ensure that every student finds learning relevant, challenging, and thought-provoking and therefore retains it?

7. How do we ensure that our educational systems remain nimble enough to be responsive to any changes required?

8. How do we enlist new forms of student-community interaction to ensure that students themselves become part of the retention solution?

These are powerful questions, possibly exceeding the scope of our text, but as leaders in education, we need to solve some of these thorny issues and develop responses or risk giving the lead and processing of the new direction to third parties. Others, while they may have good content, which we should be adapting and integrating into our Recalculation, may not know how to teach and learn alongside our students, resulting in less-than-best new practices being introduced.

Demand for change, coming from third parties, often voices concern that the moral purpose of educators, policymakers, and teacher unions simply cannot be trusted to prevail over their respective self-interests. **Moral purpose, moral compass, or self-interest?** We believe these issues are large, very large indeed, but we believe teachers and leaders in various aspects of education need to focus and work together. By taking the lead, that is in Recalculating the Route, they will retain and salvage a great deal of trust and authority, and more importantly, by reaching out to the protagonists and naysayers—with stakes in the issues—teachers and leaders can initiate the work and establish a collaborative manner in which to develop new innovative solutions, to chart *Pathways to Career Readiness*.

Setting a Course for Recalculation

re·cal·cu·late: To calculate again, especially in order to eliminate errors or to incorporate additional factors or data.
(www.thefreedictionary.com/recalculate)

There are many competing and complementing lenses that could be applied to move the educational agenda forward. One of the most obvious but least utilized lenses is that of *Pathways to Career Readiness*. This oversight is understandable given that very little research has been conducted in this area. In other words, no one has yet been able to establish a *Pathways to Career Readiness* lens on a system-wide scale. The consequence of not establishing this lens has a detrimental impact on the growth of the economy and also on the social fabric of society. So significant has this work become that priorities are now being established in many governments' policies.

> "Tonight, I'm announcing a new challenge to redesign America's high schools so they better equip graduates for the demands of a high-tech economy. We'll reward schools that develop new partnerships with colleges and employers, and create classes that focus on science, technology, engineering, and math—the skills today's employers are looking for to fill jobs right now and in the future" (Barack Obama, State of the Union Address, 2013).

How Do We Go From Policy to Implementation?

The McKinsey report (Mourshed et al., 2012, pp. 57–77) highlights the innovative strategies/programs that are experiencing success, across the globe, in addressing the current school–work disconnections. Based on the findings of the report, a recalculated education-to-employment system, where education and business/industry are called upon for shared responsibility, would need to operate differently on three levels:

1. Better data to enable stakeholders (students, teachers, parents, educational institutions, employers) to make informed choices and manage performance.
2. Collaborative approaches where solutions involve multiple stakeholders with sector-specific foci.
3. System integrators to work with education providers and employers to develop skill solutions (Mourshed et al., 2012, pp. 20–21).

How Might We Apply This to a Recalculated Route?

Would not these same three levels of implementation apply? Where do we see examples of success using this model? What can we learn from each other as we Recalculate the Route for large-scale sustainable change and determine **What Matters Most?**

It is through small-scale innovative strategies/programs, such as those captured in our research and experiences, where we, the authors, looked for common denominators to determine **What Matters Most** for large-scale change. These common denominators capture the problem solving, creativity, and innovation that may assist us in developing a road map to respond to the 21st-century learning needs of our students, teachers, system leaders, and community partners. A narrative runs throughout the chapters in this book. This narrative, supplemented by data from districts across the United States, Canada, the United Kingdom, and Australia, provides direction as to what educators consider to be the key conditions to improve student achievement. For example, turning to Ontario, Canada—a top performer in the Program for International Student Assessment (PISA)—its school district "stories" illustrate **What Matters Most** to transition from one classroom to system-wide programming for *Pathways to Career Readiness*.

These shared professional experiences reveal instructional conditions identified as common to all, as well as challenge the reader to identify conditions yet to be uncovered—in other words, **What Matters Most** to improve the trajectory for each student we encounter. In addition, for instructive (albeit highly contextual) advice, we will examine the decades-old highly successful European models that bridged the youth unemployment and retraining issues. German and Swiss models of labor-education partnerships at secondary and university levels actually work—well.

In *Realization* (Sharratt & Fullan, 2009) and *Putting FACES on the Data* (Sharratt & Fullan, 2012), we looked at improving student achievement and engagement at the classroom, school, and system levels from the perspective of having proven that our high-yield assessment and instructional strategies work for teachers and leaders in the United States, Canada, the United Kingdom, Australia, and elsewhere. We have found localized examples of new systems and structures when we asked people to tell what they offer differently that furthers teacher and student engagement within the context of a very changed world. Now we, as educators, policymakers, elected officials, community partners, and parents who will create the citizens of tomorrow in our classrooms starting today, need to find ways to move from the environment of the local content—or micro "edusphere" of yesterday—to the global content—or macro "edusphere" of the future.

The proposals and recommendations in this book come out of our lived experiences and ongoing research. Evidenced throughout our research is the notion that educators are not the only stakeholders who must be involved in getting a Recalculated Route right. There are other stakeholders who matter (see Chapter 3).

Mapping *Pathways to Career Readiness*

We begin to Recalculate the Route by looking at a refreshed *Pathways to Career Readiness Frame—Finding TrueNorth* to guide us, as we build on what has been effective practice over time and the innovative approaches currently being explored (see Figure 1.1 on page 12).

Finding *TrueNorth*

We are mindful—as with any journey—that if you are trying to "navigate your way" to get from one point at the bottom of a map to one at the top, you need to know how to find *TrueNorth*. For metaphorical purposes, it is important to understand that *TrueNorth* is the geographical direction represented on maps and globes by lines of longitude. Each line of longitude begins and ends at the earth's poles and represents direct north- and southward travel. Compasses, on the other hand, direct you to magnetic north, a point that continually shifts location based on the activity of the earth's magnetic fields. Because the earth's magnet isn't perfectly aligned with the geographical poles, there is a difference between *TrueNorth* on a map and the north indicated by your compass. That difference is called the magnetic declination. Magnetic declinations vary from place to place, depending on the intensity of the earth's fields (Conger, n.d.).

We are of the stance that *Finding TrueNorth* in a Recalculated Route is essential for accurate navigation. *TrueNorth* is a constant. It is always present. Knowing *TrueNorth*, one can always navigate one's way, regardless of one's starting point. For students to find the right course and proceed in the right direction, they need to locate and follow the right longitudinal lines—their individual *Pathway*. To determine how far east or west of the course they are at any time, they need to read the lines of latitude. Together these coordinates provide the accurate starting point toward *Finding TrueNorth*.

Sometimes students think they are heading to *TrueNorth* but are inadvertently following magnetic north. They get off course and struggle to make the necessary adjustments for the magnetic declinations. In the end, they arrive at a destination but not necessarily the one they had in mind, not their *TrueNorth*. In life's journey, we are often uncertain where we stand, where we are going, and what is the right path to follow. We all have our own *TrueNorth*; we just need the right supports, resources, and guidance systems to get us there.

To do so, we propose adopting ***a structured, collaboratively planned approach***, in which education, business/industry, and other community partners design *Pathways to Career Readiness* that work. ***A structured, collaboratively planned approach***, by its very nature, would require that educators, employers, and other community partners become familiar with each other's world. Myopic policies, good only for the short term, would fall away as a result of the problem solving and creativity engaged in by a more diversified group of stakeholders. Silos would disappear across departments, grade divisions, and schools. Students would be engaged not only in the learning but in the planning of the learning.

Figure 1.1 represents a "process of flow," a journey defined by longitudinal lines, or individualized *Pathways* for each student. Building upon his or her innate creativity, each student on that journey will experience opportunities that ultimately inform student *Career Readiness*, and develop *The Literate Graduate*, as he or she moves along the Curriculum Knowledge Continuum from preschool and kindergarten to beyond Grade 12. To do so, we highlight five Guiding Principles:

- Guiding Principle 1—**an inclusive, equitable learning community** is overarching, supporting and nurturing students' learning.
- Guiding Principle 2—**a robust, relevant K–12+ curriculum**. The + on the curriculum continuum represents the interdependent continuum between high schools and postsecondary destinations (i.e., dual credits, articulation agreements).
- Guiding Principle 3—**a broad base of community partners** who are representative of the postsecondary destinations, and provide expanded opportunities for embedding Experiential Learning.
- Guiding Principle 4—**the skilled teacher** is cognizant of the learning constructed "for and with" his or her students, while best supported through a Collaborative Inquiry process. This reminds us of the importance of building on knowledge from previous grades while keeping abreast of the skills and abilities required for each student to become *The Literate Graduate*.

FIGURE 1.1

Pathways to Career Readiness Frame–Finding TrueNorth

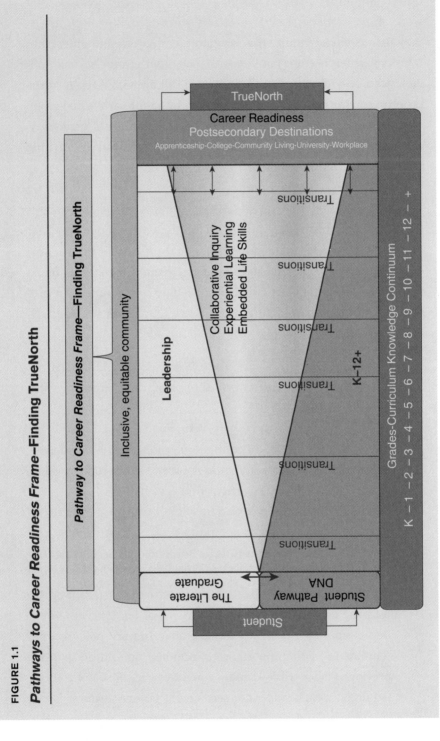

- Guiding Principle 5—**Good to Great to Innovate leadership (K–12+)** signals strong and innovative leadership is ongoing and supports the critical work necessary to Recalculate the Route.

We frame these five Guiding Principles or Recalculations in Figure 1.1 and will be examining their respective roles in the following chapters.

Taking a Closer Look at Finding *TrueNorth*

The five Guiding Principles are not new. They have been explored, considered, and written about in depth by many experts in the field, and will be in the chapters of this book using our *Pathways* lens to provide additional clarity. What we propose is taking a closer look at the structures—at the cellular levels if you will—that are most effective in supporting these Guiding Principles.

By applying a *Pathways lens*, **three structures** are shown (see Figure 1.1) to coexist and support the five foundational Guiding Principles outlined above:

Lens 1: *Career Readiness*—refers to the skills, knowledge, and abilities that would afford each student or *The Literate Graduate* the opportunity to

- pursue interests and passions regardless of postsecondary destination of choice;
- engage in the community and global world; and
- establish meaningful relationships.

Lens 2: *The Literate Graduate*—embraces multiple forms of *multiliteracies*, often simultaneously, while being responsive to the ever-evolving new technologies.

Lens 3: *Student Pathway DNA*—at the cellular level, there are three DNA strands, forming a unique triple helix that make up a *Student Pathway DNA* to *Finding TrueNorth*.

Figure 1.1 illustrates the relationship between the *Student Pathway DNA*, the development of *The Literate Graduate*, and ultimately *Career Readiness*. It is important to note that *The Literate Graduate* and *Career Readiness* are not parallel initiatives. Each exists and is supported and developed by the three *Student Pathway DNA* strands. As a student moves along the K–12+ curriculum, toward his or her postsecondary destination and beyond, the three strands of the *Student Pathway DNA* serve as the longitudinal lines that will provide the direction to *Finding TrueNorth*. There are small-scale innovative strategies/programs where significant inroads have been made in student achievement utilizing the *Pathways lens*. Their stories will be illustrated throughout the text so readers can consider the global issue of going to scale.

In the following, we clarify the terms to build a collective understanding of the three key structures to which we will be referring. The first two lenses, *Career Readiness* and *The Literate Graduate*, while not less complex than *Student Pathway DNA*, are more universally recognized. Each will be explored in greater detail in following chapters, but for now we provide the reader with a summary of our terms of reference in an attempt to clarify the role they play in the *Student Pathway DNA*.

Lens 1: Career Readiness

Career Readiness refers to the skills, knowledge, and dispositions that would afford each student, or *The Literate Graduate*, the opportunity to successfully pursue his or her interests and passions regardless of postsecondary destination of choice, be that the workplace, technical training, an apprenticeship, community college, university, or community living. It is not a narrow interpretation in the sense of strictly referring to an occupational pursuit, but rather a much broader interpretation, encompassing all the experiences that make up one's life journey on individualized *Pathways*.

The *Pathways to Career Readiness* approach is not about getting a student a job; it is much more holistic. It is about *Finding TrueNorth*. While being able to work is a key end product of students' in-school career, so too is students' learning, their ability to engage in the community and global world, and their ability to establish relationships with family, friends, and colleagues. It is these skills that fully enable their capacity to find and hold meaningful work experiences. This holistic view of *Career Readiness* can best be achieved when all three strands of *Student Pathway DNA* are addressed (see Chapter 5).

Lens 2: The Literate Graduate

Assessment literacy reminds us to begin with the end in mind, and we did just that. We asked what literacy skills do our high school graduates need to become contributing world citizens (adapted from York Region District School Board, 2004a). We found that *The Literate Graduate* embraces multiple forms of *multiliteracies*—often simultaneously—and therefore must be able to

- write with purpose and clarity,
- communicate effectively using a variety of text forms,
- read for purpose and pleasure,
- think critically,
- locate and access information from a variety of sources,
- use oral communication appropriate to purpose and audience,
- "read" and interpret multiple text forms,
- articulate a point of view,
- question and respond using higher-order thinking skills, and
- problem solve.

We begin with literacy instruction as a must in kindergarten; continue with support for strong classroom instruction, including a balanced literacy approach and cross-curricular literacy; and conclude with Collaborative Inquiry. Clearly, for the 21st-century learner, these skills represent the new "essential" foundational skills required to work and learn with ever-evolving new technologies (adapted from Sharratt & Fullan, 2012, pp. 94–150). As students move along the K–12+ continuum, opportunities to learn, refine, and practice these skills, through the application of the *Student Pathway DNA*, broaden and deepen. The two-way arrows on the frame (Figure 1.1) serve as a reminder that new skills are emerging and it is our ability to respond and evolve, which will ultimately ensure that *The Literate Graduate* has the requisite knowledge, skills, dispositions, and attributes as reflected through *Pathways to Career Readiness*. We extend our picture of *The Literate Graduate* to include 21st-century learning skills in Chapter 4.

Lens 3: Student Pathway DNA

The *Pathways lens* puts the **FACES** on each student, recognizing that everyone is on his or her own unique educational journey—each in search of his or her *TrueNorth*. It is this personalized educational journey that is referred to as a *"Pathway."* At the cellular level, there are three DNA strands, forming a unique triple helix that make up a student *"Pathway"*:

1. Skill Development
2. Curriculum Knowledge
3. Knowledge Application

Just as in the human DNA double helix, where differing combinations of base pairs or "ladder rungs" create and code for our genes—which define us as individuals and give us our unique characteristics—the triple helix of the *Student Pathway DNA* also has base pairs or "ladder rungs." It is these latitudinal "ladder rungs" and how they are applied to the Guiding Principles and supporting structures that will determine

- the "genes" of *The Literate Graduate*,
- his or her respective *Career Readiness*, and ultimately
- his or her ability to find *TrueNorth*.

Understanding the *Student Pathway DNA* is a foundational piece to the *Pathways to Career Readiness Frame—Finding TrueNorth* if we are to serve (EMPOWER) each student. Figure 1.2 represents a *Pathways to Career Readiness* Concept Map—illustrating the interrelationships and interdependencies of the Guiding Principles and structures.

The three strands—Skill Development, Curriculum Knowledge, and Knowledge Application—and their interactions and linkages weave together to form a unique genetic makeup, which we refer to here as *Student Pathway DNA* (see Figure 1.3).

At its very best, the perfectly "genetically coded" *Pathway* is a symbiotic relationship among

- the **Skill Development Strand**—the development of a student's skills, interests, and aptitudes (Self-Knowledge Learning Journey in Figure 1.3);

FIGURE 1.2

Pathways to Career Readiness Concept Map

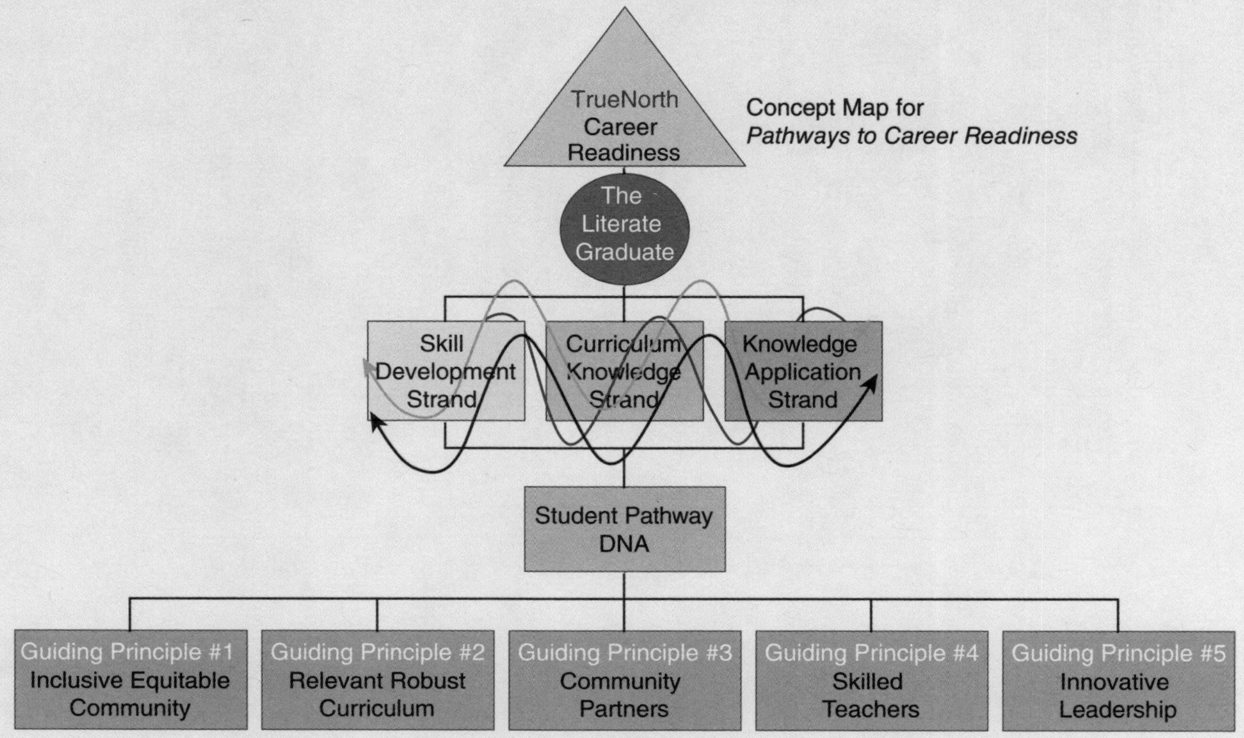

Concept Map for *Pathways to Career Readiness*

TrueNorth Career Readiness

The Literate Graduate

Knowledge Application Strand

Curriculum Knowledge Strand

Skill Development Strand

Student Pathway DNA

Guiding Principle #1 Inclusive Equitable Community

Guiding Principle #2 Relevant Robust Curriculum

Guiding Principle #3 Community Partners

Guiding Principle #4 Skilled Teachers

Guiding Principle #5 Innovative Leadership

FIGURE 1.3
Student Pathway DNA

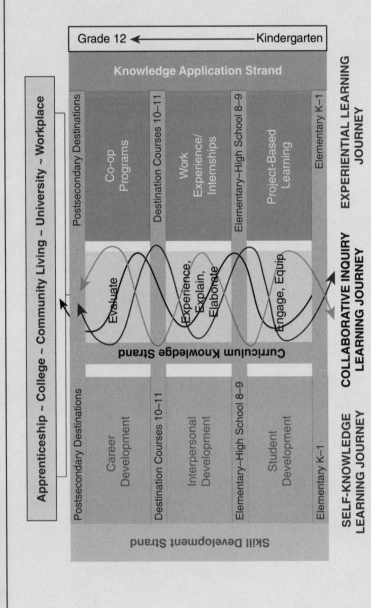

- the **Curriculum Knowledge Strand**—the appropriate instructional starting points on the curriculum continuum for a student (**Collaborative Inquiry Learning Journey** in Figure 1.3); and
- the **Knowledge Application Strand**—the opportunities the student has to practice, refine, and reflect upon the learning (**Experiential Learning Journey** in Figure 1.3).

Figure 1.3 provides the genetic coding for *The Literate Graduate* and *Career Readiness* characteristics. It illustrates the interwoven three-way educational journey that students are on from kindergarten to beyond Grade 12. The genetic makeup of *The Literate Graduate* and ultimately his or her *Career Readiness* is made up of experiencing

- three strands, Skill Development, Curriculum Knowledge, and Knowledge Application, supported by **a robust, relevant K–12+ curriculum**—our Guiding Principle 2;
- "ladder rungs" that pair up with other "ladder rungs," serving as latitudinal lines, and that help students to locate themselves relative to their *TrueNorth*, as framed in the Learning Journeys described above; and
- **skilled teachers**—our Guiding Principle 4—who master the instructional challenge of ensuring alignment among these three strands. Student disengagement and underachievement can easily occur if the appropriate alignment is not considered and addressed.

Because of our common DNA, human beings, as a species, should technically be capable of the same things. It is our genes and how they are represented, coded for, and passed on through heredity, however, that provide the human race with the member uniqueness we witness on a daily basis. Due to this understanding, we would argue that we are all innately creative learning creatures—all with the potential for growth and development given the right time and supports. Our students are no different when it comes to learning (Sharratt & Fullan, 2012).

The ways in which we "turn on" and "activate" key parts of the *Student Pathway DNA*, using the three structural strands and their respective "ladder rungs," will determine the student's respective mastery of the knowledge, skills, and dispositions. Each of the three strands is complex and layered. Often there are programs and strategies available in the genetic makeup of individual strands or across all strands to support and extend the student learning. Examples of how districts have used high-yield programs and/or strategies to support student *Pathways* will be shared as part of this book's narrative.

Figures 1.4, 1.5, 1.6, and 1.7 depict each of the strands.

Strand 1: Skill Development

There are three latitudinal "ladder rungs" to the Skill Development Strand:

- **Student Development**—students' ability to self-assess, to know their interests and aptitudes and goals;
- **Interpersonal Development**—how students get along with others, inside and outside of the school; and
- **Career Development**—the decision-making capability of the students (adapted from Ontario Ministry of Education and Training, 1999).

Implicit in all three components is a focus on *Career Readiness* (Lens 1) and the development of the essential skills required for each student to be successful in the future, in other words to be *The Literate Graduate* (Lens 2). These essential skills are often referred to as the workplace skills; we prefer to think of them as the ultimate life skills. It is when all these components come together and are aligned with instructional starting points on the curriculum continuum that students are most successful on their educational journey.

Mismatches occur when students' interests, aptitudes, goals, and skills are not aligned with where they are on the curriculum continuum. This manifests in students being either over- or underchallenged, often resulting in behaviors synonymous with disengagement and being disenfranchised. If we recognize the mismatch, we can be aware of how far off from *Finding TrueNorth* the student may be at any given time. If we, or the student, fail to recognize the signals of a mismatch, the student will further disengage and possibly continue to wander further away from *TrueNorth* and ultimately from future success.

FIGURE 1.4

Student Pathway DNA–Skill Development Strand

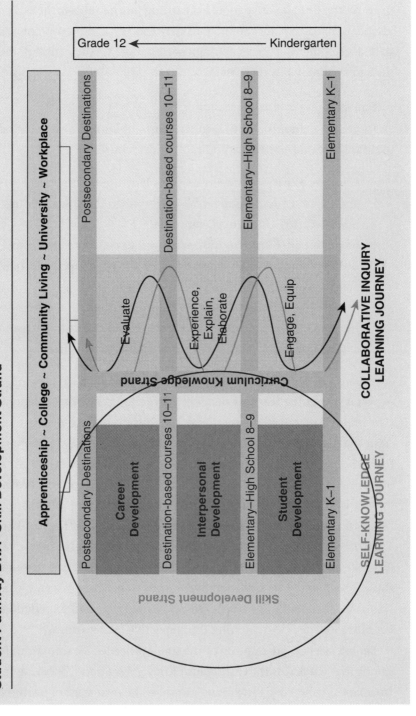

Matching the rungs on the Self-Knowledge Learning Journey with those on the Collaborative Inquiry Learning Journey allows the skilled teacher to make explicit connections between curriculum content and skill development. This matching/coordination further ensures the student's *Pathway* is "on course."

Strand 2: Curriculum Knowledge

Figure 1.5 demonstrates that in the Curriculum Knowledge Strand there are three supporting latitudinal "ladder rungs":

- **Engage, Equip**—students and teachers use multiple data sets and focused questions to research answers to their "wonderings" related to curriculum expectations;
- **Experience, Explain, Elaborate**—they collaborate to explore, gather relevant data, and pause to consider what is possible, new, and innovative; and
- **Evaluate**—they apply their findings, determine what represents the learning, and mobilize the knowledge for others to learn and extend (Saskatchewan School Library Association, 2014).

Where they exist in state curricula, curriculum grade/course expectations guide teachers in their instructional **K–12+** Collaborative Inquiry practice. Instructional starting points are determined from the data, which teachers analyze for *individual students* and vary from class to class and grade to grade. Teachers need to be mindful of where *each* student is on his or her Collaborative Inquiry Learning Journey, giving daily consideration to the assessment information that determines the structured instructional strategies they utilize. The curriculum content becomes the material by which the teacher facilitates student engagement in the learning process. It is through the content and the Collaborative Inquiry Learning Journey that skilled teachers build the respective Self-Knowledge and Experiential Learning Journeys by matching the respective ladder rungs.

Skilled teachers are mindful of the support needed for smooth transitions that cut across the Curriculum Knowledge Strand, checking for "roadblocks" and laying the foundations for the next stage of learning.

FIGURE 1.5

Student Pathway DNA–Curriculum Knowledge Strand

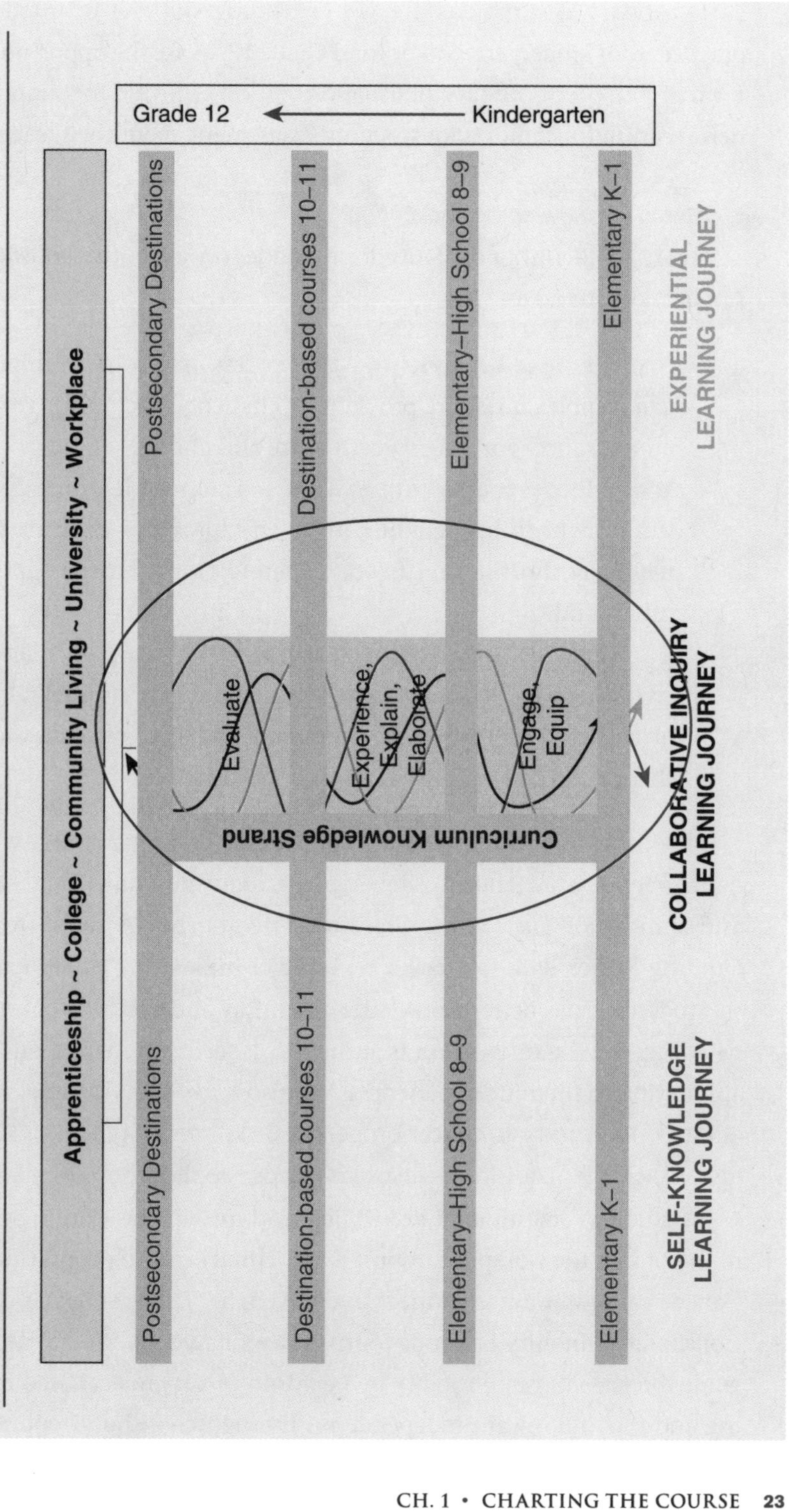

Postsecondary destinations are woven throughout the instructional practice from kindergarten to beyond Grade 12, as are the opportunities a variety of postsecondary destination options provide for supplying rich meaningful contexts for students' excitement about their learning.

Strand 3: Knowledge Application

Figure 1.6 identifies the latitudinal "ladder rungs" in the Knowledge Application Strand as

- **Project-Based Learning**—the process of inquiry in response to a complex question, problem, or challenge, including rigorous projects incorporating student voice and choice;
- **Work Experience/Internships**—a planned learning opportunity, within any credit course, that provides students with relatively short-term, subject-related work placement opportunities; and
- **Cooperative Education (Co-op) Programs**—a planned, credit earning, learning experience that forms an integral part of a specific course and/or program and integrates classroom theory and learning experiences at a workplace.

The three rungs frame the Experiential Learning Journey students need to undertake to develop the requisite knowledge, skills, and abilities of *The Literate Graduate*. This journey is supported by Guiding Principle 3—**a broad base of community partners**.

Students have better knowledge retention and are more likely to be engaged if the instruction is authentic, is feedback driven, and has application to their life experiences. We also know that learning, without an opportunity to reflect on personal skill development, is really just knowledge acquisition versus knowledge application.

As students mature and are eligible to broaden the learning environment into the workplace, robust Experiential Learning opportunities provide very real ways to connect students to the "ladder rungs" on their Collaborative Inquiry Learning Journey (see Chapter 6). We scaffold the gradual release of responsibility by beginning with project-based learning and moving toward independence through cooperative education

FIGURE 1.6

Student Pathway DNA–Knowledge Application Strand

Apprenticeship ~ College ~ Community Living ~ University ~ Workplace

Grade 12   Kindergarten

Knowledge Application Strand

Postsecondary Destinations

Destination-based courses 10–11

Elementary–High School 8–9

Elementary K–1

Co-op Programs

Work Experience/ Internships

Project-Based Learning

EXPERIENTIAL LEARNING JOURNEY

Curriculum Knowledge Strand

Evaluate

Experience, Explain, Elaborate

Engage, Equip

Postsecondary Destinations

Destination-based courses 10–11

Elementary–High School 8–9

Elementary K–1

COLLABORATIVE INQUIRY LEARNING JOURNEY

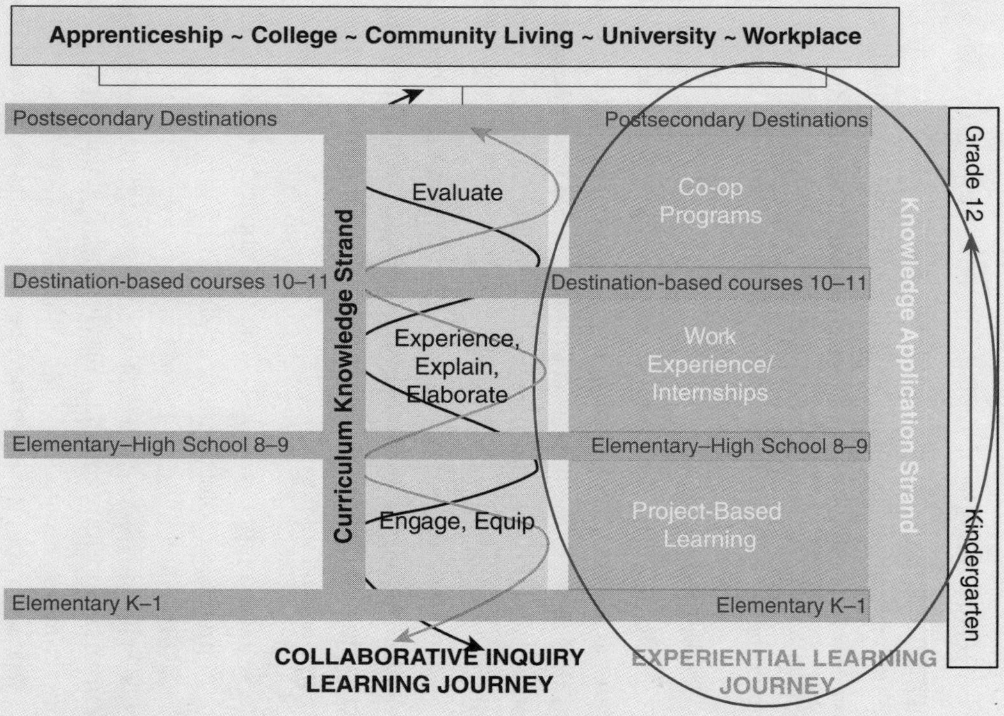

opportunities. Further, learning is enhanced when matching structures are constructed from the Experiential Learning Journey, the Collaborative Inquiry Learning Journey, and the Self-Knowledge Learning Journey because the diligent teacher, or route master, will know from the data that the student is on course to *TrueNorth*. Only then is the genetic coding for *The Literate Graduate* fully activated.

Students choosing a *Pathway* directly into the workplace or an apprenticeship have an even greater need for this fully activated journey as their transitions are more immediate, often into a limited competitive market. By scaffolding the Experiential Learning opportunities across grades and curriculum content, focused school-to-work transition programs become an excellent strategy to provide this level of learning.

Transition Planning

In Figure 1.7, the structural supports running across *all three strands* serve as anchors. They identify key transition periods for the students as they move to the next level of learning and *Career Readiness*. They offer stability. Typically there are six possible transition periods. The four most common are represented in Figure 1.7.

Given that students don't necessarily arrive at high school with the requisite foundation for a successful *Pathway*, much of the groundwork needs to be established in the K–8 years, as represented by the bottom two structural supports:

- Elementary Grades K–1—The first support represents a series of transition points starting as early as kindergarten/preschool and extending to Grade 1.
- Elementary–High School Grades 8–9—This support represents the transition from middle or elementary school to high school.

Framed within these two transition periods, as modeled in Figure 1.1, are two other possible structural supports:

- Elementary Grades 3–4—This support is for students who require a smooth transition from primary (ending in Grade 3) to junior division (ending in Grade 6).

FIGURE 1.7

Student Pathway DNA–Transition Planning

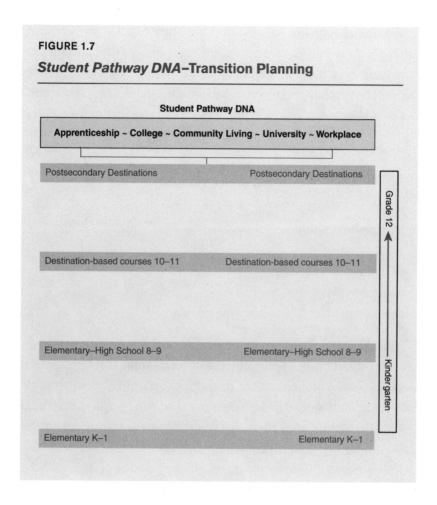

- Elementary Grades 6–7—This support is for students who require a smooth transition from junior division to intermediate.

The two upper structural supports represent the key transition periods for high school students:

- Destination courses, Grades 10–11—This support represents the transition from Grade 10 to Grade 11 or that point in time when students start considering course and/or program selection based upon their preferred destination.
- Postsecondary destinations—The final support is the transition from high school to postsecondary destination of choice.

Additional supports and resources are often required at these transition points to ensure students have deeper understandings of themselves and how those understandings might better inform their next steps as they explore the opportunities afforded them. Those opportunities might be course choices, course levels, and/or programming choices.

Postsecondary Destinations

Running across the top of Figure 1.8 are the five most common postsecondary destinations for students:

- Apprenticeship
- College
- Community Living
- University
- Workplace

Ultimately, as an outcome of a successful education system, all students should find opportunities for work—some through apprenticeship, some through college or technical training, some through university, and some through fast-tracking to the workplace. In a small number of cases, there are students whose transition will be into community or independent living. They too require very specific and targeted *Pathway* planning. Notice how the destinations are placed along Figure 1.8. There is no ranking. We no longer live in a world that ranks university at the top and workplace at the bottom. In today's world, students move laterally among postsecondary destinations. Educational opportunities are increasingly becoming more seamless, across and within the institutions. While the postsecondary and concurrent possibilities are numerous, each possibility requires reasoned and informed planning and instruction if students are to make informed choices about their *Pathways*.

Navigating *Pathways to Career Readiness*

In a Recalculated Route, **skilled teachers** masterfully weave together the five Guiding Principles and structures (Figure 1.2) to

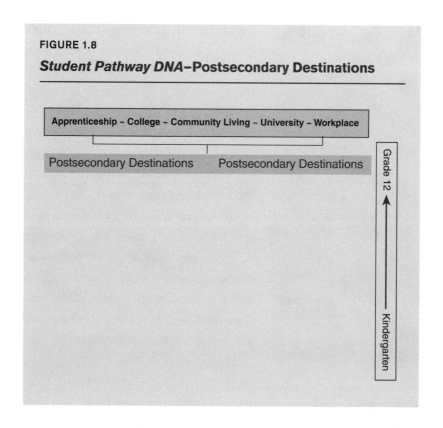

FIGURE 1.8

Student Pathway DNA–Postsecondary Destinations

Apprenticeship ~ College ~ Community Living ~ University ~ Workplace

Postsecondary Destinations   Postsecondary Destinations

Grade 12

Kindergarten

Finding TrueNorth. They use the curriculum as the starting point from which they introduce students to the practical applications of the learning. At the same time, they scaffold the learning, ensuring that the foundational skills of *The Literate Graduate* are acquired. As students move from kindergarten to beyond Grade 12, the number of opportunities for teachers to authenticate the classroom knowledge using Collaborative Inquiry approaches (see Chapter 6) broadens and deepens. Greater opportunities for authentication arise when teachers with their students offer practical, experiential opportunities from a range of community partners.

Explicit connections to the opportunities tied to each postsecondary destination increase the relevance for students as they reflect upon their own skills, interests, and abilities. Character education, service learning, and community service, to name a few, are ways in which the **skilled teacher** engages students in learning about themselves in relationship to a larger community. Every teacher understands that character development and building agency and civility in each student are not done in isolation of the curriculum knowledge. Teachers weave them seamlessly into the instructional practice and intentionally look for them in the knowledge application.

In Figure 1.1, the two-way arrows remind us of the need for continuous dialogue and feedback with key stakeholders regarding student preparedness and achievement outcomes. Recalculations must be anticipated and welcomed, as "change" is the only constant.

We noted that along the K–12+ curriculum continuum there are key transition periods that require attention as students prepare for the next level of learning. Transitions serve as "yellow caution lights," indicating new levels of learning or new directions. It is a time to slow down, secure an anchor, and pay careful attention to the **FACE** of each student. Doing so will enable informed choices to be made, building capacity for students to find *TrueNorth*. We need to be mindful! The ways in which students are supported, guided, and anchored through transition periods will either enable or disable them. If the anchors are not secured, students run the risk of "drifting away."

The old silo approach leads to parallel and distinct *Literate Graduate*, *Career Readiness*, and *Pathways* approaches, with no points of intersection, and results in students not clearly understanding *why* they are learning what they are learning. It eliminates any chance of the student "experiencing" learning and, from that, building his or her own sense of relevance to the curriculum. To maximize student achievement, the more intersections and intentional connections, the better. Hope is not a strategy!

From GOOD to GREAT to INNOVATE

Examples from practice help us to better understand the interconnectedness of our guiding principles and structures (Figure 1.1). One example of *The Literate Graduate*'s skill development is when students shift from "learning to read" to "reading to learn." Every teacher must use the corresponding curriculum (Curriculum Knowledge Strand) to support the learning but must also pay careful attention to the individual starting points of students—in other words by connecting the Skill Development Strand to students' skills, interests, and abilities. This might be reflected in

- choice of reading material and modality;
- medium for delivery—e-reader, paper text, iPad, handheld device, and so on;
- complexity or authenticity of text;
- practicality of and critical thinking involved in the assessment task;
- students' capacity for peer and self-assessment; and
- varied ways for students to choose how to demonstrate their learning: presentation, skit, diorama, writing, singing, dancing, and so on.

At the high school level, "reading to learn" is given "context" when a student, interested in pursuing a trade, has an opportunity to use the highly technical training manuals as learning tools and knowledge application. Parents of that student also get a new appreciation for the learning when they ACTIVELY STEP into their child's world and realize that the complexity of a technical training manual requires a blending of the literacy and numeracy skills being profiled as critical components of *The Literate Graduate*. Thus is dispelled the myth that technical training is a "less than" learning opportunity!

At Scuola per Sportivi d'Élite in Locarno, Switzerland, we see how the Curriculum Knowledge Strand and Knowledge Application Strand are woven together to provide timely, relevant learning for the students and the teachers (see Chapter 3). Vocational school curriculum is developed by a partnership created from members of the funding ministry and relevant industry representation. For example, the curriculum for an automotive school is developed by a team with representatives from the ministries of economics and transportation, the association of automobile dealers, the mechanics trades,

(Continued)

(Continued)

and manufacturing. An important concept, within the curriculum expectations, is the notion of learning skills in the classroom and then immediately applying them—that is, learning skills on the job through cooperative work learning experiences. The partnerships ensure that students are constantly learning the latest in technologies being used in the "real world" and that, as technologies change, the curriculum incorporates the changes and coordinates the new learning from the work experience in the related courses.

Another powerful example is in mathematics. For some students and parents, the mere word *math* conjures up many insecurities and anxieties. Most students struggle to understand mathematical principles in isolation of some context—that is, something to which they can relate. Students who struggle in math are the first to ask, "Why do I need to know this?" The fact that the question is asked is an indicator that math, as part of *The Literate Graduate* profile, is often not taught with connections to the *Student Pathway DNA*. Student achievement in math is enhanced when intersections to the *Student Pathway DNA* are constructed.

One secondary math teacher constructed such intersections. Every Friday he would come to his class dressed to represent a different occupation. The lesson on that day was constructed and deconstructed through the lens of that occupation. For example: In what ways does a house painter use measurement? Why might a doctor need to know fractions? Why is probability important to astronauts? Through a structured Collaborative Inquiry instructional approach, the teacher not only engaged the *Student Pathway DNA* Skill Development Strand to support *The Literate Graduate* skill development but enhanced the intersections by embedding life skills. Needless to say, student engagement and achievement were enhanced simultaneously. Students' attitudes changed as they now saw math as relevant to their life experiences and could appreciate firsthand and articulate "why they were learning it."

The *Pathways to Career Readiness Frame—Finding TrueNorth* (Figure 1.1) serves as the first recalculation, providing a new series of lenses through which to consider educational programming, relationships, and priorities. We fit these lenses with others, creating a multilens prism or telescope. When all lenses focus together, they create a very clear vision of the road ahead for students, teachers, and leaders. It is critical that we consider, as part of the recalculations, **What Matters Most**—to bring about large-scale system change. Our first consideration, found in Chapter 2, is that **Leadership Matters Most.**

Reflective Pause by Avis Glaze

The clarion call for educators to revisit and reclaim their leadership by grappling with and solving the problems related to the new realities is a timely and necessary one. So many educational issues and concerns have persisted over time. We could go back centuries in the history of education to find that complaints voiced by the public about education and students have not changed much even though, as educators, we have worked very hard and have paid assiduous attention to what the public feels about the education system. We have made progress. There are many pockets of excellence.

STEPS TO STUDENTS' SUCCESS

1. Assess all learners.
2. Rally your allies around a common and compelling moral purpose.
3. Be "tuned in" to the social and economic realities.
4. Establish a K–12+ *Pathways lens*, supporting **an inclusive, equitable learning community.**
5. Establish *a structured, collaboratively planned approach* building upon the assets of **a broad base of community partners.**
6. Leverage **a robust and relevant curriculum** to engage the students in their learning.
7. Invest time in acquiring and training **skilled teachers** who can turn on and activate student learning.
8. Lobby and build capacity for system integrators, to work on the skill solutions that are required.
9. "Design down" assessment, instructional practices, and programming from postsecondary destinations.
10. Build a climate of mutual respect that will allow innovative thinking, problem solving, critical thinking, and creativity to grow and flourish.

This book's authors, Lyn Sharratt and Gale Harild, build upon the work of key researchers and offer new *Pathways* into the future. They importantly deconstruct the notion of a strong moral purpose and heightened professionalism, highlighting the need for widespread collaborative efforts to address the demands imposed by the social drivers they identify. Sharratt and Harild document cogently and persuasively many educational innovations of which we can be proud, while noting the need to address a new educational model to overcome the seemingly intractable problems.

The authors recommend the alignment of economic and national policies to address the "jobs without people" and "people without jobs" conundrum. They ask provocative questions for us to ponder as we revisit our focus on preparing students from secondary school for the myriad *Pathways* they are presented with today. It becomes very clear that students need support to become the solution finders that are needed in the 21st century and beyond. Cleverly, Sharratt and Harild offer new *Pathways* into the future in order to determine **What Matters Most**, drawing upon successful practices across the globe.

One of the strengths of this book is the strong focus on a K–12+ curriculum continuum. It is a welcome approach for a discussion of the knowledge, skills, and attitudes that will enhance the skills and life chances of *The Literate Graduate*. The three ladder rungs of Student Development, Interpersonal Development, and Career Development, previously identified by the Ontario Ministry of Education as a focus in its guidance programs, highlight the importance of curriculum knowledge and knowledge application.

Including strategies such as project-based learning, work experience, internships, and cooperative education programs helps to broaden the view of what good education entails. As well, the discussion of areas such as mathematics in the profile of *The Literate Graduate* is essential in today's context of concern for the state of mathematics education. Debunking the myths about the value of a technical education by valuing all destinations is one of the many contributions of this chapter to our knowledge base.

Using the metaphor of a compass as they map *Pathways to Career Readiness* is very effective. Sharratt and Harild provide much-needed guidance for us to assist students in finding their way to the *TrueNorth*. They identify the need for intensive supports, targeted resources, and systematic guidance systems to help students discover multiple desti-nations. As someone who believes strongly in the need for develop-mentally based career guidance programs for schools, I consider this focus to be well overdue.

Chapter 1 appropriately sets the stage and offers educators new insights into the postsecondary choice making and transition plan-ning for all students as they map their *Pathways* to opportunity.

About Avis Glaze, PhD

From classroom teacher to superintendent of schools and director of education, Avis Glaze has experience at all levels of the school system. She was one of five commissioners on Ontario's Royal Commission on Learning. As Ontario's first Chief Student Achievement Officer and founding CEO of the Literacy and Numeracy Secretariat, she played a pivotal role in improving student achievement in Ontario. Avis served as Ontario's Education Commissioner and Senior Advisor to the Minister of Education. She was a professor in residence in the faculty of education at the University of Ottawa. Her most recent appoint-ment was as Advisor to the Minister of Education of New Zealand on national standards. Avis coauthored *Breaking Barriers: Excellence and Equity for All* with Ruth Mattingley and Ben Levin (Pearson, 2012). Her most recent book, *High School Graduation: K–12 Strategies That Work*, with Ruth Mattingley and Rob Andrews (Corwin, 2013), identifies the research-informed strategies to improve graduation rates for all stu-dents. Avis's international contributions to education were recently recognized when she received the Robert Owen Award, the first of its kind offered in Scotland, from Mr. Michael Russell, Cabinet Secretary for Education and Lifelong Learning.

LEADERSHIP MATTERS!

U nderstanding the *Pathways to Career Readiness Frame: Finding TrueNorth* is the first step in Recalculating the Route. It provides us with a series of lenses through which to consider new educational programming that responds to economic and social drivers. When all of the lenses are aligned and focused, they create a very clear vision of the road ahead to the benefit of our students, teachers, and leaders.

Next, to bring about large-scale system change such as we are suggesting is required to set the stage for Recalculating the Route, it is vital to understand **What Matters Most** in providing leadership within a "good to great" system. We offer that leadership within schools must be aligned with the system vision while constantly feeding back information about schools' progress to the system.

To consider how we move leaders from good to great in education, it is important to understand that when we discuss leaders, we include system leaders, school leaders or principals, teachers, and community partners—all are leaders. We know there is a vast amount of research literature that addresses the factors that impact leaders who make changes in classroom practice a priority in their work—only some of which we reference here. Then what is necessary for leadership that fosters innovation to emerge once these factors are in place?

Innovation leadership is defined by Gliddon (2006) as synthesizing different leadership styles in organizations to influence employees to produce creative ideas, products, services, and solutions. As an approach to organization development, **innovation leadership** can be used to support the achievement of the mission or vision of an organization or group. In a world that is ever changing with new technologies and processes, it is becoming necessary for organizations to think innovatively to ensure their continued success and stay competitive.

What does it take for a principal or a teacher in a school

QUESTIONS THAT MATTER MOST

1. Do the leaders in your system have high predictability for **innovation leadership** capacity?

2. How are you fostering this "innovation mind-set"?

3. What does a collaborative, lateral, peer-to-peer community look like in your classroom, school, system, or state?

4. What strategies do you consider for bringing your community partners into the learning process? What strategies do you consider for breaking down the operational barriers of doing so?

5. What needs to be improved at your school? How might you use *a structured, collaboratively planned approach* to improve it?

6. How is your school, system, or state ensuring that teachers and system leaders are keeping attuned to the economic and social drivers of the workplace?

7. How are you developing and making room for students, teachers, and leaders to become "thinkers"?

8. Do your classrooms look like lenses or silos?

9. How do you build capacity for common understanding and shared values in your classroom, school, or system?

10. How do you build time for stakeholders to meet and plan?

system to become good, great, and then innovative to ensure students have optimum learning opportunities? How can community partners add to **innovation leadership** in education?

We have discussed the need to change the way educators provide *Pathways to Career Readiness* for our students. We have said that Recalculating the Route needs to fit into or be easily adapted within the current curriculum, and yet interplay with it, changing the relationship between teachers and students. Figure 1.1, our *Pathways to Career Readiness Frame: Finding TrueNorth* (see Chapter 1), shows how highly we value leadership in K–12+ teaching and learning. Notice that we made *Leadership* the watermark that underpins our thinking—beneath the entire framework.

In this chapter, under "Leadership Context Matters," we focus on leadership in strong systems—those whose success in impacting student learning is acknowledged. Then under "Leadership Roles Matter," we look closely at the roles of senior leaders, principals, and teachers within systems, and under "Motion Leadership Matters," we set out specific strategies for understanding teaching and learning. Finally, under "Innovation Leadership Matters," we consider what is involved in a move from good—to great—to innovate.

Leadership Context Matters

Writing a commissioned paper for the Council of Ontario Directors of Education and the Institute for Educational Leadership, Leithwood (2013) reports on finding nine key characteristics or conditions operating within strong districts as shown in Table 2.1. Leithwood notes that other researchers such as Campbell and Fullan (2006) had reported eight similar characteristics. Reading the list of characteristics shows how powerfully the characteristics are embedded vertically within the entire organization of a strong district. The characteristics are meaningful and provide accountability for leaders at every level within the strong district.

Leadership Roles Matter

From Table 2.1, it is clear that the nine characteristics are applicable at senior system leadership levels and at principal and school leadership

TABLE 2.1

Characteristics of Strong Systems or Districts and Their Leadership

Characteristics of Strong Systems or Districts (Leithwood, 2013)	Our Detailed Commentary
Broadly shared mission, vision, and goals founded on ambitious images of the educated person	The vision includes raising the overall achievement bar to close the achievement gaps, and nurturing student engagement and well-being. Note the end point—the educated person—is the basis of the mission, vision, and goals. See Chapter 4, Figure 4.3, "A Profile of *The Literate Graduate*," for details.
A coherent instructional guidance system	The focus of curriculum standards and frameworks, instructional practices, Professional Learning (PL) emphases, and assessment tools is on achieving the mission, vision, and goals. Strong districts encourage schools to be innovative and differentiate resources to schools in response to variability in student performance. Coherence in a system is intended to provide some boundaries within which schools can be innovative.
Deliberate and consistent use of multiple sources of evidence to inform decisions	*Putting FACES on the Data* (Sharratt & Fullan, 2012) speaks to multiple forms of intelligence gathering regarding each student, each school, each family of schools, and the system as a whole. Some data sources reflect teacher-developed assessments, and some sources are from standards-based assessments. All are used to make wise system- and school-based decisions, such as diagnosing areas

(Continued)

(Continued)

Characteristics of Strong Systems or Districts (Leithwood, 2013)	Our Detailed Commentary
	of need, setting targets and monitoring progress, differentiating support, and clarifying and guiding improvement strategies.
Learning-oriented organizational improvement processes	A singular or very small number of key improvement goals are introduced slowly and consistently pursued over a sustained time period in manageable steps, so as not to overload schools with an excessive number of initiatives. New approaches build on foundational work and are integrated into what have become existing routines.
Job-embedded professional development for all staff members	As learning organizations, strong districts understand and live the value that everyone can and should be a continuous learner—regardless of position within the system, it is everyone's work. More learning is accomplished in school-based sessions with collaborative introduction and collective discussion about how the improvements will work best.
Budgets, structures, personnel policies and procedures, and uses of time aligned with the district's mission, vision, and goals	Nothing is invested in any program, resource, or asset that does not align precisely with the mission, vision, and values as expressed by curriculum expectations and PL to ensure the students' individual goals are met. Planning is built across departments to ensure all are aligned.

Characteristics of Strong Systems or Districts (Leithwood, 2013)	Our Detailed Commentary
A comprehensive approach to leadership development	Effective school leadership makes a difference to all students' achievement; school leadership development can be positively leveraged to influence large numbers of teachers and students; having high expectations of school leaders is key; ensuring everyone in central departments takes responsibility in his or her roles for increasing student performance alone is a powerful strategy—everyone seeing him- or herself in this work is critical.
A policy-oriented board of trustees	Growth in student achievement and well-being is encouraged when elected officials focus their attention on board policy and budgets that ensure the district mission and vision— to increase all students' achievement— drive the district's improvement efforts.
Productive working relationships with staff and other stakeholders	The relationships that matter most lie within the central office, between the central office and the schools, and among the system, schools, parents, local community groups, and the department of education. Communication within the system and within schools is nurtured by structures that ensure built-in time within the school day for collaborative work.

Source: Commentary is adapted from Leithwood (2013, pp. 13–29).

levels, and have implications for classroom teacher-leaders. All levels have a shared responsibility for student learning, and each also has specific accountabilities and responsibilities to support the others. Next, we will discuss three levels of leadership: system leadership, principal leadership, and teacher leadership.

System Leadership

At the system level, with their experience, senior leaders may have additional administrative or system responsibilities that are enormous and cannot be delegated, yet the fundamental goal remains *student learning* with the data available from a much larger source base and analyzed from a broad system perspective. The concept that system leaders must also continue to be instructional leaders is captured in at least five of the characteristics: (1) vision, mission, and goals; (2) a coherent internal instructional guidance system; (3) learning-oriented organization improvement processes; (4) job-embedded professional development for all staff; and (5) a comprehensive approach to leadership development.

The leadership literature shows the best system-wide practice approaches to building leadership capacity in a school, between schools, and across systems can work. While there are some strong systems, being strong is not the norm, as not every leader within most systems could be defined as "good," let alone "great." Good is, however, a baseline upon which teachers and school leaders need to build and scaffold to improve in their systems. While becoming innovative may be an eventual goal for some in leadership, we must achieve a high level of baseline "good" leadership performance first across systems. And that takes a lot of work not only to develop but also to sustain.

Leithwood (2013) calls the balance between the capacity to lead and manage "system thinking," and the capacity to think about new concepts that are required to move the system and its related systems and governments ahead "proactive." More specifically, "people who are proactive effect environmental change; they identify opportunities and act on them, show initiative, persevere, until they bring about meaningful change. They transform their organizations' mission, find and solve problems, and take it upon themselves to have an impact on the world around them" (Leithwood, 2013, p. 46).

As the strategic planning process is often long term, this "system thinking" involves foresight, experience, and collaborative thought. For senior leaders, there are multiple opportunities to become innovative. There is abundant research concerning how to create innovation and the specific training required for students so they understand a structured inquiry process and how teachers can foster creativity—but for system leaders, the important skills and attitudes that define one as causing innovation to happen are related to

- understanding the student learning and achievement data,
- understanding the content and experiential needs of changing economic and employment conditions,
- having strong interpersonal skills, and
- developing strong community contacts with whom the leader is willing to share and question.

Finally, innovation is about being willing to lead where no one has gone before—to take calculated risks informed by research about what works—trying alternative approaches to achieving student success when no one else believes there is a problem that requires a solution. Without **innovation leadership**, organizations are likely to struggle. This new call for innovation represents the shift from the 20th-century traditional view of organizational practices, which discouraged employee innovative behaviors, to the 21st-century view of valuing innovative thinking as a potentially powerful influence on organizational performance (see Appendix A). This leads us to consider principal leadership and innovation at the school level.

Principal Leadership

Principals who are good leaders carry the day-to-day responsibility for instructional leadership, and not only are supported in this effort by senior leadership but are accountable to senior leadership for demonstrating their in-school and in-class leadership. Key to this leadership responsibility is understanding what is going on in the school by reviewing and analyzing the various forms of data available that, once understood, can impact the school's capacity to improve achievement for all students (Sharratt & Fullan, 2012).

On the premise that we always start with data to inform our direction, we asked 507 educators in our survey, "What are the top three leadership skills needed to put **FACES** on the data?" (Sharratt & Fullan, 2012). The results, highlighted as follows, are applicable and instructive here as we attempt to move more principals to becoming instructional leaders in their schools:

- Forty-five percent said that, to lead with credibility, leaders must first model knowledge of classroom practice—assessment and instruction—what we call *know-ability*. Principals need to have a strong and compelling message, but they also must "know their stuff."
- Thirty-three percent said that the ability to inspire and mobilize others through clear communication of commitment was essential—what we call *mobilize-ability*. Principals model leadership and "learner-ship" by taking responsibility, accountability, and ownership for student learning. In that way, they "mobilize" teachers *to* action and *for* action by providing the right Professional Learning and multifaceted resources to support that learning.
- Twenty-one percent said that knowing how to establish a lasting culture of shared responsibility and accountability was crucial—what we call *sustain-ability*.

To summarize, we defined three factors, *know-ability*, *mobilize-ability*, and *sustain-ability*, which represent a specific focus by leaders to get the desired results for all students (Sharratt & Fullan, 2012). The vast trove of leadership literature available refers to modeling expected practices and behavior (being knowledgeable), to opening and maintaining communication within the school and with external sources of power and resources (mobilizing self and others), and to honest collaboration with staff as individuals and in teams (sustaining the work)—parallel commentary to the results we found in our **FACES** survey. We will not elaborate further on these baseline skills, which are not yet visible in every school or system despite decades of work by researchers and highly skilled system leadership teams.

Hattie (2012) refers to recent research that highlights three characteristics of school leaders that have a positive impact on increasing student learning. Student achievement increases when leaders

- promote and participate in teacher learning and development, which has the highest impact on student outcomes of all leadership dimensions identified in the research of Robinson, Hohepa, and Lloyd (2009);
- focus their relationships, their work, and their learning on the core business of teaching and learning (Robinson, Hohepa, & Lloyd, 2011); and
- understand and take action to become pedagogical or instructional leaders.

In his meta-analysis, Hattie (2009) determined that the overall role of leader has a .39 effect on student achievement; however, an instructional leader has a more significant effect than a transformational leader.

Hattie (2012) suggests that transformational leaders are attuned to inspiring teachers to new levels of energy and commitment toward a common mission, which develops the school's capacity to work to overcome challenges, reach ambitious goals, and then ensure that teachers have time to conduct their teaching. Instructional leaders, he reports, attend to the quality and impact on student learning of all in the school. These leaders ensure that

- disruption to learning is minimized,
- teachers have high expectations for their students,
- daily visits are made to classrooms, and
- there is concern about the quality and nature of learning in the school.

The critical difference, according to Hattie (2012), is the overall impact each nugget above has on making a difference to student learning. The overall instructional leader impact on students' achievement is significant with a positive effect size of .42 when leaders

1. observe in classrooms,

2. interpret test scores with teachers,

3. focus on instructional issues,

4. ensure a coordinated instructional program,

5. are highly visible,

6. communicate high academic standards, and

7. ensure class atmospheres are conducive to learning.

One can argue that both transformational and instructional leadership are necessary for aligning system and school capacity building, and that instructional support is valuable in leading the work of increasing all students' achievement.

V. Robinson (2006) takes on what needs to change in the role of the principal as an instructional leader when she calls for a return to the roots of the education business—that is, teaching and learning—and to get back into the classroom to determine what is impacting student learning there. In her conclusions, Robinson highlights three clarion calls to school leadership as imperative:

1. School leaders need opportunities to extend and update both the breadth and the depth of their pedagogical content knowledge. Principals, for example, cannot competently and confidently lead instructional improvement, even with substantial delegation of responsibilities, without in-depth and up-to-date knowledge of at least one curriculum area. Even though this specialist knowledge base is not directly transferable to other subject areas, it provides principals with a rich appreciation of the type and depth of expertise they need in other curriculum and instructional areas.

2. School leaders need a balanced program of professional preparation and development to support them in this new work. While there will always be a place for generic leadership, the balance between generic and educational leadership needs to shift in favor of the latter if school leaders are to get the

learning opportunities they need to support this work. It is no longer helpful to assume that it is only classroom teachers who need to learn about teaching and learning.

3. Rather than treating instructional leadership as an additional responsibility, school leaders need to adapt existing leadership practices so they are better aligned to the overall goal of instructional improvement.

While reading these quotes from Leithwood, Hattie, and Robinson, one might be forgiven for thinking there is a divide in their thinking regarding senior leadership and principal leadership. While Leithwood speaks of senior district leaders having their primary goal as the establishment and maintenance of the nine characteristics and their distal goal as student learning, it is precisely because of the emphasis in strong districts that instructional leaders are able to be deployed in schools to ensure that student achievement is their first priority as Hattie and Robinson support. The differences between the large strong systems Leithwood writes about and most other systems are very real as are the political policies and management functions between systems in Canada and the United States and those in the United Kingdom, New Zealand, and Australia. Whereas large systems are seen in the former two countries as partners or extensions of government and therefore having a stewardship role to play, in the latter group of countries, districts have largely been eroded or gutted, permitting local school management autonomy. In this situation, it is vitally important to drive home the notion that local administration, while important, is not as important as continuing to be, as Robinson says, an instructional leader in supporting classroom practice.

Teacher Leadership

Much research has been conducted about the power of teacher-leadership and distributed leadership, which we won't review here. We know that teachers who are expert teachers and ongoing learners contribute daily to creating students as self-directed problem solvers as we discuss in Chapter 6, "Skilled Teachers Matter!" It is important to note, however, that all teachers see themselves as leaders of learning alongside formal leaders. That is, everyone is a leader. Hattie (2012) adds to this vision that teachers need to consider not only the feedback that they give students but also that very feedback becoming feedback for themselves as teachers. He reiterates that as teachers derive feedback information from assessments that they set for their students, there can then be important adjustments to how they teach, how they consider what success looks like, how they recognize students' strengths and gaps, and how they regard their own effects on students. We believe that this thinking should have a profound effect not only on teachers but also on teacher-leaders, school leaders, and system leaders. Reflective evaluation of how well we are doing as teacher-leaders, school leaders, and system leaders becomes "What impact is my leadership having on increasing all students' learning?"

Motion Leadership Matters

Fullan (2013b) coined the term *motion leadership*—the state where the principal and senior leaders are regularly moving and observing—an educator's very smart take on the early business phrase *management by walking around*. The powerful concept here is that by being "in motion" in schools, specifically by being in classrooms and watching for evidence of student improvement, system leaders and school leaders can be of great assistance to the teachers in schools.

> "I am an independent public school principal from Queensland who attended your session last week. Thank you for such a wonderful learning experience. I started to read your book FACES a few days before

We present here three structures that support leadership in motion, focusing it on the evidence that students are learning and improving:

1. Learning Walks and Talks
2. Data Wall Building
3. Principal Learning Teams

Learning Walks and Talks

Daily Learning Walks and Talks are a must. It is an approach for system leaders, principals, and teacher-leaders to engage in reflective inquiry with teachers to impact student achievement and support the development of a culture of learning. Leaders and teachers must create an explicit framework of expected instructional practices to observe and talk about in and across classrooms, schools, and the system that promotes

- leader learning,
- increased use of high-impact classroom strategies, and
- decreased variation in practice between classrooms.

Learning Walks and Talks do that and are most effective when they occur daily and briefly, to collect data over time that give a complete picture of whole-system and individual-school improvement. Learning Walks and Talks assist instructional leaders' understanding of how they can best support assessment-based instruction in all classrooms.

More specifically, the purpose of Learning Walks and Talks is to

- collect data;
- understand impactful classroom practice;

the session and found it compelling reading. I could not put it down. Since the session we had, I have gone back and reread much of it. All that you say makes sense to me, and it fits in with my desired model for my school—Nambour High. I know that as a school we have the base for what you spoke about, and with some changes we can be the high-performing center with all students learning that you have shown me to believe in from my inner thoughts. One of the basic things for us will be **Data Walls**. We have used these in increasingly effective ways but nowhere as well as you described. We can make those changes with everybody believing in the direction. **Learning Walks and Talks** are another good example—they are being done but have not been done with the clearest purposes that you outlined.

Thanks again for all that you have done to raise all the issues and provide new directions that I can follow."

Wayne Troyahn, Principal
Nambour High School
Queensland, Australia
Personal Communication,
June 8, 2014

- build a common language;
- reflect on developing patterns and trends in a school;
- determine what teachers are teaching and students are learning by their responses to students' five questions asked:
  - What are you learning?
  - How are you doing?
  - How do you know?
  - How can you improve?
  - Where do you go for help? (see Figure 2.1);
- ask reflective questions of teachers about their practice;
- give constructive feedback to formulate a plan for the next level of work, which can be observed in subsequent walks; and
- define the support that an administrator (lead learner) can provide to teachers and students (Sharratt, 2013a).

Relating to Leithwood, Robinson, and Hattie, relationships are built on a shared platform of positive system capacity building when many educators care about the focus and work in each other's schools. As Sharratt (2013a) says, walking in classrooms daily and talking about assessment that drives instruction are the two keys to becoming not only an instructional leader but also a lead learner—focused on all **FACES**'s increased achievement. In a Recalculated Route where classroom walls are extended out into the community, the need for Learning Walks and Talks, in these new learning environments, not only strengthens the assessment of the learning but also broadens the instructional knowledge of the teacher.

Learning Walks and Talks culminate in reflective conversations that engage leaders and teachers in elaborating, extending, applying, and evaluating their thinking to create new knowledge. Teachers must be able to articulate what they do to impact student learning in their classrooms and why they teach the way they do by thinking about the criteria they use to make decisions every single day in their planning and teaching (Sharratt & Fullan, 2009, 2012). Administrators need to be able to do the same to ensure that every **FACE** of every student is moving forward and that all teachers are making a difference.

FIGURE 2.1

Asking Five Questions of Students to Determine Their Thinking and Teachers' Teaching During Learning Walks and Talks

SOURCE: Mayfair Community School. Used with permission.

Data Wall Building

Data sets provide leaders with a broad overview of the situation at all times and offer a lens to set new, precise expectations that increase student achievement results. System leaders need to ensure that the data sets used to measure improvement are aligned with the vision and purpose that is set by the organization, and that strategic targets for the system are supported by school plans that are based on data for each school and are the result of **structured, collaboratively planned approaches**. Collectively, all schools work toward a singular common goal through shared responsibility and accountability (Sharratt & Fullan, 2009).

Learning leaders need to immerse themselves in the data—community-based and student-based—especially data that reveal the most about individual students. Handling the student achievement data and other decision-making information at the school level can be, and has often been, a solitary activity performed by the principal. But student data are too important and too powerful to be locked away and privately held. Indeed, solitary analysis will fall well short of what is created by a team of learning leaders.

In the past few years, Sharratt has influenced hundreds of schools and systems in Canada, the United States, Australia, and Chile to create a transparent, collaborative

> "Can't tell you how useful the **Learning Walks and Talks** are to us. They have been pivotal in focusing the work of our leadership team—with relentless consistency! If I wasn't Walking and Talking in a high school this week, starting at the **Data Wall**, how could I have drilled down to the center to ask questions about a particular **FACE**? If I hadn't been Walking and Talking with the principal, I would not have seen evidence of sporadic implementation with little teacher take-up of the instructional decisions made at the follow-up case management meeting for this student. We are keeping up the intentional improvement agenda here by being across all schools through Learning Walks and Talks and the Case Management approach."
>
> Sue Walsh, Associate Director of Education Diocese of Parramatta, Australia Personal Communication, June 7, 2014

approach to data use by constructing a visual story of their data, called a Data Wall as seen in Figure 2.2. As the evolution of Data Walls continues in systems and schools that have deployed them, the concept of the Data Wall has also evolved. They are housed in discreet places for teachers and leaders to have focused conversations about instructional strategies needed to improve student learning. They must focus on collaborative problem solving and how to show growth over time of each **FACE**. The openness of principals and senior leaders in systems that have deployed Data Walls has also evolved. Leaders have learned to

- reflect on the analysis,
- ask each other hard questions,
- consider the reallocation of resources where needed in a triage approach,
- engage in problem solving for each student or school in need, and
- plan for Professional Learning sessions to revisit areas of learning need identified in the data.

Data Walls are a critical part of the case management approach that puts **FACES** on the data so that each student is known, and instructional strategies are relentlessly pursued and monitored. At the system level, the case management approach is used so that schools in challenging circumstances, using data to build system Data Walls, are identified and resourced in a differentiated approach to improvement on an ongoing basis as in Figure 2.2.

Engaging in Learning Walks and Talks and Data Wall building sessions, at both system and school levels, using collaborative dialogue, generates new ideas and typically deeper, more satisfying solutions— sometimes with heated debate—which is very good!

Experienced leaders need to maintain that immersion in student data and that singular focus on student achievement with their teachers, supporting each of them to become as effective as they can become. The third way that we know as leaders we are making a difference in increasing student achievement is to engage in Principal Learning Teams that lead to thoughtful discussion on improving practice.

FIGURE 2.2

An Example of System Data Wall Building in the Diocese of Parramatta, New South Wales, Australia

SOURCE: Catholic Education Diocese of Parramatta. Used with permission.

Principal Learning Teams

In Ontario, the Leading Student Achievement (LSA) project developed by the provincial principals' associations (OPC, ADFO, and CPCO), in partnership with the Literacy and Numeracy Secretariat (LNS), encourages and supports the development of Principal Learning Teams (PLTs). Principals work in teams and networks to increase their capacity (or collective principal efficacy) as leaders, impacting teaching and learning that leads to improved student learning.

It is no surprise that principals have always formed informal networks to

- network with other principals to help them with workplace challenges;
- seek advice from trusted and significant colleagues;

- create a safe space for reciprocal influencing—especially in the social domain;
- find new ways to think about and make meaning of their work; and
- find support in learning what they need to know more about and commit to take action—often together (Sharratt, Hine, & Maika, in press).

The challenge is to move these informed networks into PLTs by addressing a few key questions: What do effective PLTs do? How do we universalize the remarkable things that some PLTs do so that all PLTs can benefit from and demonstrate this learning? In response, the LNS built a digital resource called *Snapshots of Effective Practice* that offers images from the field and expert opinion. It can be accessed at http://resources.curriculum.org/secretariat/snapshots/principal.html.

Innovation Leadership Matters

One of the most important characteristics employers see today and into the future is creativity. Creativity—not necessarily artistic creativity but the ability to find new ways and directions and possibly even to be innovative—is key (Conference Board of Canada, n.d.). Clearly we can't continue to teach from the front of the class, or even act as "guides on the side," if we are attempting to produce creativity and an "innovation mind-set." We can't lead our staff teams the same way either and expect them to be creative in the classroom. We must become innovative leaders.

Moving Us From Good to Great to Innovate

We believe that system leaders, principals, and teacher-leaders must think, behave, and model 21st-century learners' skills (see Chapter 4) if they are going to lead teachers and students to be creative and innovative. It is possible to make all students, K–12+, believe they can participate in the workplace and society and achieve their own personal potential. Leaders must model that belief for and with their teachers.

Is there a factor like *imagine-ability*? Where does it come from? How does one teach it or learn it? How do we create the right learning environment that fosters a culture of innovation for teachers, students, leaders, and community partners?

The answer, we think, is that teachers as well as aspiring and successful leaders at every level need to learn and to constantly employ *a structured, collaboratively planned approach* with their colleagues and students. Being intentionally (or purposefully) collaborative enhances the *ability to imagine* by eliminating many self-imposed barriers to open-minded thinking. Being collaborative may be the key factor or condition that enables students and teachers to see or to develop a broader sense of "what is possible" from the perspective of multiple collaborators, which in turn then permits every student to be confident enough to feel she or he can change the world. In short, we believe from our observations, from the literature, and from our experiences as teachers and leaders that there are two key dimensions that together enable innovation:

Structured Collaboration + Ability to Imagine = Innovation.

Now we have added a fourth dimension of leadership to those mentioned on page 44:

1. Know-ability
2. Mobilize-ability
3. Sustain-ability and
4. **Imagine-ability**

Combined, these are the actions that leaders must consider to act in an ever-changing system and school context as the **Innovation Leader.**

Grose and Freedman (in press) describe the impact of globalization and the resulting globally contextualized learning opportunities. They refer to structured Collaborative Inquiry as interdisciplinary inquiry-based approaches, and they speak to using collaborative technologies that support distributed learning—through which to build knowledge together. Grose (2014) refers to the Six *C* Skills:

1. Character Education
2. Citizenship
3. Communication
4. Critical Thinking and Problem Solving
5. Collaboration
6. Creativity and Imagination

This essentially reflects our above equation Structured Collaboration + Ability to Imagine = Innovation.

In this context, Grose and Freedman (in press) found not only that a focus on the Six Cs strengthens students' academic motivation and self-confidence but that a more fluid, innovative, and adaptive participatory learning culture for all emerged where

- **critical thinkers and problem solvers** use evidence and data, analyze, think critically and manage projects, solve problems, and make informed decisions using digital tools and resources;
- **collaborators** work together in all media and settings, in both face-to-face and virtual environments, to support personalized learning and to contribute to the learning of others;
- **communicators** make and share meaning and their point of view using a variety of digital tools with real and online audiences; and
- **creators and innovators** demonstrate creative thinking, construct knowledge, and develop innovative products and processes using technology.

These findings support a wide body of research grounded in the learning sciences.

What Matters Most in Leading Innovation?

We discuss six areas of **What Matters Most** in considering innovation as part of what leaders do to support increasing all students' *Pathway* opportunities to success:

1. Individualized *Pathways* and Programs
2. Collaborative-Lateral Leadership Structures

3. Creating a Culture of Innovation

4. Engaging Community Partners

5. Operational Underpinnings Make or Break Innovation

6. What Is Needed to Combat These Systemic Barriers

Individualized *Pathways* and Programs

By having put **FACES** on the data using focused approaches like Learning Walks and Talks and Data Wall building, system leaders, principals, and teachers now are beginning to recognize that all students are already on their own individualized *Pathways*, framed by the experiences and opportunities afforded them. Those leaders who are more innovative may try to think creatively about the breadth and depth of the experiences and opportunities they provide at their schools so as to ensure that *all* students can see themselves in the learning.

These leaders ensure **an inclusive, equitable learning community** (Guiding Principle 1) that recognizes the value of all postsecondary destinations. They problem solve the operational issues that create roadblocks, and they encourage risk taking in exploring new programming yet to be charted. They understand that by opening their doors to **a broad base of community partners** (Guiding Principle 3) through collaborative planning conversations, they will be able to enhance learning opportunities for their students and staff. What is interesting about **innovation leaders** at schools generating new ideas is that for these schools to be successful, there must also be someone who is equally innovative or "proactive" (Leithwood, 2013, p. 46) who can find ways to support the school-level innovations to create bridges to outside community partners. This concept of a need for a "system integrator," as we are naming the position, is also supported by the findings of the McKinsey report (Mourshed, Farrell, & Barton, 2012, p. 21).

While embracing an effective leadership framework recognizing Curriculum Knowledge as an important strand of each *Student's Pathway DNA*, the leader in our model also prioritizes the remaining two

DNA strands. The leader appreciates how explicit, authentic assessment and intentional instructional strategies support and facilitate the student Skill Development Strand and the corresponding Knowledge Application Strand.

In support of our thinking, Leithwood (2013) comments on the importance of balanced assessment and informed instruction saying that as much time as possible in the classroom must be academically engaged time and this often depends on the effective use of classroom management strategies by the teacher. The leader recognizes that out-of-the-classroom instruction demands no less effective use of time. As structured Collaborative Inquiry and Experiential Learning shift responsibility of self-assessment to the student, the **innovation leader** supports the teacher in constructing "safety nets" to "catch" students should they stumble in meeting these responsibilities. These safety nets are not punitive but rather are opportunities to pause, regroup, examine gaps in skills, and then develop plans to close those gaps.

Collaborative-Lateral Leadership Structures

Jeremy Rifkin calls for a distributed, collaborative-lateral, peer-to-peer school community where silos and teacher isolation are removed to embrace a more multidisciplinary, diverse, problem-based approach with multiple solutions. He believes "the primary mission of education is to allow our young people to take responsibility to collaborate in larger communities to serve the better good of the community" (personal communication, November 15, 2012).

Leadership needs to be collaborative and lateral, which is not the same as delegating responsibilities. Collaborative-lateral leadership is far more dynamic and supportive. It implies collective responsibility for all learning and all learners. Teacher isolation is a huge barrier to moving forward. Good leaders build collaborative-lateral learning structures where teachers co-learn, co-teach, mentor, coach, and engage in meaningful professional conversations that are personalized to the improvement of their individual practice.

In Finland, teachers work collaboratively with other teachers and their principals. Time is built into the school day for planning across subjects and content areas and for ongoing professional conversations. Principals are required to have instructional teaching time. This keeps them up-to-date on the latest instructional practices and technologies. It is evident in Finland that one of the most valued qualities and skills is innovation. This is reflected in the language of the school—there is no such thing as a problem as an entity unto itself. A problem is something that presents itself and requires a solution. Innovative approaches are then encouraged with the understanding that it might take many attempts and iterations to get to the most appropriate solution.

For example, in one of his daily lessons, the principal presented the class with a ruler. Through a series of prompts using a Collaborative Inquiry learning model (see Chapter 6), he posed thoughtful questions: "What is this?" How do we use it?" "How might we use it?" This provoked thinking on the part of *all* students. Conversations emerged, and no "one right answer" was entertained. Thus, the principal ensured that he had not only engaged the students in conversation and argument but also captured everyone's thinking in a risk-free, solution-focused environment.

Creating a Culture of Innovation

Creativity and problem solving, balanced with an ability and willingness to take informed risks and then to evaluate the outcomes and process, matter. By opening the doors of classrooms and creating collaborative experiences, the role of teacher shifts to activator and evaluator of learning (Hattie, 2012) and the agent of change, not the "guide on the side" who stands back and waits. Good instructional leaders support this stance and know what it takes to encourage this in classrooms. Rifkin says "we must manage the environment to break open virtual space [to become] global classrooms." He calls for "leveraging service learning and moving more experiences out into the community" (personal communication, November 15, 2012).

We believe that to do this successfully, leaders and community partners need to have the system structures and operational pieces in place to support learning in new structured contexts. While there are increased risks associated with moving student learning outside of the classroom, these should not be perceived as barriers. Keeping student safety and accountability in the forefront of robust programming must be critical considerations to extend student learning beyond the walls of the classroom.

The old adage applies: "Practice what you preach." Students need to see the very qualities and skills of *The Literate Graduate* (that we determine to be vital for them) modeled by our teachers and administrators. Whatever we want to see as *The Literate Graduate* outcomes—innovation, creativity, problem solving, teamwork, entrepreneurship, excitement for the process and for the end result—also needs to be what we see embedded in our teacher and leadership expectations, assessments, and Professional Learning programs.

We are not offering a review of the literature concerning creativity and innovation in this text; we are presenting the view that an "innovation mind-set"—trying something new that responds to the relevant data sets available within the school and community and is then supported by ongoing Collaborative Inquiry—is a valid option for good and great leaders who want to innovate.

There have been countless new ideas and creative directions taken by people who have not used any analysis to set their course, and whose outcomes therefore have been erratic—some good, most not so good. Again, rather than list the negative, we present only a potentially positive way forward toward what we call the Recalculated Route. Similar to Thomas Edison and other great inventors, the leaders' world is one of multiple trials, but trials where good thinking is applied first, where intense observation and measurement are attached to every stage, and where, when the trial has proven successful, the leaders know why. That is, **innovation leaders** constantly monitor, deeply understand the parameters of the innovation, and Recalculate the Route, thereby increasing the likelihood of success

(A. Scott, personal communication, November 19, 2013). But when proven unsuccessful, innovation leaders also know why. Innovation leaders learn from every action, enhance all innovations through Recalculation, and focus on the lessons learned for the future (A. Scott, personal communication, November 19, 2013).

Engaging Community Partners

A story is perhaps most illustrative of this area. Dave Chaplin taught in the Catholic District School Board of Eastern Ontario for 12 years before becoming vice principal. He began a specialized program at St. John Catholic High School for hard-to-serve students that grew so rapidly it was moved to a church basement off campus, then again into a vacant school, and added several teachers. Chaplin became principal of St. Luke Catholic High School where the successful program was later housed and provided hands-on, project-driven learning experiences that allowed students to develop hospitality, trade, and technology skills. What started as one class of 16 students grew in the third year to over 100 students. What was the secret to this success?

The students and community literally built the new school buildings. Because of community partnerships, the highly engaged students created "legacies": built stone walls, designed a 900-square-foot building for construction work, and built classroom cupboards and added new millwork. Each year classes had a project of which to be proud. This school was established using various community partnerships— for example, with RONA, Patterson Electric, and the St. Lawrence Parks Commission—all of whom played a role in developing programming that changed students' lives. The community partners continue to provide not only materials but important professional resources and advice for the extended classrooms. The students have had remarkable success as a result of the impact of these solid community partnerships. Students enter high school academically and socially unsuccessful and leave as confident and skilled graduates, ready for employment or post-secondary training.

The success story is due to Chaplin's leadership. He articulates a clear vision and demonstrates determination that all students can and will be successful. His hands-on, student-focused approach to build a caring community and a safe school environment in which students achieve personally and academically is exemplary. It is a place where student achievement is recognized because of parental and community involvement. Chaplin's leadership is an excellent example of an innovative response to a real student disengagement problem and is sustainable and continues to be successful.

Can this type of leadership exist at the school level without also existing somewhere at the system level? Not likely. Is it a demonstration of great leadership skill at the system level to recognize there is a problem that can be solved by a very innovative leader and a leadership team who are provided with the resources required. Our wonder is whether this leadership can be replicated in large numbers across a system and across a nation.

There are many pockets of excellence like this school where skilled teachers and open-minded leaders bring core content areas to life through Experiential Learning for high school students. It can be done on a large scale if intentional. Among PENCIL principals in New York City (NYC), who worked with business volunteers on increasing student engagement, 90% agreed that partnership activities boosted student engagement, and nearly 7 out of 10 saw improved academic performance in students who consistently participated in partnership activities (Haberman, 2013). NYC is making big investments in this model, to which we ascribe, that ensures college and *Career Readiness* and community partners are involved at every level. Schools are partnered with businesses such as P-Tech and IBM, Aviation High School, and JetBlue Airways, among others, that are creating access to on-the-job-training—led by leaders who inspire teachers to move out of their comfort zones so that students can create, develop, and implement new ideas with no barriers to what *is* possible.

Rhetorically we ask: Does this model of community/corporate participation mean a "sellout" to corporate need by public education? Or is it a one-off opportunity for specific learning and *Student Pathway DNA* needs to be satisfied, while at the same time providing a synergistic education/workforce development project to occur within the public education context? Is it a win-win model? Might it be replicated with other industries given the "will" to initiate new projects and to deal with the political fallout from public resources being applied to a limited number of seats available, and who decides who gets a seat?

We would suggest that the success of these models is based upon *a structured, collaboratively planned approach*. In the beginning stages of collaborative discussions, it will become apparent that education and business leaders may have very different languages for similar thoughts, but as they work together, they can come to express the same purpose. It is generally argued and very often agreed that we need better-prepared graduates and employees, with demonstrated skills, specific qualities, and the focused preparation needed to support a thriving economy. Our Innovation Leadership Prism (Figure 2.3) and Appendix B illustrate how recognition of the critical nature of community partnerships needs to be at every level of the system and school effectiveness work.

Figure 2.3 is a graphic of the Innovation Leadership Prism showing the relationships necessary at every level. The critical constant in our work and writing, we believe, is the community partnership role in each prism piece, one that we do not see as the constant in any research we have investigated.

In Appendix B, each of the prism sections is broken out for a detailed discussion of the collaborative and **innovation leadership** skills needed at every level to produce a new innovative program with community involvement.

As the metaphor of prism lenses suggests, only by working "together," across sectors, can we focus all the lenses—one at a time in succession—and then view the resulting accomplishment that is making a positive difference for all students. It is happening in pockets of

FIGURE 2.3

Innovation Leadership Prism

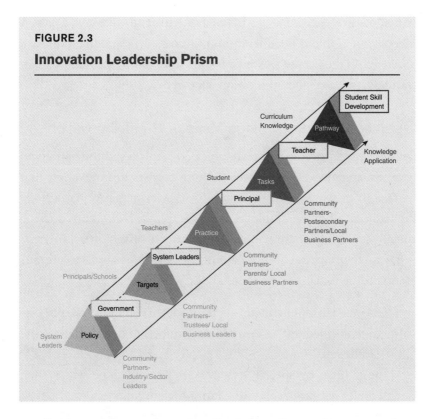

excellent practice as we have described. As authors, what we are advocating for in Recalculating the Route includes

- a refreshed mind-set—one that reaches out to and draws in community partners;
- consistent practices across all schools to ensure equitable access to partnerships where students' skills are career and college ready;
- Experiential Learning through inquiry (Chapter 6) as a required component of the curriculum delivery where students experience real-world problems, explore multiple solutions, and experience what it takes to be job ready upon graduation; and
- leaders with open mind-sets to cultures of learning that honor risk taking and innovation.

Innovation leaders essentially require the organization to listen to ideas, build on the innovations brought forward by staff members, and allow everyone to share his or her expertise with colleagues. A school system that is filled with innovation leaders working to make a difference in the lives of all students they serve is unstoppable (William Gartland, personal communication, October 27, 2013).

Operational Underpinnings Make or Break Innovation

Our text would not be complete unless we considered the barriers to what we are advocating. What are those barriers to innovation that we face in many Western societies? Two key examples of barriers are the tradition of union/employee versus employer dichotomy, and the equally damaging lack of political will. Both are driven by self-interest. What are the consequences of permitting these two barriers to prevail?

According to recent popular analyses, jobs have

- migrated to lower-cost jurisdictions within countries and offshore,
- gone unfilled due to insufficient numbers of qualified domestic candidates,
- been filled by special visa workers from offshore where such employees have been trained in sufficient numbers, and
- produced a continuous reduction in the standard of living for unskilled workers, with what is seen as an unsettling decline in the national economic picture.

Postsecondary-workplace solutions need to scale up and work against these present alarming barriers to Recalculating the Route. How do we take successful trial practices and scale them to serve millions? What are the operational considerations of which leaders need to be cognizant, and then responsive?

In a Recalculated Route, all institutions need to work together, more frequently and more efficiently than in the past, to provide the best conditions for learning and increased student achievement. This shift to a collective responsibility will require government and societal incentives in school systems where this has not been the collective practice. This critical interconnectedness is shown through the two-way arrows on the *Pathways to Career Readiness Frame: Finding TrueNorth* (Figure 1.1).

To support our position, the Royal Commission on Learning (1994) states, "If school-level integration of services and resources is to be achieved, changes will have to be made in the way services are funded, in who undertakes co-ordination of efforts between the school and the community" (p. 148).

Current challenges to this supposition are identified in the McKinsey report (Mourshed et al., 2012) as

- constraints on the resources of education providers,
- insufficient opportunities to provide youth with hands-on Experiential Learning,
- hesitancy of employers to invest in training, and
- lack of integration among all stakeholders.

What Is Needed to Combat These Systemic Barriers?

Innovative leaders—principals and system leaders at every level—find the human and material resources to support the classroom teachers' focus on what should be their top priority: meaningful, authentic student learning in every classroom.

Our survey participants identified practical, high-yield conditions that contribute to their successful pursuit of effective programming and strategies (see Figure 2.4). They recognize that attending to these high-impact conditions requires creativity, problem solving, and innovative approaches to operational decisions, such as

- a focused strategy for building alliances with other partners and agencies who can work with schools;
- a commitment to ongoing Professional Learning for teachers and leaders together—particularly in the area of technologies, Collaborative Inquiry, and Experiential Learning;
- embedded time for teachers to plan collaboratively; and
- flexibility in programming, timetables, and schedules.

Breaking Barriers

What does it take as an innovative, proactive leader to remove the systemic barriers identified by Mourshed et al. (2012) so that conditions teachers need and identify can flourish? We have identified three areas as our work to break the barriers: Focus—Align—Feedback. They have

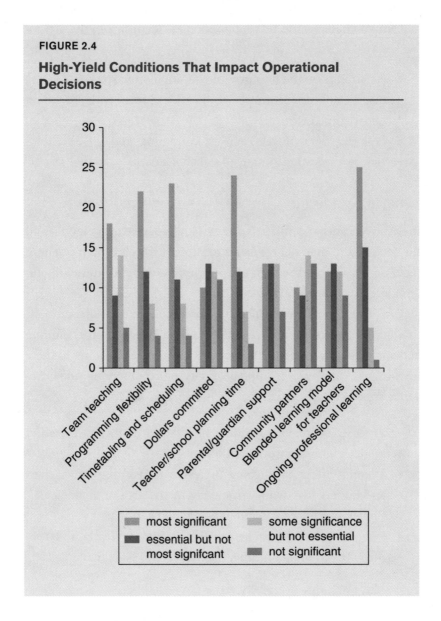

FIGURE 2.4

High-Yield Conditions That Impact Operational Decisions

been discussed in a global education study titled *Six Drivers of Student Success* (Battelle for Kids, 2012). They are discussed in greater detail here:

Focus

Systems and schools must focus their efforts on a singular priority or at the very least on a very small number of priorities in order to do this challenging work of increasing all students' achievement. This entails

- recognizing that structure drives behavior—so breaking down silos and walls between classrooms, between schools, and between elementary and secondary panels as a first step in embracing structured Collaborative Inquiry and Experiential Learning stances (see Chapter 6);
- taking time to explore learning possibilities beyond the four walls of the school; and
- establishing an environment focused on learning that is safe enough to look for new ways of doing things.

Align

After systems and schools have identified a priority, then measured steps must be taken to ensure the alignment of the priority. This includes

- creating the narrative or story line to get focused on the work and align it at every level;
- getting the balance right between multiple efforts and coherence as one of the main tasks of leaders; and
- explaining to everyone in the organization what the components of improvement are and how they fit together.

Feedback

Giving and getting descriptive feedback is critical to our growth and improvement as students, teachers, and leaders. Tasks demand

- ensuring that the feedback loops for students, teachers, and leaders are frequent, constructive, detailed, and insightful to support innovative thinking; and

- embracing the moral purpose issues to ensure that not only teachers receive feedback but policymakers and bureaucrats who, for example, do not administer standards-based, criterion-referenced assessments, also get feedback to move ahead as they have in New York City, Ontario, and Australia.

Descriptive Feedback is critical to move beyond measuring the "what" of learning to assessing the "how" of knowledge acquisition by each learner.

Leaders at every level must focus, align, and "give and get" feedback on the authentic, relevant learning provided through various *Pathways* to *imagine*, to believe in, and to measure what students can and will contribute to society. As Fullan (2014) says, we need to stop depending on Band-Aid remedies (to improvement) and instead focus on changing the culture itself (so learning is the work). And here, principals (working with other leaders and community partners) have a key role to play.

Arguably, public education is facing critical challenges and a shaky future. Can public education continue to be underfunded, as many suggest, or continue to operate in vertical silos without respect for the future economics of nations and future citizens' success? Can the stakeholders in public education make the necessary hard decisions on a large scale to break down the barriers and drive ahead for the future benefit of all students? Or are only small compromised forward steps acceptable to elected officials and to the unions?

Can this model be one that all leaders work toward? Can we bring business and other teams of professional unionized labor to our planning tables to build a genuine focus on "our customers" and build the programs our students need to become *Literate Graduates* and therefore successful citizens? Can we make hard decisions regarding public spending that coordinate the learning across elements of education, higher education, and workplace training?

Many educational leaders, politicians, and business forums are pressing in different ways to move ahead in a coordinated fashion. Governor Mike Pence of Indiana recently created a new body to coordinate the work and spending of the State Board of Education and 11 workplace councils across the state. Many Australian states link primary, secondary, college, and university policies with training under a department of education and training. The Canadian Council of Chief Executives recently called for better integration of the spending policies both to ensure the future of a skilled workforce supply for businesses and to ensure future jobs for students.

As we consider the transition from traditional to **innovation leadership** styles (see Appendix A), we look for examples to provide clarity. The following narrative demonstrates that there are those innovation leaders who have seen a need and will stop at nothing to make their dreams and solutions work on behalf of students. This is a story worth telling, one in which an innovative individual has made a major difference in education in his country by driving ahead with his vision of engaging community partners to increase all students' learning and opportunities.

From GOOD to GREAT to
INNOVATE

Taddy Blecher was not a "great student"; however, with time, dogged determination, and encouragement from his family to continue his studies to become an actuary through the international exams of the Institute of Actuaries out of the United Kingdom, and supported by his daily practice of Transcendental Meditation (TM), he graduated as an actuary in South Africa, achieving the highest marks in the country in his university honors and winning a gold medal for top qualifier and in record time too. Just when he could have become personally successful and wealthy anywhere in the world, he turned down the best job offers his international consulting firm could make, and five other international offers received from three continents.

Why? He looked around at the young people in South Africa and decided he wanted to make a difference. Taddy became focused on the needs of

(Continued)

disadvantaged Black youth. He became a pioneer of the free university movement in South Africa. He created a university model that enables poor Black students to acquire a free, high-quality, professional education and simultaneously be employed by the university itself to gain practical experience and an income.

Taddy's story is one of innovation, where, as hero, he truly learns and demonstrates *knowledge-ability*, exemplifies *mobilize-ability*, ensures *sustain-ability*, and is a master of solution-creating *imagine-ability*.

When Taddy first became engaged in finding solutions to South Africa's problem of youth unemployment, he went back to teaching TM in schools with his colleagues in the Community and Individual Development Association (known as CIDA). Using his business analysis skills, he learned with others about teaching and learning. When he began to imagine CIDA City Campus, as the first free university in South Africa, he reached out collaboratively to his previous business partners and the community for advice, information, and resources.

He started with data as his research indicated that education is one of the main avenues through which the poor can enter the labor market in South Africa. However, the low quality of education that is available in previously disadvantaged communities limits the upward mobility of these individuals. Taddy created a free university model based on a "learn and earn" methodology, whereby students have to contribute to running and maintaining the university while completing their studies. They also commit to teaching young people in their home villages during their holidays (*knowledge-ability*). Once they have graduated and secured employment, they pay for the university costs of another student who will follow in their footsteps (*sustain-ability*).

Taddy founded South Africa's first free university, CIDA City Campus, in 2000. To maintain a low-cost and sustainable model, Taddy created the CIDA Empowerment Fund by tapping into a local and international pool of donors. This $19 million (U.S.) education fund is 100% reinvested in the advancement and expansion of the model. Despite its success, it became imperative for Taddy to progress from the CIDA higher education model to one that placed greater emphasis on students taking greater responsibility for unlocking their full human potential. Therefore, Taddy created the Maharishi Institute in

2007, which adds consciousness-based, character education to his "learn and earn" methodology, thereby enabling students to focus on their development as human beings, in addition to their professional training (*mobilize-ability*).

Thanks to this model, over 5,500 graduates, to date, have gone on to claim promising jobs in the business field. Besides CIDA City Campus and the Maharishi Institute, Taddy has already helped to found at least five other free colleges and universities in South Africa. More than 600,000 young South Africans in high schools have been educated in life skills and general business courses through the students at these higher education institutions. Taddy's academic focus has now extended beyond business training as he has opened a university inside a nature reserve to apply the "learn and earn" methodology to the natural sciences field (Ezemvelo Eco-Campus), a powerful example of our Experiential Learning approach (see Chapter 6). In the future, Taddy plans to spread the model throughout Africa, and is currently helping similar models grow in other countries in Africa and Asia.

One particularly revealing anecdote he mentioned (personal communication, November 15, 2008) concerned the late acquisition and subsequent arrival of the personal computers and keyboards for his first CIDA City Campus class. He did not have the computers that he had promised all his students; however, he was able to photocopy one keyboard and create a touch-typing class using paper keyboards to which the students provided rhythms and songs for cadence. Interestingly, when the real keyboards and computers eventually arrived, the students were able to transfer their skills readily and accurately type at 30 words a minute, a professional typing speed—a real example of *imagine-ability* and *mobilize-ability*. Operational challenges can be overcome!

Source: Adapted by J. Coutts, as published on Ashoka–Innovators for the Public (http://ashoka.org).

Taddy Blecher's actions, character, and perseverance demonstrate that we all have a stake in implementing what it takes to be an **innovation leader.** Our actions must always relate back to closing the gap to raise the bar (A. Hargreaves, personal communication, December 3, 2012) to increase all students' achievement—our moral purpose as leaders. So let's get to work and lead with the belief that each student can and will change our world—for the better, as we discuss in Chapter 3, "All FACES Matter!"

STEPS TO STUDENTS' SUCCESS

1. Be knowledgeable about what works.

2. Mobilize staff around the singular goal of increased achievement at every level.

3. Promote knowledgeable leaders who will continue to sustain improvement work.

4. Imagine what is possible, be passionate, be open-minded, and take action.

5. Focus a concrete strategic plan on *all* students achieving.

6. Align student achievement work at the system, school, and classroom levels.

7. Give and get feedback daily from internal and external partners.

8. Build intentional, mutually beneficial community alliances.

9. Establish trust as an operating norm, and model appreciation.

10. Model the 21st-century qualities you aspire to for your staff and students.

Reflective Pause by Ken Leithwood

This chapter provides much food for thought. As any piece that is successful in stimulating us to think outside the box, this chapter not only presents a compelling Recalculation to our current way of doing school; it also prompts readers to consider their own problem solving and creativity—to be innovative, as leaders are encouraged to be by the chapter. My own reading of the chapter prompted me especially to consider the nature and size of several challenges even the best of our current schools and systems face in moving from good to great to innovative.

1. The Challenge of School Leaders Contributing to Substantial Instructional Improvement

This is a patently obvious challenge, a challenge painfully understood by almost all practicing school leaders and so a good place to begin. Historically, the principalship has been described as hectic and fast paced, with those in the role making about 150 decisions in the course of a typical day. Now add in the complexities associated with the much greater demands for accountability and related reporting requirements that have arisen over the past decade.

To date, a small but determined percentage of principals are able to focus substantial efforts on instructional improvement. However, if large-scale change is to be successful, it has to be doable by most members of the organization, not the most talented or driven. Some might offer a "distributed leadership" solution to this challenge. While this lens offers us a more comprehensive picture of the nature and sources of leadership in schools, it does leave principals to manage the same set of operational matters that have always consumed so much of their attention. Both the structures within which principals work and their job descriptions will need to change if increasing all students' achievement is ever to be seriously achieved. However, "in the final analysis, whether a principal or a director of education, leaders have responsibility for improving student learning" (Leithwood as quoted in Zegarac, 2012, p. 6).

This will need to be the discussion and decision making behind the **structured, collaboratively planned approach** as put forward by the authors.

2. The Challenge of Collaborative Work That Improves Student Learning

This chapter encourages collaboration across most levels of the school system writ large.

If collaborative practice is to stand much chance of even approximating the ambitious outcomes used in its justification, both "social loafing" (Dobelli, 2013, pp. 99–100) and "groupthink" (Dobelli, 2013, p. 100) will need to be at the forefront of the challenges surfaced when any team or group begins its work. Given that teacher and school planning time were reported to be one of the high-yield conditions impacting operational decisions, we need to pay explicit attention to this. Without explicit attention to this by group leaders, most group work will absorb significant amounts of time no one in schools can afford to squander and produce much more heat than light. Thus, "a principal today needs very solid team building skills—skills that build teacher capacity to work together collaboratively" (Leithwood as quoted in Zegarac, 2012, p. 4).

3. The Challenge of Identifying a "Great" School System

I don't actually think there is a "great" school system if improved student learning is the metric by which we judge such things. Such a designation can only be made using highly selective data sets.

The lesson here is that any claims about what works on a large scale needs to be assessed and examined within the context in which it worked. Any large-scale change strategy, using a *Pathways* lens as the authors support, might be just fine as long as those in the trenches get adequate support for their work and there is a mechanism in place, on a large scale, for tracking progress. "So I think leadership right now is more about taking control over improving your own practices, but in a larger context. Along with this is a sense of responsibility not only for the students in your school but also for the improvement of all the children and youth in your district, and in the province [state or nation] as well. This means expanding our horizons. That, I think, is what the future is about" (Leithwood as quoted in Zegarac, 2012, p. 22).

4. The Challenge of Knowing You Are Making a Difference

The authors remind us that there are currently relatively few large-scale things about which to conduct robust research (districts, states, provinces, countries) using a *Pathways* lens, so meeting the normal canons of good science becomes virtually impossible.

We are left with what is euphemistically called in medical research "clinical evidence" (evidence based on small, unrepresentative samples with no baseline measures and no controls for competing explanations). And this means great uncertainty about what works on a large scale.

As the chapter acknowledges, it cannot be only or largely that kind of evidence that is used to move schools from "great" to "innovative," or we will be left with debilitating uncertainties about even what works on a small scale. Twenty-first-century schooling must certainly aspire to innovation but not for its own sake and not at the expense of ignoring what is, by now, a robust body of empirical evidence about many aspects of teaching and learning. "I think innovation really does depend on people feeling a strong sense of both autonomy and responsibility for the mission, and for devising ways to accomplish the mission, and a sense of shared ownership in the purposes that are going to be accomplished" (Leithwood as quoted in Zegarac, 2012, p. 19).

"What I think we want our leaders and teachers to be doing is to have a careful understanding of the best evidence in the field informing their practice, and using that as the starting point for working out what practice might look like in their own schools and classrooms" (Leithwood as quoted in Zegarac, 2012, p. 11).

If most educators actually implemented what we know now from robust evidence, in a locally sensible manner, the current performance of students would be dramatically better in even "great" schools and school systems.

In conclusion, "Initiative taking is the supreme indicator of this constellation of qualities [optimism, resilience, and efficacy]. I do think that many of our school and district environments are risk-averse. Taking initiative in school and district contexts is not something a lot of people are prepared to do. So if you see someone stepping out in front of the band, advocating for something dramatically new to take place, you're probably looking at someone with a lot of psychological resources. Promote them quickly before they leave and go to some other system!" (Leithwood as quoted in Zegarac, 2012, p. 15).

About Ken Leithwood, PhD

Ken Leithwood is Professor Emeritus at Ontario Institute for Studies in Education of the University of Toronto and advisor to the Leadership Development Branch of Ontario's Ministry of Education. His research and writing is about school leadership, educational policy, and organizational change. He has published extensively on these topics. For example, he is the senior editor of both the first and second *International Handbooks of Educational Leadership and Administration* (Kluwer, 1996, 2003). His most recent books include *Linking Leadership to Student Learning* (Jossey-Bass, 2012), *Leading School Turnaround* (Jossey-Bass, 2010), *Distributed Leadership According to the Evidence* (Routledge, 2009), *Leading With Teacher Emotions in Mind* (Corwin, 2008), *Making Schools Smarter* (3rd ed., Corwin, 2006), and *Teaching for Deep Understanding* (Corwin, 2006). With colleagues, he has recently completed one of the largest studies of its kind about how state-, district-, and school-level leadership influences student learning. Professor Leithwood is the recipient of the University of Toronto's inaugural Impact on Public Policy Award, the American Educational Research Association's 2011 Outstanding Leadership Researcher Award, and the 2012 Roald F. Campbell Lifetime Achievement Award from the University Council for Educational Administration. He is a Fellow of the Royal Society of Canada.

ALL FACES MATTER!

Relentless Pursuit to
Excellence and Achievement Matters!

I n "shifting" from the Industrial Age to the Knowledge Age (and arguably to what is anticipated to be the Innovation Age), it is becoming increasingly evident that "to have expert innovative knowledge workers, every country needs an education system that produces them, thus education becomes the key to economic survival in the 21st Century" (Trilling & Fadel, 2009, p. 6). While each of these shifts has been precipitated by social and economic drivers that together have powered change, there has also been a required and "forced" corresponding "up-shift" or very real change in perceptions, attitudes, and acceptances throughout the broader community. The necessary changes have not always been accepted equally or rapidly by all community sectors, with some leading, some following, and some never accepting the new elements.

1. How are your shared beliefs and understandings constructed, shared, and acted upon using *a structured, collaboratively planned approach*?

2. How does your **comprehensive communication plan** represent the diversity of the stakeholders?

3. What evidence of "up- shifts" do you see happening in your classrooms, schools, and system planning tables?

4. Does the language used in your classrooms, schools, and system planning tables reflect the values you are trying to strengthen?

5. How are you building trust within your classroom, school, and systems?

6. To what extent are students involved in co-constructing their learning?

7. To what extent are students involved in decisions regarding programs and courses offered?

8. To what extent are students involved in the operational decisions governing the classroom, school, and system?

9. Who are the **FACES** at your planning tables?

10. What is your definition of excellence and achievement? How do you measure success?

Based on experience, reviewing data and information supplied to us, and surveying popular news and announcements in the media, what we propose—a Recalculated Route to *Pathways to Career Readiness* for our 21st-century knowledge worker, *The Literate Graduate*—also requires a significant "up-shift" or change in mindset. The rationale underlying **FACES** is to constantly use assessment data to inform, personalize, and drive differentiated instructional practices, ultimately resulting in *The Literate Graduate*. We show in Chapter 1, in our discussion of *Student Pathway DNA*, that **skilled teachers** depend on many forms of individual student assessment to drive differentiated Experiential Learning. We show that these teachers need significant contacts within the community to access authentic, relevant, and substantially challenging learning opportunities for their students. We posit here, then, that in addition to skilled teachers, leadership teams, and elected officials, our community partners matter.

Currently, system effectiveness frameworks, such as the 14 Parameters (Sharratt & Fullan, 2009, 2012), are utilized by educational organizations to capture a flow of process and accountability, within their schools, districts, and systems. Substantive organizational achievements are noted where there is alignment between the system plan and individual school plans. Working toward specific targets, using high-impact strategies, ensures that everyone is moving forward toward the same goal. To have such a framework in place would be an indication, for many, of a high-performing school system. The question is—is this enough to ensure innovation at all levels? How do we know if we have the right targets and the right strategies if community partners are not represented at the planning tables? What are the other possibilities yet to be considered? What conversations do we need to have?

Community Partners Matter!

Community partners bring their own set of resources to the planning table. They keep us abreast of the latest trends, technologies, and skill sets required by *The Literate Graduate*. A well-functioning partnership is collaborative, a "win-win" for all. In other words, it is not about "What can you do for me?" but about "What can we do more effectively together?" It is not about yielding authority or control of the stakeholder group represented. It is about respecting the expertise of each stakeholder and seeing where there is alignment, common ground, and synergy. These partnerships are not top-down relationships. For example, students, and rightly so, are now self-emerging as not only users but teachers of technology devices. This has created a bottom-up push, compelling postsecondary and workplace partners to respond.

The McKinsey report (Mourshed, Farrell, & Barton, 2012) found that the most innovative and effective programs in the world had two common elements between the education providers and the employers (community partners). They could both

1. **"ACTIVELY STEP** into one another's world" (Mourshed et al., 2012, p. 20), and

> 2. work **COLLABORATIVELY** with their students **EARLY** and **OFTEN**.

Community partners are critical stakeholders in attaining our educational outcomes. All require their own supports, resources, and conversations to support their own input to "up-shift" or change their collective mind-sets. There is no denying the complexity of bringing so many stakeholders to the planning table. We can choose not to ask or invite them, but by not doing so, we will forever lose the impactful opportunities these stakeholders have to offer *The Literate Graduate*, and we will lose the ongoing feedback this involvement will give to the Curriculum Knowledge Strand and to the Knowledge Application Strand—making both much stronger. Or worse yet, we as educators will quickly lose our momentum or any leadership power we may wish to have in mapping our way forward.

The *Pathways to Career Readiness Frame—Finding TrueNorth* (Figure 1.1, p. 12), supported by the Innovation Leadership Prism (Figure 2.3, p. 65), further defines community partners and the roles they have to play in Recalculating the Route. Each prism segment is represented by the stakeholders: leadership, skilled teachers, and community partners. The lenses of the prism demonstrate, from policy through *Pathways*, that only by collaborating can we make a difference for *all* students. To achieve *a structured, collaboratively planned approach*, the following components need to be in place:

1. **Shared beliefs and understandings**—supported by comprehensive data sets, clear targets, and intentional assessment and instructional approaches framed by a strategic plan reflective of stakeholders' diversity to know every learner (Parameter 1, Sharratt & Fullan, 2009, 2012);

2. **An inclusive, equitable learning community**—in which every student not only sees but has access to an individualized *Pathway*, supported by **a broad base of community partners**; and

3. **A culture of innovation and mutual respect**—where new approaches are welcomed with processes in place to enable everyone to be responsive and nimble enough to reset the course as needed.

Shared Beliefs and Understandings

We know from our research of the 14 Parameters (Sharratt & Fullan, 2009, 2012) that educational system coherence can be achieved if we *collectively have an end in mind in each of the 14 areas.*

The 14 Parameters to Align, Focus, and Increase System and School Improvement

1. Shared Beliefs and Understandings
2. Embedded Instructional Coaches
3. Large Blocks of Time Focused on High-Impact Assessment and Instruction
4. Principal as Lead Learner
5. Early and Ongoing Intervention
6. Case Management Approach
7. Focused Professional Learning at Staff Meetings
8. In-School Grade/Subject Meetings to Moderate Student Work
9. Book Rooms of Leveled Texts, Varied Media, and Resources
10. Allocation of System and School Budgets for Literacy Instruction and Resources
11. Collaborative Inquiry Focused on Data to Make Intentional Decisions
12. Parental and Community Involvement
13. Cross-Curricular Literacy Connections
14. Shared Responsibility and Accountability

Source: Sharratt & Fullan (2009, 2012).

In other words, as we state in Parameter 1, it is foundational that teachers and leaders in schools believe and take action to demonstrate that they share a belief and understanding that

- *all* students can achieve high standards, given time and "just in time" support;

- all teachers can teach to high standards given the right assistance;
- high expectations and early and ongoing intervention are essential; and
- all teachers need to be able to articulate what they teach and why they teach the way they do (adapted from Hill & Crévola, 1999).

We defined these as quintessential dimensions of Parameter 1 in *Realization* (Sharratt & Fullan, 2009) and *Putting FACES on the Data* (Sharratt & Fullan, 2012) as we know that system and school improvement does not happen unless there are shared beliefs and understandings as the underpinning for moving forward. Strategic leaders, from the members of the elected board to the chief superintendent and assistant superintendents, "walk this talk" and stay the course in modeling these four beliefs, even when things are chaotic in their schools and system.

From our research, we noted that school leaders clearly understood and, most importantly, lived the shared beliefs and understandings (Parameter 1) in the design of their improvement plans. School teams did constant self-evaluation, striving to align beliefs and understandings between the principal and the leadership team who worked with all staff to model and make beliefs come alive. This involved *accountable talk* and corresponding action, with each other and with teachers, in an ongoing way—during the school day. System and "school leaders did not let the 'distracters' divert their energies and focus—they stayed the course toward all students' improvement—holding their nerve until improvement results were realized—no matter what!" (Sharratt & Fullan, 2012, p. 14).

The same proposition—*collaboratively having an end in mind*—holds true when drawing upon the collective knowledge and skills from **a broad base of community partners**, our Guiding Principle 3.

To do so, we need to

- engage strategic leaders from all stakeholder groups who will "walk the talk" with a deep understanding of and commitment to *Pathways to Career Readiness*;
- ensure that systems, schools, and community partner leaders understand and live the shared beliefs and understandings;

- support accountable talk and corresponding action in an ongoing way;
- ensure all stakeholders stay the course; and
- engage stakeholders in constant self-evaluation to ensure alignment of practice with Parameter 1 and its four dimensions of the beliefs and understandings.

Finding Common Ground

By ACTIVELY STEPPING into another's world, we start to get a sense of the values and motivations held by each stakeholder. Finding the common ground, rather than living in parallel universes, is the first step in establishing clarity to the shared beliefs and understandings that will frame a Recalculated Route. Ultimately, all stakeholders need to be compelled forward by the **FACE** of each student and the shared beliefs and understandings that frame the collective purpose and vision. For example,

- **Educators**—want to know that they are making a difference in students' lives by examining students' thinking and challenging their perceptions;
- **Parents/Guardians**—want the best possible outcomes for their children. They want them to have skills, experiences, and opportunities that enable them to be successful for life;
- **Community Partners**—want a skilled workforce that can bring innovative approaches to their businesses and institutions; and
- **Students**—want multiple choices and a voice in responding to social issues and global concerns.

On the surface, these may seem like diverse or competing interests, but central to all are the *students*, the individual **FACES** of our future. We *all* have a role, through *a structured, collaboratively planned approach*, in determining and acting on

- how we get them there,
- how we collectively support them on their journey,

- how we nurture and sustain them to be the best they can be, and
- how we take feedback from their achievements, at every stage, to make the collaboratively planned process even better.

Creating the Mind-Set "Up-Shift"

*A **structured, collaboratively planned approach*** to developing shared beliefs and understandings seems a simple enough "bill to fill." However, as educators, we know that any change is complex and messy. Between elementary and high school panels, there are already differences given variances in size of student/staff populations, operational complexity, and subject and institutional silos. Add to this the dimension of additional stakeholders, and the task may seem insurmountable.

> "People ask us why we invest so much to develop the skills of our people," a Siemens executive explained. "I ask them instead, 'How much is it going to cost you to not have skilled workers?'"
>
> Mourshed et al., 2012, p. 65.

Finding TrueNorth on the Recalculated Route requires an "up-shift," a new mind-set where all stakeholders see themselves as having a responsibility to excellence and increased student achievement. Educators are not the only ones with a responsibility or mandate to promote learning. Community partners, postsecondary partners, and parents/guardians also share in this responsibility. The current disconnect between education and work opportunity serves as a reminder that the cost of not sharing in this collective responsibility is too high.

This new mind-set also requires that we clarify what is meant by "excellence" and "achievement." We need to be clear about what we are pursuing. Is it measured performance against tabled scores, dropout rates, or percentage grades, or is it a much more holistic picture of the learner, capturing the social-emotional capacity of the student along with the academic achievements, or perhaps a combination of both? These are important questions that must be addressed to arrive at the shared beliefs and understandings that will frame the foundation for achievement and excellence.

In Ontario, in the old paradigm, prior to the launch of the Student Success Strategy in the early 2000s, it was not uncommon to hear high schools measure their success by

- the number of student graduates obtaining an 80-plus average,
- the number of graduates going on to attend a university,
- the number of clubs and sports teams offered in the school, and
- the number of other specialized programs the school provided.

This was occurring against the provincial backdrop of

- declining graduation rates,
- changing labor market trends, and
- changing outcomes for postsecondary graduates.

Questions were asked against this backdrop of a changing global economy. Is this kind of information inclusive of the student population in our schools? Are we saying that if you are not going to university, you are not successful? Are academic marks the only indicators of success? Do all of our students have equitable learning/*Pathway* opportunities?

Let's Be Clear About What We Value

When talking about the "Third Industrial Revolution," Rifkin speaks of the need for hierarchical, top-down structures to shift to lateral, collaborative structures (personal communication, November 15, 2012). We are already seeing evidence of this move to an "up-shift" in our educational structures—that is, a new paradigm where

- students with a university/college education, exclusive of professional training programs, can expect to do further training to prepare them for the workplace (CBC Television, 2013);
- technical training programs at colleges, and apprenticeships, are quickly becoming the "gold collar" jobs driven by technology and skilled trade shortages;

- project-driven, part-time, and contract jobs are becoming the norm versus permanent work; and
- knowledge is viewed *as just one* of the attributes required for success, with increasing credence given to one's ability to create innovative approaches by thinking critically, being creative, problem solving, applying collaborative approaches, and using technology everywhere in every way.

Students, in response, are interested in seamless transitions as they move laterally from one postsecondary destination to another. Growing student pressure is compelling postsecondary institutions to respond as students and their parents seek out value-added educational experiences. Recent growth in shared programming between colleges and universities is breaking down the silos of these institutions, opening the doors to a more collaborative lateral approach. Dual-credit programming, articulation agreements, and advanced standing are examples of lateral capacity building between high schools and college/university programs.

In the CBC documentary *Generation Jobless*, futurist Thomas Frey speaks to part-time and temporary work as being the new normal. He indicates that, in today's economy, the average person has 11 different jobs by the time he or she is 30 and that, in the next 10 years, the average person will have anywhere up to 300 projects by the time he or she is 30 (CBC Television, 2013). A shift is happening. However, perceptions and value systems are slower to respond.

The underlying challenge in the mind-set or "up-shift" we are currently undergoing is that old value systems often get in the way of change. For most parents, educators, and elected officials, this lateral structure was not their educational reality. In their reality, postsecondary destinations were ranked hierarchically, and jobs and careers were for life. As a result, many university-trained high school teachers, stuck in the old paradigm, are hard pressed to relate current and relevant postsecondary learning opportunities and employment outcomes to their students. Parents, still under the impression that a university degree is "success insurance," are uncomfortable considering different

Pathways for their sons and daughters and so default to what worked for them, in their traditional contexts.

Collectively, we need to "up-shift" our thinking—we need a new mind-set. More challenging does not mean preparation for university. Challenging can be anything that stretches students' thinking and pushes them to learn more deeply, in preparation for *any* postsecondary destination. If part-time, contract jobs are the reality of the workplace, then students will need the requisite skills that enable them to excel in flexible work environments. They will need many opportunities to practice those skills along their *Pathways*, building on their Experiential Learning Journey. This needs to happen **EARLY** and **OFTEN**.

An Inclusive, Equitable Learning Community

Let us be clear. If we are to successfully Recalculate the Route, then the "up-shift" requires a broader definition of community partners (Figure 3.1) expanding from the traditional parents and local public service sectors to include our economic associates (business and industry sectors) as well as postsecondary educational partners.

Constructing Pathways Together Matters!

Educators have long understood the positive and impactful relationship between parent/guardian involvement and student success. What is the relationship to **a broad base of community partners**? How will those relationships impact student success? What are the roadblocks to constructing *Pathways to Career Readiness*? What are the experiences that need to be shared to help us "up-shift" our approaches?

Parents as Partners

Human nature is such that parents nurture and care for their children. They want the best for them, and they certainly don't want to "close any doors" to their future opportunities.

FIGURE 3.1

Community Partners in a Recalculated Route

Parents

Public Sector

Student

Post-secondary Destinations

Business/ Industry

Challenges arise in course selection, programming choice, and *Pathways* when parents make uninformed decisions based upon their own assumptions or experiences. Uninformed decisions result in mismatches between students' current skills, interests, and abilities (their Skill Development Strand) and the correct starting point on the Curriculum Knowledge Strand. The mismatches result in academic challenges, disengagement, and discouragement for students.

Given the rapid rate of change in workplace opportunities, it is not surprising that parental assumptions and experiences quickly become outdated. How, then, do we design clearer road signs, marking a more delineated *Pathway* for each child? This is particularly challenging in high school settings where parents are far less visible than in elementary school settings. Innovative approaches and a multitiered communication system are required. If parents are more visible in elementary school, then this is where the road signs need to be most visible, **EARLY** and **OFTEN**, particularly around the caution signals—transition periods highlighted on the *Pathways to Career Readiness Frame—Finding TrueNorth.*

 A school district in Ontario, Canada, was finding that parents of its Grade 7 and Grade 8 students were reluctant to direct their children into anything other than academic high school programs. As a result, a significant group of students were starting high school with a mismatch between their current skills and abilities and the curriculum content. In other words, *Student Pathway DNA* was not being recognized—and activated. This mismatch manifested itself in low credit attainment scores, higher absenteeism, and increased behavioral issues.

Confident that parents were not intentionally setting up their children for failure, the district adopted a new communication approach. The objective was to provide sufficient information, in an interactive way, which would empower students and their parents to make informed choices, and "up-shift" parent perceptions regarding the value of various postsecondary destinations.

A webcast, *Talking Opportunities,* was developed to invite parents and students to consider what students might like to "try" as they grow up, shifting away from the old notion of "What do you want to be?" The webcast provided information on all the postsecondary destinations and the opportunities available (York Region District School Board, 2004c). The resources provided "Tips for Parents" (see Appendix C) on strategies families might consider for developing and enhancing their son's or daughter's self-knowledge.

Communication was tiered with the presentation available online and in paper format, with multiple language translations available. Teachers developed an innovative approach, viewing segments of the webcast with their classes and then asking students to view or read it over with their parents at home using a series of question prompts to guide them. Part of the homework assignment required a parent or guardian response, which students brought back for class discussions. Parent forums were also provided for those wishing for a face-to-face session. In the end, not only were students and parents better informed of choices they had, but teachers also learned through the process. They became more comfortable with the postsecondary conversations and better able to provide direction and informed choice at subject selection time.

Parents are a valuable school resource in providing connections to the workplace. The majority of parents are likely engaged, or have been engaged, in some form of employment and as such provide a network base for the school from which Experiential Learning opportunities might be developed. Proactive schools achieve this by inviting their parent community to share business cards and expertise. These opportunities might include classroom presentations, guest speakers, work placements, and/or mentorships. These opportunities are but a small representation of what is possible. They serve as a reminder that by ACTIVELY STEPPING into our parent community, and inviting them to join us in *a structured, collaboratively planned approach*, we can find new and creative ways to support student learning.

What would our planning conversations look like if we broadened this approach to the other stakeholders, as represented in Figure 3.1?

Postsecondary Destinations as Partners

The *Pathways to Career Readiness Frame—Finding TrueNorth* identifies the most common postsecondary destination *Pathways* as being

- the workplace,
- college or technical programs,
- universities,
- community/or independent living, and
- apprenticeship.

The two-way arrows on the *Pathways to Career Readiness Frame* serve as a reminder of the interdependence of this partnership.

Postsecondary partners, regardless of destination, represent the next level of learning for students. Currently, postsecondary destinations exist as silos. They have their own guidelines for job entry skills or standards for admittance, curriculum, instruction, assessment practices, and accreditation. A mind-set change, from viewing only the hierarchical educational structures to also viewing lateral collaborative structures, would require establishing a greater interdependence between and across all postsecondary destinations. Lateral structures, where interdependence exists, would enable schools and postsecondary partners to build *Pathways* and program bridges by connecting elementary and middle schools with high schools and high schools with postsecondary destinations.

The existing silo structure presents challenges in building *Pathways* and program bridges, as each partnership must be individually constructed. As well, each silo is in competition with the other for students and funding. Such competiveness does not lend itself well to a collaborative culture that a Recalculated Route requires.

Currently, small-scale *Pathways* and program bridges are being developed through collaborative planning conversations among individual postsecondary institutions. This is time-consuming and repetitive, not a cost-effective approach. The success of the partnership rests solely upon the energy of teachers, schools, and partners involved in the planning and implementation. In addition, the fragmentation created by the silos results in inevitable mixed signals and messages to parents and students regarding the actual opportunities available and the benefits accrued.

Pathways to Career Readiness require a well-thought-out government educational strategy. The two-way flow of information (Figure 3.2) is foundational to *a structured, collaboratively planned approach* and a functioning funded program that works to the long-term benefit of students and state. As part of the *planned approach*, it is critical for information sharing and program planning to be among all three panels: elementary and middle schools, middle and high schools, high schools and postsecondary destinations, and postsecondary destinations and elementary and middle schools.

FIGURE 3.2

FIGURE 3.2

Information Sharing Across Lateral Structures—Where Interdependence Exists

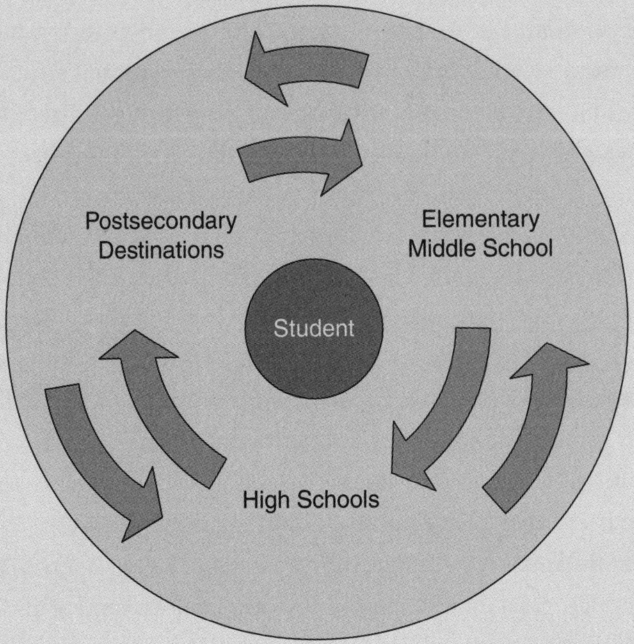

As part of that plan, teachers of all grade levels must be attuned to

- the transition requirements—our caution lights,
- curriculum content demands, and
- labor market predictors for each postsecondary destination.

Skilled teachers then use this combined knowledge to successfully activate *Student Pathway DNA* as they differentiate their instructional practice.

Within the plan,

1. postsecondary partners need to ensure their programs are relevant and timely. To do so, they need to be cognizant of middle

school/high school programming, as well as the evolving skill sets of students; and

2. high schools need to ensure that parents and students receive timely, relevant information so that they can make informed choices regarding *Pathway* planning across the educational spectrum. Given that the majority of their information gathering occurs in the elementary school where parents are most visible, transition conversations—our caution lights—need to occur, **EARLY** and **OFTEN**, as part of the *Pathway* planning.

Our research highlights a range of innovative strategies and approaches utilized by schools and districts to bridge knowledge gaps and build lateral capacity across the system. They do this by ACTIVELY STEPPING into each other's world. For example, plans include

- postsecondary destination tours for teachers, regardless of grade division;
- teacher skill training offered by postsecondary destination partners;
- school-based *Career Readiness* activities supported by representatives of the various postsecondary destinations;
- co-teaching and instructional support across all three panels;
- reach-ahead opportunities for students, such as college and university visits, industry tours, and so on;
- internships for students and teachers;
- dual-credit programming and opportunities for students to attend college while earning credits that count toward their high school diploma as well as the college program;
- elementary and middle school events held at high schools and postsecondary destinations; and
- business and entrepreneurship mentors.

In the most successful programs and strategies shared through our research, a communication loop, in the form of explicit feedback, was evident. This explicit feedback helped the partners to identify any recalculations that needed to occur within the organizational structures and the institutions themselves to activate student learning. Building capacity for informed choices, resulting from the "upshift," requires an effective **comprehensive communication plan** that is reflective of the diversity of all stakeholders.

Where we have seen smaller *Pathway* initiatives (individual articulation agreements between one school and one college) being adapted for use on a larger scale (articulation agreements extended among multiple stakeholders), there is evidence of strategic planning supported by collaborative approaches and an effective **comprehensive communication plan**. In Ontario, dual-credit programs are in place, building lateral capacity across institutions. High school students have opportunities to attend college and earn credits that also count toward their high school diploma.

The same trend is taking place in pockets within the United States. Columbia High school, in East Greenbush, New York, runs a school-based, business education program where a combination of college-credit courses and high school credits is leading to success in college and career readiness. In each instance, colleges and high schools **ACTIVELY STEP** into one another's world, earlier than they normally would have. College instructors get to learn more about the instructional strategies and programming used in the high schools and vice versa. Students see a clearer, more visible *Pathway* for themselves.

Postsecondary destinations are opening their doors to elementary and middle school students. In Ontario, York Region District School Board is offering Promoting Skilled Trades and Technologies (PSTT) programs in collaboration with a cadre of local colleges. Students in Grades 7 and 8 have opportunities to visit the colleges and experience "hands-on" activities that are intended to open their eyes to future possibilities—to create a "spark"—as they consider their transition into high school.

Given the rising cost of education, in relation to the resulting earnings to be gained, students and parents are becoming more attuned to "value-added" education. Increasingly, the ability of colleges, universities, and apprenticeship training programs to retain students through to program completion is a metric for their success, status, and funding.

In today's economic reality, it is becoming important for these institutions to demonstrate not only program completion but also transition opportunities into the workplace.

In a high-stakes, innovative approach, the University of Regina(UR), in Canada, has instituted a UR Guarantee Program whereby it offers to support the students enrolled through every step of the university experience to successful employment. One step of the program involves offering programming options for students that enable them to gain valuable work experience (through private sector partnerships) while building a career portfolio that will assist them in standing out from the competition.

The UR Guarantee states that if a student in the program does not secure career-related employment within six months of graduation, he or she will be eligible to come back for another year of undergraduate classes free of charge (tuition and course fees). The university also offers high school students opportunities to get a "head start" in their postsecondary training by allowing Grade 11 and 12 students to take full-credit university classes. Currently, the university covers the expenses for one course per term, and in return, students get to lighten their future university course load while getting a head start on developing the skills required to excel (University of Regina, 2014).

This example of a postsecondary institution, considering a design-down approach in collaboration with the private sector, highlights the interconnection of destinations and the power behind planning conversations.

> **"** *"I have been blessed to be part of the co-op student program! The students have exceptional knowledge and experience in the social networking world via the Internet and have created, designed, developed, and maintained sites and advertising for Maple Leaf Mortgages, which has been instrumental in the growth and development and has significantly increased business in our company. Students learn all about our world of financing while we benefit from their wealth of knowledge via computers and the Internet. This is a win-win program for both employers and students!"*
>
> R. Morad, personal communication, September 27, 2013. **"**

Business Associations and Industry Sectors as Partners

The private sector is not a familiar world to education providers. However, the growth and success of high school cooperative education and work experience programs (see Chapter 6) have created intersections where the value of these relationships to the private sector is visible. We can cite many instances where the relationship has had a major impact on individual students, teachers, and industry.

The *Pathways to Career Readiness Frame—Finding TrueNorth* illustrates how the Experiential Learning opportunities broaden as students develop and mature. These real-world experiences give them opportunities to apply their knowledge in authentic applications by ACTIVELY STEPPING into another world.

In a Recalculated Route, both educators and business/industry partners own the responsibility to develop the skills and training of our youth for the greater good. These community partners are naturally cautious about investing in training for high school students. Often cited are concerns associated with costs, productivity, and long-term employability benefits to their organization (Mourshed et al., 2012). Add to the mix the reality of employee turnover, unions, and economic downturns, and one gets a sense of the challenges associated with building sustainable relationships over time.

Wherever we see examples of sturdy bridges being built, there is a high degree of trust and cooperation, and well-articulated expectations and outcomes communicated between partners.

A unique example of vocational schooling and programming is the Scuola per Sportivi d'Élite in Locarno, Switzerland, that we mention in Chapter 1. It brings a limited number of highly skilled young athletes with world-class and Olympic Games participant potential together for both academic and "vocational" training. This school is a partnership of the Federal Ministry of Culture and Military and a select group of national sport federations.

The school and athletic complex is composed of world-class training facilities built by the Federal Department of Defence, Civil Protection and Sport and partially funded by the military, which is then managed by professionals from the selected sports federations. Coaches and other personnel are supplied by the sports federations for the portion of the day that is not reserved for academic learning. The fact that not all of the students will become world champions or have an income from their sports is the rationale for ensuring all the students have a strong foundation that would permit them to work within sports management, tourism, or perhaps the military in a training capacity.

The school in Locarno is effectively managed by partner sports federations for triathlon, gymnastics, swimming, ice hockey, freestyle skiing, cycling, soccer, and tennis. In this case, the curriculum partnership includes representatives of these sports federations and the canton that is responsible for funding the academic component for the 120 students who live on site. The Swiss government supports the full cost of the facilities through the sports and military departments. Students are selected by the sports federations from all their athletes who apply to attend.

Students spend three to four years at the school and, upon graduating, receive a diploma that enables them to work within sports federations, in clubs, in stores, or advance to a management technical university should they qualify and want to do so.

The Swiss model is a solid example of how partnerships can be employed to provide very effective and relevant education for students who wish to work in a specific field. By continuously involving partnerships of all key stakeholders in an industry, the Swiss ensure their students in vocational schools receive totally relevant academic and applied learning. The partnerships keep the in-school trainers fully up-to-date—in fact ahead—with new technologies that are being investigated and deployed. No traditional model where teachers continue to teach only what they know could expect to provide such up-to-date learning. No government-funded technology schools whose teachers are not in such close, deliberate, and interdependent contact with industry stakeholders could expect to provide this highly relevant learning to their students.

With partnerships, industry leaders have a responsibility to provide descriptive feedback to the teachers on the quality of the transitions their students are making into the "field," and in return, the teachers can provide descriptive feedback on evaluations of the work experiences too, thereby upgrading the in-field work of industry professionals. In a broad analysis, the Swiss model, which parallels many European models, such as the German model, is an intelligent investment in the country's economic future with an ongoing review of the return on that investment. Isn't that what anyone might define as intelligent use of public funding in education?

Building on this model of shared responsibility and collaboration, we turn, once again, to Ontario, Canada, where we see programming reform in all high schools taking place in the development of the Specialist High Skills Major (SHSM) program (see p. 125). Similar to the Swiss model, sector-specific programming is offered, one of which is sports.

The Ontario Ministry of Education invited business and industry sector representatives to join in roundtable discussions, regarding effective, experiential programming for Ontario students. Sector representatives identified not only the projected growth and needs in their sectors, but also the additional certifications, essential or workplace skills, and experiences that would enhance student placement for employment.

The program has been so successful in terms of student engagement and credit completion rates that by 2010 it caught the interest of the Bill and Melinda Gates Foundation and U.S. Secretary of Education Arne Duncan, resulting in the sharing of effective practices across countries—an example of nations, collectively, finding solutions that work by ACTIVELY STEPPING into one another's world.

Similarly, in the United States, Career Academies have developed where targeted career fields are identified as "schools within a school." According to the College and Career Academy Support Network (CCASN), academy career themes are selected locally, based on an industry that is healthy and able to provide a cadre of partners interested in supporting the program. Employers work as partners in the academy, serving on a steering committee (along

FIGURE 3.3

Innovation Leadership Prism (Government, System, and Principal Lenses)

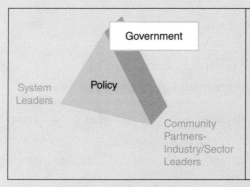

Through *a structured, collaboratively planned approach*, the ministry and sector/industry association stakeholders and system leaders developed the Specialist High Skills Major (SHSM) program.

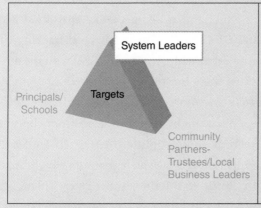

System leaders and principals with their school leadership teams collaborated with community partners, trustees, and business leaders to determine the appropriate sector foci for the school communities as well as to set achievable targets for the schools and system.

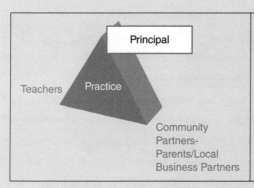

Schools implementing the program engage with their local sector business/industry partners to plan for work placements and contextualized learning opportunities and additional certification training.

with teachers, administrators, and often parents and students) that governs the program's development and operation. Networking opportunities are developed for the student, school, and teacher by engaging business and industry sector participants as

- guest speakers,
- field trip and job shadowing hosts,
- individual mentors,
- work experience and internship supervisors, and
- community service and service learning partners.

Students transitioning to the workplace may find employment with the academy partners or may benefit from course articulation or concurrent enrollment options with postsecondary institution partners (CCASN, n.d.).

In another example of the benefits accrued by **ACTIVELY STEPPING** into one another's world and working **COLLABORATIVELY** with students **EARLY** and **OFTEN**, California has been tracking the performance of its California Partnership Academies (CPA) with the most salient findings showing that there is a higher graduation rate for CPA seniors, compared to the state as a whole (Stern, Saroyan, & Hester, 2013).

What might educators learn from concepts such as those captured in the 20 Under 20 Thiel Fellowship? The fellowship, which began in 2010, was founded by Peter Thiel, best known as cofounder of PayPal and Facebook's first investor. Through a rigorous application process, 20 students under the age of 20 are eligible for $100,000 and two years of independent project work (Thiel Foundation, 2014). The opening question on the application is **"Tell us how you would like to change the world."**

The fellowship brings together some of the world's most creative and motivated young people, and helps them bring their most ambitious ideas and projects to life. They are mentored by a network of visionary thinkers, investors, scientists, and entrepreneurs who, with a "pay it forward" attitude, provide guidance and business connections that can't be replicated in any classroom. Rather than just studying, the students are *doing*. Though the Thiel Fellowship only helps a handful of students each year, their focus has translated into the creation of over 50 companies (Averbuch, 2013).

Regardless of the availability of funding dollars, the notion of supporting entrepreneurship and innovative thinking is powerful. It is critical that we engage students in their interests and passions, guide them through a process of inquiry and action, and support them with connections to knowledgeable stakeholders.

Public Sector as Partners

Public service is the sector most likely to be connected and associated with the day-to-day business of our school communities. There seems to be a greater affinity, among educators, to work with these like-minded, not-for-profit organizations. Perhaps it is easier to find a shared moral purpose given that social service agencies already play a role in supporting youth as they transition through life. With the increase in mental health issues that are being reported by schools, they are an example of partners who have become vital resources.

The Canadian Mental Health Association (2014) reports that 1 in 5 Canadians will personally experience a mental illness in their lifetime with anxiety disorders being the most common. In the United States, 1 in 8 children are affected by anxiety disorders (Anxiety and Depression Association of America, 2014). It remains to be seen if anxiety is a by-product of the current societal cultural and technological revolutions and the resulting uncertainties they are creating. We do know, however, that we can mitigate these problems by

- adding clarity to uncertainties,
- building visible *Pathways* for students, and
- teaching the life skills our students need to be resilient, emphasizing areas such as problem solving and conflict resolution.

Some would argue that underfunding has been detrimental to building these partnerships. Others would argue that the societal "taboo" associated with acknowledging mental health issues has taken pressure off the political decision makers to commit dollars. Regardless, increased incidents of student suicides, acts of violence in schools, and school-related cyberbullying have now created their own groundswell of new attitudes and perceptions. This groundswell frames the new mind-set that is required to bring about change.

 We see examples of this new mind-set and related programming through *a structured, collaboratively planned approach*, taking shape through the policy implementation of Ontario's comprehensive mental health and addictions strategy: *Open Minds, Healthy Minds* (Ontario Ministry of Health and Long-Term Care, 2011). The policy puts a focus on partnerships. It anecdotes district stories such as in Sault Ste. Marie, Ontario, where school boards, community-based mental health and addictions agencies, and health care services are working together to provide strengths-based, person-centered services for children and youth to build resiliency and improve mental health. The network of services starts in kindergarten. Junior and senior kindergarten teachers in 27 elementary schools have been trained to teach children skills, including how to make friends, to express their feelings, and to solve problems. Over 500 children have engaged in the program, and schools are seeing the difference of starting **EARLY** and **OFTEN**.

 Northern Lights Secondary School and the James Bay Lowlands Secondary School Board in Ontario focus on the health and well-being of their students as the fundamental overarching priority for student success. Superintendent of Education Tom Steele comments:

If students are not physically, mentally, socially, or emotionally well, all of the other strategies and programs we have to offer are of limited value. We initially determined our need for a very approachable, caring, and well-qualified "Student Success Counselor" and hired a graduate of our school (someone who knows the context, knows the students, and in many cases knows their families) and is connected and able to mobilize a wide variety of community resources to help students.

This position helped tremendously and shed light on the "real and immediate life needs" of our students. Our counselor and the entire Student Success team was risking burnout once we began to realize and address the true source of our students' struggles and disengagement. Realizing that we were on the right track but needed more front-line assistance, our school board supported us and made the addition of a Student Success Outreach Counselor a major priority within the overall strategic plan.

Our Student Success team now includes the principal, guidance lead, Student Success teacher, special education, and two Student Success Outreach Counselors with slightly different roles. We support students well beyond the time and space limitations of our school day and assist and engage them in positive activities . . . and **it is working.** (personal communication, January 17, 2013)

In summary, *a structured, collaboratively planned approach* brings many voices to the planning table. It is an approach that needs to be *inclusive of all postsecondary stakeholders*, collectively committed to developing innovative solutions to build lateral capacity across the educational and economic systems. It is an "up-shift" or change in mind-set. It is a mind-set that values community partner interdependence and collective responsibility and, as such, understands that every partner has a stake in the success of the other.

Whether these solutions are driven by government, educational institutions, community partners, or a combination, the fact remains that our students need and deserve *Pathways* that are clearly marked, with ways to merge from one *Pathway*—one postsecondary destination—to another so that they can find their *TrueNorth* in an efficient, cost-effective way.

There is no denying that such an approach requires an "up-shift" from what has been standard practice for all stakeholders in the old paradigm. It cannot be relegated to one individual or to one organization. To be successful, it has to become the way of "doing business," not just for educators but for all stakeholders. There has to be common understandings and shared beliefs. This requires a **comprehensive communication plan** that is responsive to the diversity of the stakeholders.

A Culture of Innovation and Mutual Respect

Our words and actions, as educators, can be powerful tools in framing the new mind-set. In Recalculating the Route, we need to be mindful that our words and actions reflect our shared beliefs and understandings. While understanding the changing workplace realities and how these social drivers connect to our work is important, equally important is the language we are using or not using to express this new value system expressed through a **comprehensive communication plan**.

"Up-Shifts" in Ontario

Following the release of the Student Success Strategy, there was recognition that student "success" was much broader than grade percentages and numbers of university attendees and, as such, needed to be defined in a more inclusive, representative way. Newly revised shared beliefs and understandings were identified as conversations shifted to the individualized learning needs of *each* student, recognizing that

- any student can become "at risk," academically or socio-emotionally;
- all students can achieve, given the right time and support; and
- the role of a caring other, to monitor student progress and keep an eye out for changes in performance, is essential.

Redefining student success required taking a critical look at potentially outdated values held by students, parents, teachers, system leaders, and community partners. It entailed spotlighting the disconnection between the current opportunities and realities and old belief systems. Through the process, it became evident that student *Pathways* were not visible to a large portion of the population. Not only were the breadth and depth of current postsecondary destination opportunities not clearly understood, but current student *Pathways* for many were feeling like "the road to nowhere." The challenge quickly became how to assist all stakeholders in developing the knowledge and skills required to support *Pathways to Career Readiness*.

Examination of past practices revealed that sometimes, in very subtle ways, what was being expressed through words and actions in the schools and classrooms was contrary to a more inclusive school. As a corrective measure,

- guidance and career centers began working toward ensuring that all the resources and displays were representative of all postsecondary destinations;
- graduation ceremonies and scholarships were broadened to honor all destinations including apprenticeships, college, technical training, community living, workplace, and university;
- the writing of curriculum units for elementary students highlighted the trades and technologies as student experiences and possibilities expanded;
- transition conversations occurred across elementary and high school panels; and
- teachers considered whether students who were interested in pursuing a career in apprenticeship or technical training saw evidence of these opportunities in the instructional practices in their classrooms.

The York Region District School Board responded with a "Power of Language" poster campaign, illustrated in Figure 3.4. The poster and supporting instructional activities were workshopped with school staff. Through a series of exercises, staff members were encouraged to reflect on the *Pathway* language they used with their students. They were challenged to consider whether their words represented the shared beliefs and understandings of the organization and whether they were judgment-free.

In a Recalculated Route, how we define success, the words we use, and the recognition that we give to student achievement need to be inclusive of all postsecondary destinations. It is important to be

FIGURE 3.4

Power of Language Poster

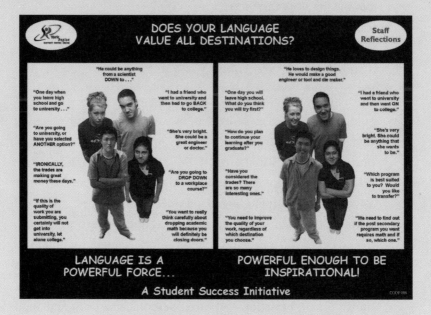

Source: York Region District School Board (2004b).

mindful that sometimes actions speak louder than words. Just as students' skills, abilities, and dispositions are unique, so are the success criteria unique for apprenticeship, college or technical training, community living, university, and the workplace. As educators, we need to recognize achievement for each of these destinations. In doing so, we take a step forward in creating Guiding Principle 1—**an inclusive, equitable learning community** for our students, or places where all students can see opportunities for themselves.

It would be incomplete to discuss reform and change, particularly under the *Pathways to Career Readiness Frame—Finding TrueNorth*, without acknowledging the importance of trust. Trust must exist between all partners as we work toward the best possible outcomes for our students. There needs to be trust at the government, system, school, classroom, and community levels. If we do indeed value relationships, then structures of trust need to be inclusive of all our communities whether among

- government, system, and community partners;
- systems, schools, and community partners;
- schools, teachers, and community partners; or
- teachers, students, and community partners.

Trust is the glue. Without it, relationships become unstable. Because trust can take years to build and seconds to destroy, we need to embrace an innovative culture where we understand that we are all on a learning journey, where there will be successes and failures, where small failures are not treated punitively, and where collaboration and mutual respect are foundational.

In a Recalculated Route, there needs to be an understanding of the importance of building "safety nets," not only for our students but also for teachers and leaders. If our goal is to develop innovative, creative thinkers, then students, teachers, and leaders must be comfortable with taking risks and understanding the value of "learning from failing." We must give them the voice to do so.

The degree to which we, as educators, see ourselves in a relationship business or curriculum delivery business will determine to a large extent the degree to which we let other partners come to our planning tables. As Hargreaves and Fullan (2012) note, "if you want to change human behavior, you need to help people obtain what they most care about: the respect of their peers" (p. 151).

Educators know that teaching is much more than job readiness for students or delivering curriculum expectations. We are in the relationship-building business. Most countries, such as the United States, Canada, and the United Kingdom, have taken a more holistic view and embrace the social and emotional development of students as an integral part of the learning journey. As any teacher will attest, this certainly adds to the complexity of the work.

The first element in developing well-being comes with understanding and delivering on solid classroom practice, based on knowing the **FACES** of each and every student. With the resulting success comes a sense of value and increased student self-esteem, both of which support the student's well-being. Skilled teachers build community in the classrooms and create environments where students' voices flourish.

Student Engagement Matters!

Student engagement is a term that is frequently heard but ill defined and with no comparative measures. Initially, student engagement was viewed as a student's sense of belonging and level of participation in school life. This was broadened by a study done by the Organisation for Economic Co-operation and Development (Willms, 2003) to include measuring institutional engagement through student truancy. More recently, Douglas Willms, Sharon Friesen, and Penny Milton in *What Did You Do in School Today?* (2009) introduced intellectual engagement as a new variable for consideration. They define three areas of engagement:

- Social Engagement—meaningful participation in the life of the school;
- Institutional Engagement—active participation in the requirements for school success; and
- Intellectual Engagement—a serious emotional and cognitive investment in learning.

While students report their number-one reason for attending school is to improve their future job opportunities (Mourshed et al., 2012), we as educators know that is not enough. Many students need something more immediate and tangible to keep them engaged in the learning over time. What, then, is the "hook" or "spark" for students' intellectual engagement? What is important to students?

To build an emotional connection to and have cognitive insights about learning (Sharratt & Fullan, 2012), we need to know what students care deeply and passionately about. We then need to be able to take those emotional connections and cognitive insights to propel students forward to develop the skills and knowledge required to learn a living. Who knows better what their passions are than students themselves?

Moving From Student Engagement to Student Empowerment: Voice and Choice

Student voice is a powerful resource in educational planning and in empowering students. Systems and schools that give priority to student voice use qualitative and quantitative data to keep a pulse on what students are thinking and feeling. Student forums, surveys, interviews, and online tools are just some of the ways schools and systems undertake this work. They pay careful attention to the discrepancies among the various stakeholder perceptions and respond accordingly.

Student choice is also another powerful correlate to student engagement. If students are going to be engaged in their learning, then they need to be able to relate to it (see their individual *Pathway*), have ownership (course selection and program choices), and assume responsibility for it (Glaze, Mattingley, & Andrews, 2013). To do this, they need to be able to make informed choices. This includes input into the decisions that impact not only classroom learning but school life in general.

While *student voice plus student choice* has a strong correlation to student engagement, we have found that student engagement is further enhanced when the learning is grounded in the development of agency and values.

> " *"It is not enough for citizens to have access to education and 'training.' In order to shape a fast-changing world, we need learning that matches and updates skills, grows the ability to generate solutions, and also builds the capacity to create possibilities. Underpinning these needs to be a strong emphasis on developing agency and values"*
>
> Hannon, Gillinson, & Shanks, 2013, p. 140.

In a Recalculated Route, values are as important as curriculum and learning methods and are reflected in the shared beliefs and understandings of the organization. Agency, our ability to take control of our lives—to see, understand, and act on what we believe to be important—is given wings when all our stakeholders feel a sense of responsibility, have the will to act, and possess the skills to follow through.

An innovative school culture creates empowered students through values-based learning and action when teachers and school districts

- give priority to "student voice" by providing safe equitable and inclusive spaces where students have opportunities to give voice to issues they are passionate about, concerns they have, and changes they would like to see;
- use students' "passion" to activate the *Student Pathway DNA* by incorporating these issues into the Curriculum Knowledge Strand, using a Collaborative Inquiry process (see Chapter 6);
- encourage students to see value in themselves, through their Self-Knowledge Learning Journey, as they self-assess their own skills, abilities, and dispositions;
- help students develop the tools to move from "thinking about" to "action," through a Collaborative Inquiry approach;
- recognize that the combination of meaningful learning and authentic work-related opportunities, with the right set of values, makes for positive behavioral and cultural changes for all stakeholders;
- understand the importance of scaffolding the learning;
- recognize the importance of developing skills and abilities in students but at the same time appreciate that it is the values that will ultimately empower and steer them in the right direction;
- take time, at the appropriate time, to invest in character development;
- help students see that before they can contribute to the world around them, they must first understand and value themselves as learners; and
- build resilience through ongoing reflection, helping students to know who they are and are not.

Innovation leaders, teachers, and administrators, maximize student empowerment by

- leading by example;
- distributing leadership (A. Harris, personal communication, January 3, 2013);
- being inclusive;
- enabling learners to observe, interact, and empathize;

- thinking globally;
- building networks of learners within their classrooms and schools,
- making it fun; and
- creating structures that promote positive values (adapted from Hannon et al., 2013).

They recognize that school is time based and, as such, it is imperative that student voice and choice be captured and responded to, in a timely fashion, to avoid lost opportunities.

From GOOD to GREAT to INNOVATE

The Metropolitan Regional Career and Technical Center (MET, 2014) is part of Big Picture Learning in Rhode Island, and a strong example of moving from good to great to innovate. It is a not-for-profit organization, cofounded by social entrepreneurs Dennis Littky and Elliot Washor. There are now 52 Big Picture Learning schools across the United States serving some 9,000 students. All are public schools; some operate as charter schools. Similar start-ups are located internationally in Australia, Canada, and the Netherlands (Hannon et al., 2013).

With a focus on entrepreneurship, the MET makes the relationship with the world of work fundamental. In practice, this translates into two days of a five-day week spent in internships. For the MET, a real-world foundation is critically important. Students, whether building particular skills or learning to solve complex problems, are supported by **a broad base of community partners** (Guiding Principle 3).

"Students work with their advisors to create individual learning plans that blend student passions and interests with core conceptual content. Learning is structured around projects that bring in other aspects of the curriculum. Collaborative learning is central to the approach" (Hannon et al., 2013,

(Continued)

(Continued)

p. 85). In addition, the MET has launched *College Unbound*, a partnership with Roger Williams University where Big Picture Learning offers three-year degrees grounded in real work that is contextualized and academically challenging (Hannon et al., 2013).

The 10 distinguishers of Big Picture Learning schools are

1. learning in the real world,
2. personalization,
3. authentic assessment,
4. school organization,
5. advisory structure,
6. school culture,
7. leadership,
8. parent/family engagement,
9. school/college partnership, and
10. professional development (www.bigpicture.org/schools).

> "When young people are given real world experience and their learning is grounded in it, they change. By engaging them and respecting them, you will change them. They become transformed"
>
> Dennis Littky, quoted in Hannon et al., 2013, p. 80.

In Ontario, Canada, students across the province are invited to be part of a student *SpeakUp* initiative. In one part of the initiative, students act as action researchers, using a Collaborative Inquiry model, to explore issues that are relevant to their school and impact their learning. Student forums, online resources, and teacher mentors provide students with the training and tools to engage in this learning. Results are shared with stakeholders. System and school improvement plans across Ontario are now integrating Student Voice as a lever to "Closing the Gap to Raise the Bar," as we will see in Chapter 4.

Reflective Pause
by Alma Harris

The vast school improvement and school effectiveness literature points toward the difference that schools make. There is no question that the "school matters," but as Sharratt and Harild point out in this chapter, no school is an island. The most effective schools are essentially communities that build strong partnerships and seek strategic alliances. They are networked, connected, and ultimately concerned with drawing upon all the expertise they can. Sharratt and Harild refer to this as **an inclusive, equitable learning community** with one core purpose of supporting students to be the very best they can be.

As do many other writers, Sharratt and Harild point toward the importance of stakeholder engagement in securing

STEPS TO STUDENTS' SUCCESS

1. Be relentless in your pursuit of excellence and achievement.
2. Be clear about what excellence and achievement look like.
3. Develop, share, and revise shared beliefs and understandings.
4. Consider whether your language and actions reflect these shared beliefs and understandings.
5. Capture student voice and support student choice.
6. Enhance the **structured, collaboratively planned approach** by drawing upon the collective knowledge and skills of your community partners.
7. **ACTIVELY STEP** into your community . . . collaborate . . . **EARLY** and **OFTEN**.
8. Share information laterally, strengthening interdependence.
9. Support accountable talk and action.
10. Stay the course but be nimble enough to be responsive.

better outcomes for young people. They are careful to note that any partnership or collaboration has to be "win-win" and not just one-way to be most effective. Research evidence shows very clearly that of all the stakeholders, parents are a critically important group. If properly engaged in students' learning, parents can have a positive impact on subsequent educational performance and achievement. The question is how best to engage them and to sustain that engagement over time.

Sharratt and Harild offer some potential solutions in this chapter and quite rightly reflect upon the types of engagement that are most productive for parents and, indeed, other stakeholders. Their central argument is that it is the student who should be at the epicenter of all the partnership arrangements among stakeholders, if there is to be a positive and lasting effect. Sharratt and Harild talk about the importance of shared values and intent so that the intersections between stakeholders are powerful and the interconnections are properly aligned. The word *partnership* is easy to say, but when stakeholders come in with different priorities, intentions, and motivations, there is always the danger that they simply talk past each other.

The authors suggest that there needs to be information sharing across lateral structures where interdependence exists along with clear communication channels. They provide useful and insightful examples of the ways in which partnerships can be authentic and can make an active difference to learners. In summary, they suggest *a **structured, collaboratively planned approach*** that brings many voices to the planning table.

This has to be the right way forward. A planned and coordinated approach to the engagement of stakeholders is often lacking in many schools despite unbridled enthusiasm for connecting with external partners or agencies. The authors talk about an "up-shift"—a change in mind-set that focuses on collective responsibility as well as collective authority to act in the best interest of the student.

Along with stakeholder engagement, Chapter 3 focuses on the importance of student engagement and student voice. So often this is glossed over as something that schools believe they have in place but in reality are neglecting at their peril. Authentic student engagement, as Sharratt and Harild make clear, is not just about representation but about participation. It means participation in decision making and planning, and it means taking student views seriously and acting upon them. Students will readily give their views and opinions, but if no action is taken, they will know their views are not taken seriously and withdraw.

In a model of distributed leadership, students have agency and influence; the challenge is to release the power of their leadership in authentic and trusting ways. It means putting **FACES** on the learners and empowering them to be leaders.

About Alma Harris, PhD

Alma Harris is a professor and the director of the Institute of Educational Leadership at the University of Malaya. She is also the pro-director (of leadership) at the Institute of Education, University of London. From 2010 to 2012, she was a senior policy advisor to the Welsh government and assisted with the process of system-wide reform. Her research work focuses primarily on leading organizational change and transformation. Alma is internationally known for her work on school improvement, focusing particularly on improving schools in challenging circumstances. She has also written extensively about leadership in schools and is an expert on the theme of distributed leadership. Her latest book, *Distributed Leadership Matters* (2013), is published by Corwin. She holds visiting professorial posts at the Moscow Higher School of Economics and Nottingham Business School. Alma is currently president of the International Congress for School Effectiveness and Improvement (www.icsei.net).

Closing the Gap to Raise the Bar

"The greatest danger for most of us lies not in setting our aim too high and falling short, but in setting our aim too low and achieving our mark."

—Michelangelo (Brainy Quote, 2014b)

Data Matters!

If we believe that every student can learn and has the right to learn, then we need to determine not just whether every student has learned but whether every student has access to optimal classroom teaching. We need to know on an ongoing basis that all students are achieving, by assessing them daily and incorporating that assessment information into individualized, small-group, and whole-group instruction—a nonnegotiable practice. All teachers can teach if supported with time to improve and the right resources. We need to offer them rich, easy-to-use tools, including how to put **FACES** on the data, so that they can do what it takes to reach the goal of every student learning in order to close the gap. Doing so is the system's responsibility to the students, and it is necessary to guarantee every teacher's right to teach well (Sharratt & Fullan, 2012).

When considering *Pathways to Career Readiness*, there are many valuable data sources that help to ensure that everyone is using the same road map as illustrated in Figure 4.1:

- Perception Data—from all stakeholders (parents, students, community partners, teachers, leaders);
- Destination Data;
- Labor Market and Trend Data (locally and globally);
- Demographic Data; and
- System and School Achievement Data.

Good systems gather data and share it internally, hoping to effect changes. Hope is not a strategy. Great systems gather data and use it to set aggressive targets. They mandate high-impact assessment and instructional practices and build in

QUESTIONS THAT MATTER MOST

1. How are you using data from all community partners to inform instructional and program planning decisions?
2. What evidence is there that programming and instructional decisions are designed down from *The Literate Graduate* profile?
3. How do you ensure your students, parents, teachers, and system leaders are aware of postsecondary outcomes?
4. Have you identified the life skills you are hoping to develop in students?
5. Do you have a means to assess these skills?
6. How do you incorporate local and national labor market trends into your programming planning and delivery?
7. What qualities and skills does your school or system work collectively toward developing in your graduates?
8. What measures do you have in place to ensure that these qualities and skills are being developed?
9. What measures does your school or system have in place to review and refresh these qualities and skills as they relate to evolving economies and world realities?
10. What would parents, professionals, and other employers in your community say about the level of skills and qualities they see your graduates exhibit?

responsibility and accountability for all students' progress. Innovative systems, in addition to what great systems do, are fearless in communicating their findings, successes, and challenges transparently with all stakeholders so that the process of innovation can be fed and nurtured. Innovative systems also continue to question, explore, and go deeper in perfecting precise instruction, carefully crafted for each student.

FIGURE 4.1

Data Sources

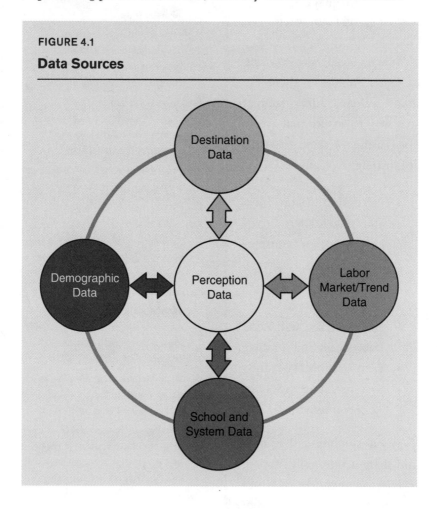

Figure 4.1 illustrates that perception data, more qualitative in nature, are shaped and influenced by other, quantitative data sources. Relevant and fully analyzed data that are gathered, shared, and communicated will determine the Recalculations that need to occur in the educational system.

PERCEPTION DATA

Perception Data: Checking for Traffic Congestion

Personnel from states, systems, and schools, interested in keeping a pulse on their effectiveness, set aside time and resources to see if the strategies and approaches they have prioritized are having the outcomes predicted. These perception data sources are particularly useful when attempting to create a nimble, evolutionary educational system. Roadblocks can be identified, and potholes can be filled, in timely ways before crises erupt. It is through the collection of perception data that we become aware of the parallel universes in which community partners, teachers, parents, and students can often reside.

Understanding the drivers of student, parent, and potential employer preferences is not only instructive but essential when considering *Pathways to Career Readiness*. In the old paradigm, a university degree boosted earnings by an average of 30% per year, as compared to a high school diploma (Hayter, 2013). It is no wonder that the perception of a university degree as the best road to success still exists. This gap, however, has been shrinking with the new economy. The investment in a university degree now varies significantly depending on the demands of the changing labor market and the degree earned (Hayter, 2013).

In gathering perception data about *Pathways* in secondary schools, one high-performing district in Ontario, Canada, the York Region District School Board, found that there was a need for more information about the various postsecondary *Pathway* options available to students, particularly those options not related to college or university. This information compelled schools to reexamine their counseling approaches, messaging, and resource allocations. Industry and workplace tours were set up for teachers so that they could experience firsthand the range of opportunities available to students. With this newly acquired knowledge, teachers were able to make explicit links between skills needed beyond high school and the curriculum expectations being taught. Students became more receptive, and parents became more comfortable in exploring *Pathways* to a wide variety of postsecondary destinations.

While it appears that everyone wants the best possible outcomes for all students in an education system, other data sources indicate that mixed directions and poor signage still exist, making *Pathway* navigation to many postsecondary destinations challenging at best. The McKinsey report (Mourshed, Farrell, & Barton, 2012) found that only 45% of youth and 42% of employers felt that graduates were adequately prepared for entry-level positions. This is in comparison to 72% of educators who felt new graduates were ready to work.

Perception data help to keep us abreast of the degree to which students, teachers, and parents don't know what they don't know. How we use other sources of data and effectively communicate them will influence the perceptions and ultimately create the "up-shift"—a new mind-set—that is now required to Recalculate the Route.

Destination Data: What *Pathways* Are Students Following?

To close the gap to raise the bar (A. Hargreaves, personal communication, December 3, 2012), it is important to find the points of intersection among our perceptions, realities, and possibilities.

It is no surprise that

- **students** are interested in finding jobs suited to their skills in a reasonable period of time;
- **employers** want to find the right, affordable talent;
- **parents** want their children to have opportunities beyond what they themselves experienced; and
- **educators** want to know that what they teach matters.

Given that schools still pride themselves as being "academic schools," it is worth exploring what is being inferred by this terminology. For many, it means holding onto the perception that most of our graduates are going on to university- or college-level training. In a more inclusive, equitable 21st-century school, as demonstrated by the *Pathways to Career Readiness Frame: Finding TrueNorth* (Figure 1.1, page 12), we need to broaden our perceptions. A truly successful academic school meets the learning needs of all learners by being responsive to all postsecondary destinations: workplace, college, apprenticeship, technical training, community living, or university.

In Ontario, a commissioned report from 2009, *Who Doesn't Go to Post-Secondary Education?* by King, Warren, King, Brook, and Kocher summarized where high school students were going after secondary school (Figure 4.2). The findings were insightful and certainly contradicted the parental and educator perception data prevalent at that time. The report also confirmed that students are inclined to change their destination, or not finish reaching the destination they intended to begin. While this has significant personal and financial expenses for families, it is also costly for society as a whole.

The data summary from Figure 4.2 shows that of 100 students who start Grade 9 in Ontario,

- 75 graduate with their diploma within four to five years, and
- 30 return for a fifth year to continue their studies.

In total, of the 100 Ontario students who started high school in Grade 9,

- 34 start university,
- 20 start college,
- 6 start apprenticeships, and
- 40 start directly in the workplace, 15 with a diploma in hand and 25 without.

The significant data set for educators was the percentage (40%) of students who were transitioning directly into the workplace upon completion of high school. Systems were motivated to look at their own local destination data. Interestingly, even in the most academically inclined systems, where a large percentage of the population was university trained, these destination data groupings held true. It appeared that a school could be "academic" and still have a high percentage of students pursuing nonacademic postsecondary *Pathways*, including a large pool of talented students who appeared to be stalled in pursuing further studies.

FIGURE 4.2

Postsecondary Destination

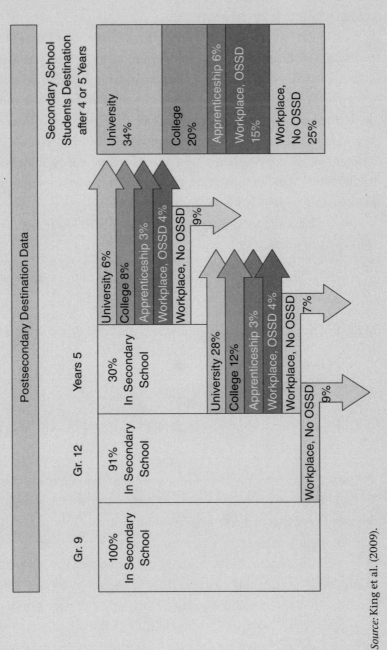

Postsecondary Destination Data

Gr. 9
100%
In Secondary
School

Gr. 12
91%
In Secondary
School

Workplace, No OSSD 9%

Years 5
30%
In Secondary
School

University 28%
College 12%
Apprenticeship 3%
Workplace, OSSD 4%
Workplace, No OSSD 7%

University 6%
College 8%
Apprenticeship 3%
Workplace, OSSD 4%
Workplace, No OSSD 9%

Secondary School
Students Destination
after 4 or 5 Years

University
34%

College
20%

Apprenticeship 6%

Workplace, OSSD
15%

Workplace,
No OSSD
25%

Source: King et al. (2009).

Note: OSSD = Ontario Secondary School Diploma.

Ontario responded using the Student Success Strategy as one way to close the gap to raise the bar. This "More Ways to Succeed" model is grounded in a Grade 7–12 policy based on the belief that every student learns in his or her own way. This means meeting the needs, interests, and strengths of *all* students, engaging them in learning and better preparing them for graduation and beyond. Structures, resources, and supporting programming components were then put in place so that Ontario's high schools could work with communities, employers, colleges, universities, and training centers to offer more ways than ever before to help students focus on their interests and to support their learning. Aggressive graduation targets were set, strategies were implemented, and expectations for core deliverables were shared across school boards (Ontario Ministry of Education, 2011).

The destination data from King et al. (2009) raised concerns about this cadre of bright, capable students who appeared disengaged. They appeared to lack focus and confidence to plan the next step of their learning. Were the barriers about cost, discouragement, lack of information, lack of preparedness, or perception of lack of opportunity? The Ontario Ministry of Education (2013b), through the Student Success Strategy, responded by setting a new *Pathway* toward a new designation on the high school diploma with the implementation of the Specialist High Skills Major (SHSM) program.

SHSM is a specialized program that allows high school students to experience a broad range of customized, career-focused learning opportunities while working toward the completion of their high school diploma. All interested students, whether their postsecondary destination of choice is apprenticeship, college, workplace, or university, are able to participate in this program. Upon completion of the program, students are granted an SHSM designation on their high school diploma.

The Ontario Ministry of Education, in collaboration with industry/ sector representatives and educators, developed sector-specific SHSM programs (for example, business, construction, health and wellness, and so on). School boards must apply to the Ministry of Education for programming approval based on set criteria and program readiness.

Ministry staff members work with the high schools to support the program implementation.

Five key deliverables for the program, regardless of sector, were established and have become the baseline for ensuring programming standardization across the province. They are

1. a preapproved sector-specific bundle of Grade 11 and Grade 12 credits made up of a major course, related courses with *contextualized learning* components, and a required 2-credit *cooperative education* course;
2. sector-recognized certifications and training courses;
3. Experiential Learning activities within the sector including *job shadowing, job twinning,* and short-term *work experience*;
4. "reach ahead" experiences in students' postsecondary destination choices, which could include *dual-credit programs, college visits,* and so on; and
5. use of the Ontario Skills Passport (Ontario Ministry of Education, 2014) to document development of essential skills and work habits.

SHSM is intended to reach students at their point of need and engage them by focusing their learning in sector-specific areas of interest while at the same time broadening their networks through experiential and reach-ahead learning models. By enabling students to develop and acquire the requisite workplace skills, training, curriculum knowledge, and certifications, the goal is to better prepare them to make an informed transition to postsecondary destinations whether the workplace, apprenticeship, college, or university. It is important to note that the networks students establish have a lasting, lifetime impact—an impact that is being experienced by over 20,000 students who have been enrolled in 740 SHSM programs in over 430 schools (Tucker, 2011).

Student empowerment is enhanced through *a structured, collaboratively planned approach*, supported through an SHSM team at each school, comprising school administrator(s), subject-specific teachers across disciplines, an SHSM school board lead, guidance and Student Success teachers, co-op teachers, technology support teams, a school advisory committee, and community partners. Dedicated funding, tied to specific Ministry of Education targets and program deliverables, ensures standardization across the province. As program planning and sustainability is contingent upon sector strength in the community, SHSM school teams are particularly attentive to labor market and trend data.

Labor Market and Trend Data: A Snapshot of Opportunities

If educators are to be successful in developing 21st-century *Literate Graduates*, then they need to be attentive to the labor markets and local and global trends. Working closely with sector representatives and local community partners helps to ensure strong connections to the opportunities. As affirmed by the destination data, parents and students need timely data about viable career options and appropriate *Pathways*. The McKinsey report (Mourshed et al., 2012) confirms that "in almost every society, occupations that require a higher level of studies tend to carry more status" (p. 31). This bodes well for the future of post-secondary education but not exclusively for the university or college trained. The realities of the global economy indicate that a shift is occurring in the skills and abilities required.

Skilled trade shortages are turning what were traditionally thought of as "blue collar" jobs into the "gold collar" jobs of the 21st century. Consider that 70% of young people surveyed in the McKinsey report (Mourshed et al., 2012) believe vocational tracks are more helpful in getting them jobs, and half said they find them more appealing than the academic track. At the same time, though, nearly two thirds of youth said that vocational tracks were less valued by society. According to the report, Germany is the only country out of the nine surveyed where students believe that the academic and vocational paths are held in equal esteem.

Labor market trends, local as well as global, provide a snapshot of current and future employment opportunities (Organisation for Economic Co-operation and Development, 2012). In addition to valuable data on jobs and sectors, these reports emphasize the skills that are required—a mirror by which educators can reflect back on the skills and abilities of *The Literate Graduate* (Employment and Social Development Canada, 2013b). It takes an effective **comprehensive communication plan** to share this information with parents, students, and teachers so that knowledge can be shared for timely *Pathway* decisions. In Ontario, local labor market boards work with schools and systems to support their communication plan. The Workforce Planning Board of York Region and Bradford West Gwillimbury, Ontario, works with a number of stakeholders to develop resources that are sector specific (see Appendix E). By working together, **EARLY** and **OFTEN**, they are able to make a difference.

Demographic Data: Knowing Your Community

Socioeconomic status (SES), first language spoken, gender, grade, age, and enrollment all provide information about the community that schools and teachers serve. These data allow schools and teachers to consider any special programming or accommodations that support our overarching Guiding Principle 1: **an inclusive, equitable learning community** (see Chapter 1). Recognizing that immigrants arrive with their own set of perceptions based on their realities and experiences, ensuring equitable *Pathway* opportunities for all students supports increased student achievement and will close the gap for many disengaged students. Working collaboratively with the communities and parent/guardians in every school system is essential. Often statistics establish negative mind-sets of what will be probable outcomes for students with low-SES data. These road bumps must be addressed. Outcomes and opportunities must defy these predetermined mind-sets!

By connecting with and through your community, you can begin to remove unnecessary road bumps. At Langstaff Secondary School in

Richmond Hill, Ontario, with a large English language learner (ELL) population, it was a challenge to convince this group of students and their parents of the benefits of extending learning through a cooperative education experiential program. These students from central Asia were more accustomed to Socratic lessons where the teacher provided all the direction within the confines of a classroom. Parent perceptions were that the only learning "that mattered" occurred within the walls of the school. The teachers set up an opportunity for the ELL students to do a job shadow experience with a co-op student from their school. By accompanying the co-op student to the workplace, with specific inquiry questions in hand, the ELL students were able to experience a new model of learning while learning about the realities of a new work culture. The resulting engagement of the ELL students sparked an interest. This spark became the catalyst to convince parents of the value of this new programming option for their children. Within a year of establishing this model, low ELL student enrollment in cooperative education programming was no longer an issue. Perceptions had been changed.

School and System Data: Closing the Gap

SCHOOL AND SYSTEM DATA

While gains in student achievement occur inside the classroom and are directly influenced by the effectiveness of the teacher, large system change, in owning every student, is only possible when everyone in the organization sees him- or herself as responsible for the success of each student. Each class contributes to the school targets, each school contributes to the system targets, and each system contributes to the state targets. Schools examine their own data, such as

- **Quantitative and Qualitative School Data**—observation notes, perception surveys, student interest surveys, and the amount of student voice heard in each classroom constitute qualitative data; percentage grades, report card comments, suspension rates, attendance records, and standards-based assessments constitute quantitative data;

- **Programming Data**—anecdotal notes about what is making a difference for individual student needs, tracking programming and *Pathway* opportunities afforded students across grades and divisions (see Appendix G); and
- **Completion Data**—credit attainment, graduation rates, and standardized or criterion-referenced asse*ssment r*esults.

Combined, these data sources can provide schools and systems with a snapshot of students' achievement as well as put a **FACE** on struggling students. By being attentive to multiple sources of data, systems, schools, and teachers can provide the opportunities for timely interventions to not only *meet students' needs but also close the gap to raise the bar.*

Once established, the habit of seeing behind the statistics provides powerful new strategies that come naturally. A case in point is Ontario's Student Success Strategy. By using a personal, focused approach on a large scale, Ontario has been able to increase its high school graduation rate from 68% to 81% in six years across the 900 secondary schools in its school system. The basis of the program is that each of the 900 schools has a "Student Success teacher" on staff whose job it is to help school staff members identify secondary students who are on the margins (at risk and vulnerable) and to take action with and on behalf of each student.

Specifically, as the schools and the system routinely paid personal attention to students, one of the central leaders in Ontario thought to identify, on a system level, how many students entered Grade 11 but did not graduate on time. Ontario identified 7,000 students who got as far as Grade 11 but dropped out before graduating. A simple and direct program—let's call it **FACES**—was developed quickly. Leaders contacted the 72 school districts in the Ontario system and gave them the list of dropouts for each school (Sharratt & Fullan, 2012).

The Student Success reengagement strategy was put in place. Schools were "provided with a small amount of money and suggestions that schools hire recently retired guidance counselors to track down each 'lost' student and figure out what it would take to invite them back to complete their program. Of the 7,000 students who had dropped out, 3,500 returned and graduated. Our point is that personalization programs—**FACES**, for short—do not occur spontaneously. Being intentional about the **FACES**, on a local and large scale, can bring dramatic results to close the gap" (Sharratt & Fullan, 2012, pp. 41–45).

Ontario has proven, locally and internationally on PISA results, that by knowing all learners and making contact in a personal way, schools can make a difference in whether students drop out or stay in school (Sharratt & Fullan, 2012). Student data inform our instructional and institutional practices. If we are to successfully guide students to find their *TrueNorth*, then assessing the skills and abilities that frame *The Literate Graduate* is essential.

Foundational Literacy Skills Matter!

Recalculations within the educational sphere are only effective if there is a vision of where you want to go, a sense of purpose that drives you, a commitment to see the Recalculations through, and a willingness to continually check your compass to ensure you are "on route." As we noted previously, the vision and moral purpose need to be reflected in the shared beliefs and understandings clearly articulated throughout the whole organization.

In *Putting FACES on the Data*, we shared the innovative work conducted in one system to develop the profile of its *Literate Graduate* as framed through its shared beliefs and understandings (Sharratt & Fullan, 2012). The graphic use of puzzle pieces—and one empty one (Figure 4.3) symbolizes ongoing learning with the finished picture still evolving and never completed. The benefit of framing such a graphic provided professional conversation points for staff and school leaders, a sense of direction for students and teachers, a growth mind-set for all stakeholders, and a point of connection with many postsecondary destinations.

We asked what literacy skills our high school graduates need so that they can be contributing world citizens. We heard that *The Literate Graduate* must be able to

- write with purpose and clarity,
- communicate effectively using a variety of text forms,

FIGURE 4.3

A Profile of *The Literate Graduate*

PROFILE OF THE LITERATE GRADUATE

York Region District School Board

Mission:
*We unite in our purpose to inspire and prepare
learners for life in our changing world community.*

LCC1003

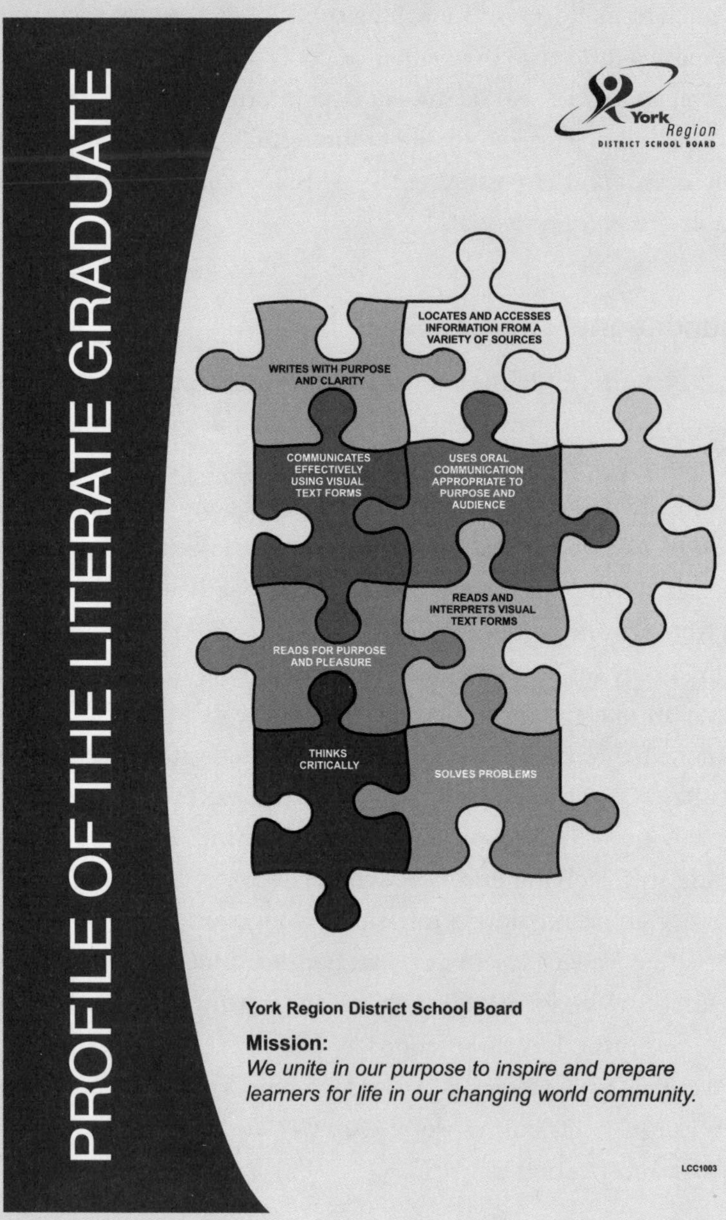

- read for purpose and pleasure,
- think critically,
- locate and access information from a variety of sources,
- use oral communication appropriate to purpose and audience,
- "read" and interpret multiple text forms,
- articulate a point of view,
- question and respond using higher-order thinking skills, and
- problem solve (adapted from York Region District School Board, 2004a).

Clearly, for the 21st-century learner, these skills represent the new "essential" foundational skills required to work and learn with ever-evolving new technologies (York Region District School Board, 2004a).

What Constitutes *The Literate Graduate* in the 21st Century?

In a Recalculated Route, the *Student Pathway DNA* (Figure 1.3, page 18) emphasizes the importance of the close relationship and the inter-connections among the Skill Development Strand (the puzzle pieces), the Curriculum Knowledge Strand, and the Knowledge Application Strand. *The Literate Graduate* is supported and developed through the three strands of the *Student Pathway DNA.*

The *Pathway to Career Readiness Frame: Finding TrueNorth* (Figure 1.1) relies on the understanding that student skill development must be explicitly taught through the core curriculum and assessed accordingly. To do so requires an understanding of not only what skills are being taught, and how they might be practiced and refined, but also a sense of how best to assess and report student progress.

Skills Data

Assessment of student achievement in literacy skills helps us to determine the extent to which we are achieving *The Literate Graduate* outcomes required for *Pathways to Career Readiness.* Foundational literacy skills are expected to be explicitly taught by teachers and demonstrated by students. The foundational pieces of *The Literate Graduate*, in our world, include mathematical literacy, specifically problem solving. We describe the Success Criteria for (1) oral communication, (2) reading, (3) writing, and (4) problem solving as follows.

Oral Communication

Students can

- focus and engage in on-task discussion;
- speak more than the teacher does in class;
- take turns, challenge others' thinking respectfully, respond to others, and revise and reflect on their thinking;
- engage in small-group discussion, make formal presentations, and think-pair-share;
- engage with each other in conversations to problem solve and think critically;
- listen actively to learn new skills and adopt new attitudes; and
- raise questions of each other that promote higher-order thinking.

Reading

Students can

- read for meaning at their instructional levels;
- access and make meaning from rich and diverse texts;
- use all reading comprehension strategies—summarizing, making connections, identifying important ideas, visualizing, predicting, evaluating, questioning, and inferring (reading between the lines);
- access and interpret information from multiple media and digital sources and text forms;
- apply information read to other disciplines and situations;
- articulate how to improve their reading;
- live the lives of authors, seeing reading as useful and enjoyable; and
- evaluate texts (print and online materials) for bias, deception, and social justice issues.

Writing

Students can

- understand the ongoing, recursive nature of the writing process;
- express themselves clearly and in a variety of genres and formats;
- self-assess against a developmental writing continuum;
- articulate how to improve their writing against an exemplar;
- respond in writing to demonstrate higher-order, critical thinking; and
- distinguish between bias and point of view.

Problem Solving

Students can

- identify multiple ways to solve problems;
- reason, using logical sequential steps;
- comprehend problems conceptually;
- carry out procedures logically;
- show solutions in pictures, words, and symbols;
- view problem solving as useful and worthwhile; and
- explain and justify the most efficient solution.

Assessment of the Foundational Skills

Beginning with the end in mind is just good assessment practice—the outcome is that we want all students to master the above foundational literacy and mathematical literacy skills. This is a given. This is the intentional way to close the gap at every level. We start with knowing the learners socially, emotionally, and academically and progress to putting **FACES** on the data, ensuring that learners know the clear expectations that their teachers have for them.

Figure 4.4 depicts the flow of formative assessment—assessment "for" and "as" learning that allows teachers to use the ongoing formative data, collected daily, to assess and teach the very next day, as we believe that data today is instruction tomorrow.

In Figure 4.4, the Learning Goals/Intentions (LG/Is) are derived from state standards or curriculum expectations of what is to be taught. Specific reflection on curriculum expectations and the Big Ideas derived from them give teachers and students opportunities to co-construct how to be successful in attaining the LG/Is. We defined Big Ideas in *Putting FACES on the Data* (Sharratt & Fullan, 2012) as "the teaching of the higher-order thinking skills of analysis, interpretation, evaluation and synthesis of a text or curriculum unit . . . providing students with the modeling of higher-order thinking skills and opportunities to think through text or essential questions critically, bringing them to levels of deep understanding, creativity and new learning" (p. 203).

Success Criteria (SC) must be clear, visible in classrooms, and easily understood by students. Students are more likely to be successful and

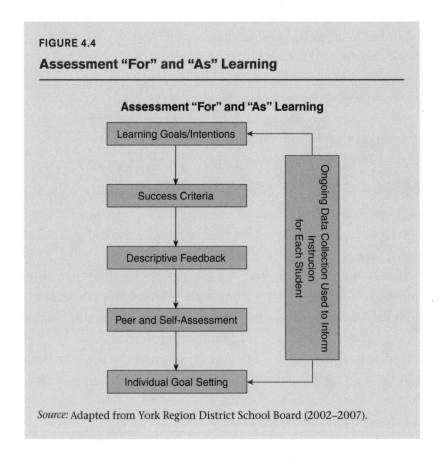

FIGURE 4.4

Assessment "For" and "As" Learning

Source: Adapted from York Region District School Board (2002–2007).

hence engaged more readily when LG/Is and SC are co-constructed by the teacher and students so that students understand, in detail, how to be successful. Success breeds success. When teachers incorporate evidence-proven teaching practices, such as making LG/Is and co-constructed SC visible, by posting them in classrooms, all students' achievement will improve. As Hattie (2012) reminds us, students who are confident as assessment-capable learners have an impactful effect size of 1.44. Thus, teachers are more confident in their professional practice as specificity breeds success for teachers, too—that is, teacher and student empowerment occurs.

Explicit Descriptive Feedback is the key element in assessment that improves instruction, and it is best used by students when they articulate what next steps they will take to improve their learning prior to a summative point in their learning. Feedback must be timely, precise, and clearly understood by students—we say one praise point and (at least) one instructional point in each verbal or written piece of feedback (Sharratt & Fullan 2009). Hattie (2012) states that feedback is most powerful when the nature of the feedback is related to the student's degree of proficiency (from novice to proficient). Hattie (2012) also reminds us that how well students are progressing (or not) is invaluable feedback for teachers in how well their teaching is increasing all

> "Big Ideas are the teaching of the higher-order thinking skills of analysis, interpretation, evaluation and synthesis of a text or curriculum unit. The term 'big idea' does not mean naming a theme unit such as 'Friendship' and selecting a bunch of books and activities that go along with the Friendship Theme, but rather providing students with the modeling of higher-order thinking skills and opportunities to think through text or essential questions critically, bringing them to levels of deep understanding, creativity and new learning. 'Big Ideas' can be addressed through the reading of individual texts or through a unit of study but they need to cause and stretch student thinking by highlighting what is essential in the text or learning experience and connecting these ideas meaningfully to students' lives and the world"
>
> M. Greenan, personal communication, August 2011, as cited in Sharratt & Fullan, 2012, p. 203.

students' achievement—and how they must craft lessons to achieve that (pp. 96–98). Skilled teachers see their role as evaluating their effect on students' learning (Hattie, 2012, p. 19).

The ability to peer and self-assess is an important goal in teaching—which begins to develop in kindergarten. Teachers must ask, "Can students apply what has been learned to new situations?" This occurs only when students can reread their work on their own volition to improve or when they use teachers' Descriptive Feedback to self-assess and improve their work, thereby becoming independent learners—taking ownership of their learning. Then, when formal, summative evaluation takes place and students are part of the process, there are no surprises because they know how they have done.

Figure 4.4 shows the "waterfall" progression in assessment and instruction of the foundational literacy skills that ultimately lead to students being able to set their individual Learning Goals/Intentions (LG/Is) and clearly articulate at any given moment how they can improve.

When students set their own individual Learning Goals, they begin to own their successes as well as their unique personal needs and improvement strategies. Then the cycle in Figure 4.4 repeats itself, in a perpetual flow of assessment data that inform teaching and learning.

One way to assess how we can make Figure 4.4 come to life and check for deep use of assessment "for" and "as" learning is to use the five questions that we first asked students and now ask teachers and leaders as well:

1. What are you learning?
2. How are you doing?
3. How do you know?
4. How can you improve?
5. Where do you go for help?

Leaders who do daily Learning Walks and Talks (Sharratt & Fullan, 2012) (see Chapter 2) gather evidence of teachers' intentional teaching and of students' improvement when they ask students the five questions above. Students who can accurately describe their learning, and how to improve, close the achievement gap. After many walks, conversations

TABLE 4.1

The Power of Five Questions to Answer "How Do You Know?"

5 Questions for Students	Teachers Do . . .	Students Say . . .	Leaders Observe . . .
1. What are you learning?	• Deconstruct curriculum expectations to develop Learning Goals/Intentions (LG/Is). • Work with students to develop LG/Is in student-friendly language. • Post LG/Is in classrooms for students' reference.	• "I am learning to discuss and use more descriptive words in my narrative writing." • "I am adding more descriptive words to my writing so the reader knows what I am thinking as an author."	• Purposeful talk among students in classrooms. • More student than teacher talk. • Whole group/small group—individual work in classrooms. • Students clearly articulate LG/Is and why they are learning them. • No students are saying "I don't know." • The five questions are posted in all classrooms to serve as a reminder of intentional teaching.
2. How are you doing?	• Co-construct with students how to be successful using age-appropriate language. • Ensure that students use Success Criteria (SC) language and they understand what they look like. • Develop SC that are not checklists. • Add to SC as lessons progress.	• "I am able to do the first SC at a Level 4." • "I am working on the second and third SC." • "Here's my work that shows how I can do the first SC."	• Anchor charts/prompts/scaffolds are clearly visible in classrooms. • These charts are marked up (not laminated) indicating frequent use.

(Continued)

5 Questions for Students	Teachers Do . . .	Students Say . . .	Leaders Observe . . .
3. How do you know?	• Give timely, relevant feedback based on LG/Is and SC. • Teach students how to peer and self-assess accurately based on LG/Is and SC.	• "My teacher and I have talked about my writing, and we decided . . ." • "I got feedback on my narrative from my friends, and they said . . ."	• Written comments on students' work are explicit and do not include "well done" or "good work" or other such platitudes. • Teachers are giving explicit oral feedback and recording it for follow-up.
4. How can you improve?	• Make anecdotal notes of written and oral feedback to give ongoing feedback. • Track and monitor feedback given to know students' progress and plan next steps.	• "I am working on being better at . . . " • "The teacher gave me this writing feedback sheet to put in my binder."	• Students can clearly articulate their next steps to improvement of their work.
5. Where do you go for help?	• Work with students on becoming independent learners by teaching them where they can go for help beyond the teacher.	• "I go to [name of classmate] as s/he is very good at . . . " • "I look at the chart we made in class to remember where I can go for help." • "I go to our class website to look again at the lesson." • "I go to my parents or to a homework help online site when I'm stuck."	• Scaffolds in classrooms show discussions of where supports are for students' learning. • Students can articulate several places where they can go for help in addition to the teacher.

with teachers ensue. Leaders ask authentic questions about why teachers make the decisions they make. Leaders also take action if teaching is not occurring at a competent or preferably high-impact level. Action must be taken if students are not progressing at an expected rate (Sharratt, 2013a). Table 4.1 gives explicit examples of how leaders, teachers, and students work together to create clearly articulated purposeful learning.

Another powerful way to assess how we're doing in increasing all students' achievement to close the gap is to collaboratively mark student work. The collaborative marking of student work is essential at all grade levels, K–12+. Cross-grade and same-grade examination of student work, based on common assessment tasks, drives the process and offers teachers invaluable data about "before, during, and after" expectations of the work. It is teacher led, and leaders are part of the team. After engaging in this approach, teachers and administrators know how to determine the instructional starting points for each learner and can clearly articulate the next steps in learning for all students by determining the Descriptive Feedback to be given to each student (Sharratt, 2013b).

The above two approaches, asking students the five questions and collaborative marking of student work, become a large and focused part of every Professional Learning session, which is critical for all teachers and leaders. Taking daily Learning Walks and Talks to ask learners the five questions and making time, bi-weekly, for collaboratively marking students' work ensure that teachers have the time to reflect on the firm foundation necessary for all students' mastery of reading, writing, oral language, and problem-solving skills—which then provides the springboard needed to incorporate the 21st-century skills into the curriculum content.

21st-Century Skills

While there appears to be universal support for the importance of what are casually and frequently referred to as 21st-century skills, there is ongoing controversy over which skills are most important for student success in the 21st century. Numerous skills' frameworks exist as illustrated in Table 4.2.

TABLE 4.2

The Evolving 21st-Century *Literate Graduate*

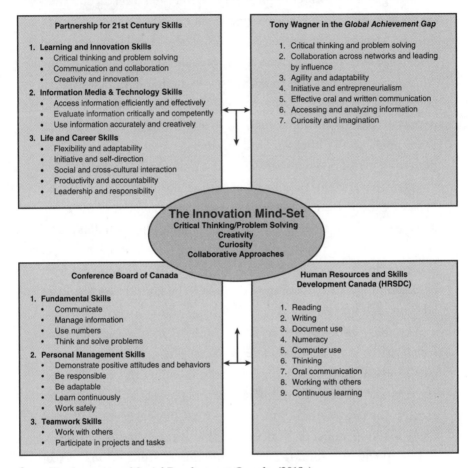

Partnership for 21st Century Skills

1. **Learning and Innovation Skills**
   - Critical thinking and problem solving
   - Communication and collaboration
   - Creativity and innovation
2. **Information Media & Technology Skills**
   - Access information efficiently and effectively
   - Evaluate information critically and competently
   - Use information accurately and creatively
3. **Life and Career Skills**
   - Flexibility and adaptability
   - Initiative and self-direction
   - Social and cross-cultural interaction
   - Productivity and accountability
   - Leadership and responsibility

Tony Wagner in the *Global Achievement Gap*

1. Critical thinking and problem solving
2. Collaboration across networks and leading by influence
3. Agility and adaptability
4. Initiative and entrepreneurialism
5. Effective oral and written communication
6. Accessing and analyzing information
7. Curiosity and imagination

The Innovation Mind-Set
Critical Thinking/Problem Solving
Creativity
Curiosity
Collaborative Approaches

Conference Board of Canada

1. **Fundamental Skills**
   - Communicate
   - Manage information
   - Use numbers
   - Think and solve problems
2. **Personal Management Skills**
   - Demonstrate positive attitudes and behaviors
   - Be responsible
   - Be adaptable
   - Learn continuously
   - Work safely
3. **Teamwork Skills**
   - Work with others
   - Participate in projects and tasks

Human Resources and Skills Development Canada (HRSDC)

1. Reading
2. Writing
3. Document use
4. Numeracy
5. Computer use
6. Thinking
7. Oral communication
8. Working with others
9. Continuous learning

Source: Employment and Social Development Canada. (2013a).

Beyond the foundational skills of literacy and mathematical literacy that we have highlighted, skills that stand out as common to all and best aligned with the demands of the workplace and an "innovator's mind-set" are

- critical thinking/problem solving,
- creativity,
- curiosity, and
- collaborative approaches.

Critical thinking and problem solving are first for a reason. They are the bridge between the foundational language literacy and mathematical literacy skills and the 21st-century skills. The four consolidated 21st-century skills demand collaboration on the part of teachers and students—and in some instances community partners—working together toward a common goal to find a solution or resolve an issue. For Collaborative Inquiry to reflect deep learning, teachers need time to formulate rich performance tasks, and students need time to work on these tasks that are relevant and authentic, and demand critical thinking and problem solving. It is through this Knowledge Application Strand of the *Student Pathway DNA* that the skilled teacher activates this level of learning.

In Appendix H, we have provided a detailed Student "Innovation Mind-Set" Self-Assessment Sheet that demonstrates how teachers and students can work together to not only know the expectations of these learning skills but also determine, together, what is needed for the student's next level of work and how teachers and other resources can be of assistance to the student. As we indicate in Chapter 6, Collaborative Inquiry is a process that is not linear but involves observable steps (Figure 6.5, page 197). Both strong communication skills and cognitive insights are necessary, observable, and measurable in this process.

Getting Started

As Nelson Mandela said, "It always seems impossible until it is done" (Brainy Quote, 2014c). What will be your frame of reference to get started? While currently there appears to be different starting points for systems and nations in terms of building a 21st-century skills framework, what is evident is a common desire to nurture and support a generation capable of formulating better innovative ideas and having the courage to implement them. Perhaps this in itself is a sufficient vision for states, systems, and schools to start the process of Recalculating the Route to *The Literate Graduate.*

Individual skill sets begin to emerge by asking educators and workplace employers tough questions, such as the following:

- "What are the qualities/skills we value in our graduates?"
- "What does a knowledge worker look like?"
- "What sub-set of skills needs to be nurtured in students in order for them to be able to generate this type of thinking?"
- "How do we go about assessing and measuring those skills?"
- "What do we envision the world to look like in 20 years' time?"
- "What skills will our youth need to be successful in this world?"
- "What would learning be like if it was designed around these responses?" (Boss, 2012 p. XXIV).

Choosing the Navigational Markers

Assessment and Teaching of 21st Century Skills (2014) offers a framework for answering the questions above by organizing the four common skills into four categories:

1. Ways of Thinking
2. Ways of Working
3. Tools for Working
4. Living in the World

This framework provides us with a useful organizer to discuss 21st-century skills that can be added to the foundational pieces of *The Literate Graduate* and not only close the gap but reach for the top with each student. Innovative teaching occurs when it is focused on students' **FACES**. It can be readily observed and assessed in classrooms through specific actions that students are demonstrating. We specifically provide these expected skills in each area of the four categories:

Ways of Thinking include the skill sets of innovation, creativity, critical thinking, problem solving, decision making, and learning to learn (metacognition) and are evident when the following SC are met:

Students can

- persevere with a task,
- fail and regroup,
- try new strategies,
- think through alternative solutions,
- demonstrate originality,
- correct in midcourse,
- improvise,
- use constructive feedback to move forward confidently,
- evaluate their own thinking and set goals to improve, and
- apply learned success critical thinking processes to future endeavors.

Ways of Working include communication and collaboration and are evident when the following SC are met:

Students can

- listen to alternatives and apply the most appropriate solutions,
- resolve differences in respectful ways,
- be flexible,
- compromise authentically,
- outline steps to group task completion with co-constructed SC,
- give and get feedback,
- take ownership of the process and product within a group and individually, and
- identify where they can go for help beyond the teacher.

Tools for Working include information literacy and information and communication technology (ICT) literacy and are evident when the following SC are met:

Students can

- use the appropriate digital media for communication, production, and collaboration;
- determine what information may be needed;
- find relevant information;

- teach others using digital media;
- self-evaluate and articulate how to improve;
- establish their own learning networks; and
- defend choices.

Living in the World includes citizenship, life and career personal and social responsibility, and culture awareness and competency and is evident when the following SC are met:

Students can

- manage time,
- consider others' perspectives,
- articulate options,
- use "we,"
- be courteous and grateful,
- be reflective to consider implications of actions,
- understand social responsibility,
- set clear goals for self and as global citizens,
- select partners inside and beyond the school,
- contribute to greater good beyond self,
- regulate self in society and within cultural norms, and
- make choices that they can live with.

These skills are universal and wanted by all for all. Some systems that have made significant inroads in building *Pathways to Career Readiness* have adopted a vision or purpose that embraces these specific skill subsets. Not only do systems weave the skill development through the curriculum, but they also use practical applications within the workplace and across postsecondary institutions to reinforce and assess the skills.

Finland, for example, has a culture of consensus building and stability, a history of relative equity (narrow gaps, low influence of socioeconomic background), and a consistency of strong educational results. There is continued Professional Learning. For instance, Finland has demonstrated a strong commitment to universal achievement and equity of outcomes in its education policy as well as overall societal infrastructure (Fullan & Barber, 2010).

Finland is committed to innovation. This is supported through a collaborative co-teaching approach (see Appendix F). In addition, the country expects its *Literate Graduates* to be multilingual. It is not uncommon for Finnish students to have acquired five languages by the completion of high school.

Both examples, Finland and the system story of constructing the puzzle of *The Literate Graduate*, model an innovative approach. By harnessing teacher and leader creativity, there is an opportunity for exploring *a structured, collaboratively planned approach* to working toward a clear understanding of what the specific skill development for students should be and how best to assess that learning. The very term *innovation* implies that while you might not get things right the first time, there is a process in place to review, adjust, unlearn, relearn, and refine—to keep working on something until precision is experienced and applied.

> "Innovation on some level is evolution not revolution. It's the idea of taking something and making it better. It is about deepening and enriching"
>
> Chris Lehmann, cited in Boss, 2012, p. 14.

> "The illiterate of the 21st Century are not those who cannot read and write, but those that cannot learn, unlearn and relearn"
>
> Alvin Toffler, quoted on Goodreads, 2014.

Teachers must take responsibility for their own learning, unlearning, and relearning as they consider the needs of *The Literate Graduate*. They search for authentic opportunities that encourage inquiry, teamwork, and big thinking. They need to know the "buzz" in their classrooms. Something as simple as our language instills innovative thinking. "What would you like to be when you grow up?" is very narrow and confining; however, "What would you like to *try*?" is open-ended with possibilities—it lends itself to much more interesting questions for students to consider on their Self-Knowledge Learning Journey: What do you find interesting about that? What might it involve? What attributes might you need? Teachers make the weather in their classroom—will it be one where curiosity and creativity flourish? One that leverages learning skills and work habits, to build a foundation for life skills and employability skills?

Higher-Order Thinking

Collaborative Inquiry, as we describe in detail in Chapter 6, is an intentional way to teach higher-order thinking skills and develop independent learners who own their own learning. By using rich, authentic performance tasks, the assessment is focused on the process as well as the product. *The MILE Guide: Milestones for Improving Learning and Education*, developed by the Partnership for 21st Century Skills (2009), helps systems determine where they are on the spectrum of 21st-century skills integration and then use that information to plan a path for future work that brings 21st-century skills into their systems of learning. To get systems to move to higher-order thinking framed within a six-step approach, the guide prioritizes

1. getting buy-in;
2. teaching through core subjects and themes;
3. raising the bar—focusing on critical thinking and problem solving;
4. assessing current status;
5. developing implementation plans; and
6. collaborating for the future.

In Ontario, the SHSM program is rewarding higher-order thinking through the development of a recognized innovation and creativity certification. Cooperative education programs in Ontario use tools such as the Ontario Skills Passport (Ontario Ministry of Education, 2014) to assess student workplace and essential skills. Career Academies in the United States have online assessment tools such as the College and Work Readiness Assessment. In elementary schools, teachers use classroom observation, Developmental Reading Assessment, and PM Benchmarks and state-wide testing to determine if our instructional practices are getting the results intended for *The Literate Graduate*. Once the student profiles are in place, teachers are in a better position to consider these 21st-century skills in the context of their lessons as they design down from the Big Ideas found by interconnecting the curriculum expectations across the content areas.

Developing Innovation Skills

Systems need a vision of what is possible, beyond a few random examples of innovative schools in each system. They need an infrastructure to support widespread "whole system" innovation. *Leaders* must become lead learners who can recognize and remove barriers to innovation and support high-yield teaching practices. *Teachers* need continuous Professional Learning (PL) sessions with strong examples of structured Collaborative Inquiry processes and ongoing formative assessment practices that go well beyond the true/false and fill-in-the-blank performance tasks often used currently. *Students* need opportunities to know themselves as learners, to take risks and become lead learners with fellow students and teachers. *Community partners* must experience multilevel collaboration to feel like contributors to the solutions to the alarmingly high "dropout" rate, highlighted by the ever-increasing number of disenfranchised underemployed or unemployed youth in our society.

> "Reading, math and science are the foundations of student achievement. But to compete and win in the global economy, today's students and tomorrow's leaders need another set of knowledge and skills. These 21st Century skills include the development of global awareness and the ability to collaborate and communicate and analyze and address problems. And they need to rely on critical thinking and problem solving to create innovative solutions to the issues facing our world. Every child should have the opportunity to acquire and master these skills and our schools play a vital role in making this happen"
>
> Michael Dell, quoted in Sharma, 2014, p. 2.

All of these urgent demands require an "up-shift" to a culture of learning and caring about the environment in which our *Literate Graduates* experience authentic, hands-on learning. As Michael Dell says, "To compete and win in the global economy, today's students and tomorrow's leaders need another set of knowledge and skills."

From Good to Great to
Innovate

In Ontario, as part of the ongoing educational reform process beginning in 2000, elementary school criterion-referenced literacy and math test scores were proving to be a strong indicator of student performance and success in high school. To confirm this, data collection included high school graduation, early leaver, attendance, and suspension rates, as well as the tracking number of credits earned in any given year. These data sets framed the expected completion outcomes for the systems. But was this enough to close the gap? With increasing concern over student engagement, schools started to take a closer look at the *Pathways* they were building for their students.

- Questions they asked included the following:
  - How were the instructional approaches used by the teachers aligning with students' engagement?
  - Were there significant gender differences in the data?
  - How did students with special needs measure up?
  - How many students were taking advantage of experiential/hands-on learning programs such as co-op and work experience?
  - How did these programs influence students' choice of destination?

- Where were students going after secondary school?
  - Was there a difference between where students thought they were going and where they actually did go?
  - Why were students not continuing on, immediately after graduation, with furthering their studies? Were students disengaged or uncertain, or was postsecondary education becoming cost prohibitive?

- Were *Pathways* being clearly articulated?
  - Was the current offering of courses and programs reflective of all postsecondary destinations?
  - What programming opportunities to which students were exposed helped them to make better informed decisions?
  - Were schools attending to the transition needs of this group of students?
  - How were parents informed about *Pathway* opportunities?

In York Region District School Board, cohort data for two graduating groups were examined and used to inform school planning and program implementation. Perception data from students, teachers, and the community were gathered through system surveys (see Appendix D). The questions and the data informed the process and the resources that needed to be applied to the next level of work. As an old business saying goes, "what gets measured gets managed." A comprehensive system improvement plan was developed with specific targets set. Individual schools were then required to develop their own school improvement plans based upon the priorities outlined in the system plan. Alignment was achieved. The overriding *Pathway* target was established in the system improvement plan for targeted percent growth in SHSM programming across all high schools.

For that performance target to be reached, it required that multiple strategies needed to be rolled out and implemented in schools. Since SHSM programming includes all *Pathways* and all learners, the attention to Experiential Learning models, differentiated instruction, Collaborative Inquiry, integration of cross-curricular expectations, transition conversations, and work with parents and community partners complemented other areas of work identified as priorities in the system improvement plan.

How we get students and teachers to move from passive learning stances to authentic Collaborative Inquiry will be very much determined by the choices they are afforded—as they move from thinking to doing, as outlined in Chapter 5.

STEPS TO STUDENTS' SUCCESS

1. Source various ways to gather perception data from staff, students, and community partners and triangulate it with qualitative data to make informed decisions.

2. Share transparent data with parents and the public.

3. Assess system effectiveness on an ongoing basis.

4. Make students aware of their own data regarding their abilities, interests, and opportunities.

5. Have the will, perseverance, and determination to provide multiple *Pathways* to opportunity, K–12+.

6. Audit the *Pathways* you provide at every level.

7. Measure success in the exactness and visibility of co-constructing learning intentions, Success Criteria, Descriptive Feedback, peer and self–assessment, and the student's individual goal setting.

8. Timetable teachers' collaborative marking of student work.

9. Graduate *Literate Graduates* who understand and can apply 21st-century skills.

10. Ask the five questions of students (page 138) on daily Learning Walks and Talks to take the improvement pulse.

Reflective Pause by Louise Stoll

How to close the gap to raise the bar—it's the million-dollar question, and the answer is data. So many reflections, so little space. Here are just a few thoughts.

1. *Evaluate what matters.* This book and chapter rightly argue that it's essential to go beyond "the usual suspects" when thinking about the necessary outcomes for *Career Readiness*. The trouble is that we always fall back on what's easily measured. It's good to see that the Organisation for Economic Co-operation and Development (OECD) is starting to address this by including comparative assessments of collaborative problem solving using technology in its 2015 Program for International Student Assessment. We're told that other skills will follow. But large-scale assessment doesn't get at the heart of what school communities value in terms of *Career Readiness*. Only a community's members can jointly determine the outcomes they value and then ensure that these are assessed. This is no easy task, but universities and other research organizations can also become partners. But never forget the qualities that

will make those career-ready graduates human as articulated under "Choosing the Navigational Markers" for *Living in the World*. I hope this includes them feeling happy and good about themselves.

2. *Take a closer look together.* Rarely applied to education, as I read the chapter the term *forensic* came to mind. Clearly, just how and why those gaps are occurring needs much greater scrutiny. Educators' lives are demanding, and many people argue that they don't have the time or skills to analyze data. But the right kinds of data can unlock doors, as we and others have found in many projects in England and elsewhere. Involvement is also a critical trigger for buy-in and change. If we're serious about *Pathways to Career Readiness*, everyone has to be more data "savvy"; inquiry habits of mind (Earl & Katz, 2006) have to become the norm. It doesn't take a huge amount of data to create a profound shift in practice (note it is important not to drown in data), but thinking of the right questions and then determining exactly what data you require to answer those community-generated questions is hard. Preservice training and professional learning of teachers are needed, including helping educators learn how best to involve other community members in the process.

3. *The power of perception.* Placing perceptual data in the center is smart. Really listening to what students have to say about their learning often provides teachers with the compelling motivation to transform their teaching strategies, but it requires being truly open to having long-held assumptions challenged. Teachers' perceptions and those of other members of the community about issues like trust, openness, collaboration, and partnership also act as indicators of how they will respond to the kinds of deep changes to practice described or implied in the chapter. In my experience, gathering these kinds of data and taking their message seriously are fundamental to meaningful change.

4. *Communication as learning.* Communication is critical, as the chapter highlights, but communication isn't just dissemination. It's hard helping people to engage with data and other evidence. Serious engagement is a process of learning, and finding powerful ways to "animate" data and other kinds of knowledge is a key feature of community learning (Stoll, 2010). Coming to grips with data and making collective meaning that can shift practice in more than one or two

classrooms depends, in part, on rich conversations about data. I was particularly struck by the *Literate Graduate* puzzle graphic (Figure 4.3). The puzzle, with its incomplete, evolving image, offers a creative trigger for conversation among community members. In England, newspapers now convey national data using diverse visual representations, and one newspaper is even offering courses in data visualisation and infographics to help participants "create compelling stories out of raw data." The question I would add to the authors' ones at the end of this chapter is "How can communities ensure that their data tell compelling stories about how they have closed the gap to raise the bar?"

About Louise Stoll, PhD

Louise Stoll's research and development activity focuses on how schools, districts, and national systems create capacity for learning and improvement, with particular emphasis on creative leadership, leadership development, Professional Learning communities, and learning networks. Louise is also committed to finding ways to help make better connections between research and practice. A former president of the International Congress for School Effectiveness and School Improvement, and an academician of the Academy of Social Sciences, she is a part-time professor at the London Centre for Leadership in Learning at the Institute of Education, University of London, a freelance researcher, an OECD expert, and an international consultant. She started her career as a teacher in London, and also spent six years as research director at the Halton Board of Education in Ontario. Author and editor of many publications, including *Professional Learning Communities* with Karen Seashore Louis, *It's About Learning (and It's About Time)* with Dean Fink and Lorna Earl, and *Changing Our Schools: Linking School Effectiveness and School Improvement* with Dean Fink, her books have been translated into five languages. She has developed research-based materials on Professional Learning communities, a simulation on networking, and *The Toolkit: Improving School Leadership* for the OECD. Co-editor of a book series, *Expanding Educational Horizons*, she is a popular international keynote presenter and workshop facilitator.

CHOICE MATTERS!

The motivators for students, the choices they have, and how they see themselves in their own future influence not only students' individual sense of belonging within the school community but the degree to which they learn. As educators, how do we take that knowledge and move from "good to great to innovate" when considering a Recalculated Route that supports *Pathways to Career Readiness* for the 21st-century learner?

The *Student Pathway DNA* (Figure 1.3, p. 18) reminds us that learning is optimized when there are personalized opportunities to connect to the learning. How does this class/course fit in with our students' skills, interests, and dispositions? What might we improve? What has sparked students' interests? These personal connections are intensified when the curriculum knowledge is practiced through authentic, timely, structured experiences.

These experiences allow students to apply their learning while serving as a metric to reflect on as they consider their future choices. What do students think about? What has this experience taught

QUESTIONS THAT MATTER MOST

1. What are the multiple ways your students have to demonstrate their learning?

2. How do your students co-construct, with teachers, the Success Criteria by which they will be assessed?

3. How do you ensure that all students see a future possibility for themselves in the courses and opportunities offered?

4. As a teacher, school, or system, how are you tapping into the creativity and innovative skills of your students, colleagues, and community?

5. How are you enlisting new forms of student-community interactions to ensure that students themselves are part of the retention solutions?

6. How do you help students find their voice?

7. How might you create safe opportunities for students to take intellectual risks, learn from their mistakes, and improve their work through revisions?

8. What is your Professional Learning plan for supporting skilled teachers?

9. What are the skills, knowledge, and mind-sets that teachers require?

10. What Recalculations need to occur in the education system to address this skill/knowledge/mind-set development?

students about themselves? In what other context could students apply this learning? Collaborative Inquiry, cross-curricular/interdisciplinary units of study, and Experiential Learning approaches are just some of the instructional practices that enable this kind of learning in context to take place.

The choices made within each strand impact student learning and skill development. How well the three strands are aligned and integrated, through guided Collaborative Inquiry, will influence whether the choices are informed choices.

The three *Student Pathway DNA* strands and their respective Learning Journeys—Self-Knowledge, Collaborative Inquiry, and Experiential—provide opportunities for students to reflect on their learning as they consider what they would like to try, who they would like to be, how they think about things, and ultimately what further learning they would like to pursue.

If students are to find their *TrueNorth*, then the *Student Pathway DNA* is dependent on a foundation of *informed student choice* particularly where students are given "choice" and "voice" over course selection, program selection, *Pathway* destinations, preferred instructional approaches, and opportunities to explore.

In Ontario, Canada, an Individual Pathways Plan (IPP) has been put in place as part of the Student Success Strategy to ensure that all students, Grades 7–12, are supported in this process. Teachers, in every curriculum area, support students in planning *Pathways* by providing learning opportunities that enable them to

> " *"Getting students ready to tackle tomorrow's challenges means helping them to develop a new set of skills and fresh ways of thinking that they won't acquire through text-book driven instruction. They need opportunities to practice these new skills on right-sized projects, with supports in place to scaffold the learning. Success will be dependent upon the student knowing how to frame problems, generate ideas, test solutions, and learn from what works as well as what doesn't"* (Boss, 2012, pp. 3–4).*

1. **explore** subject-related education and career/life options (in our model, that is matching the Skill Development Strand and the Curriculum Knowledge Strand);
2. **apply** subject specific knowledge and skills to work-related situations (in our model, that is matching the Curriculum Knowledge Strand and the Knowledge Application Strand); and
3. **become** competent self-directed planners (in our model, that is matching all three DNA strands and their respective Learning Journeys).

Learning Journeys

A Recalculated Route uses inquiry questions as prompts. Students are encouraged not only in the planning but also in building skill sets that will enable them to be responsive to the changing world around them. We look closely at the questions students must ask themselves and others in the respective Learning Journeys of our three DNA strands: (1) Self-Knowledge (Strand 1: Skill Development), (2) Collaborative

Inquiry (Strand 2: Curriculum Knowledge), and (3) Experiential Learning (Strand 3: Knowledge Application).

Self-Knowledge Learning Journey (Strand 1: Skill Development)

Students ask,

- Who am I?
- What might I try, to learn more about myself?
- What might I aspire to do?
- How will I move forward toward my goals and aspirations? (See Figure 5.1.)

FIGURE 5.1

Self-Knowledge Learning Journey

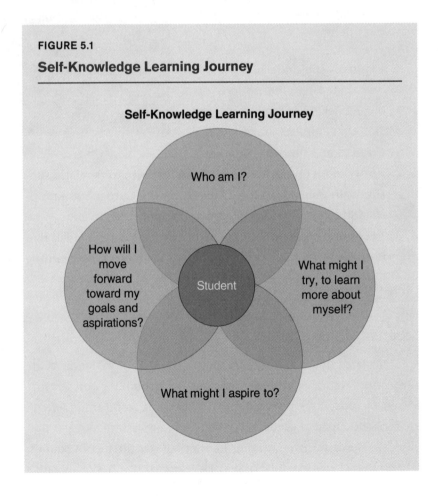

To help answer the questions, students think about and identify

- the characteristics that describe who they are,
- the factors that influence or shape the outcome of who they might become,
- how these characteristics and factors shape their thoughts and actions, and
- how they will plan for success—what they should "try" (adapted from the Ontario Ministry of Education, 2013a).

Collaborative Inquiry Learning Journey (Strand 2: Curriculum Knowledge)

Students ask,

- What do I wonder about? What questions do I have?
- What do I already know? What will I need to explore more deeply?
- Where can I go for help? What tools do I need?
- What new understandings can I apply to other situations? (See Figure 5.2.)

To help answer the questions, students explore

- the relationship among opportunities, choices, and *Pathways*;
- ways to refine and extend their learning;
- other approaches or supports they might consider; and
- how they might apply the new learning to other contexts.

Experiential Learning Journey (Strand 3: Knowledge Application)

Students ask,

- What kind of learner am I?
- What are the best ways for me to demonstrate my learning?
- What opportunities would extend and refine my learning?
- How can I apply this new learning to my future plans? (See Figure 5.3.)

FIGURE 5.2

Collaborative Inquiry Learning Journey

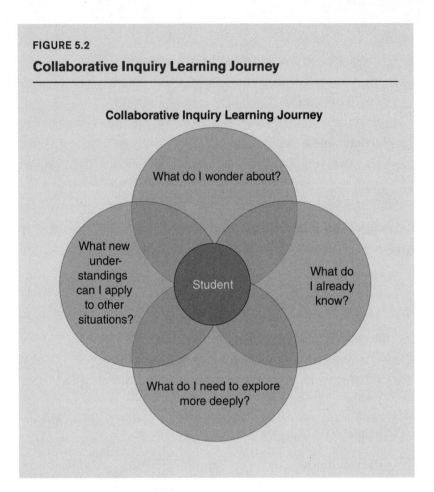

Collaborative Inquiry Learning Journey

What do I wonder about?

What new under-standings can I apply to other situations?

Student

What do I already know?

What do I need to explore more deeply?

> "Students become the architects of their own lives as they gain the confidence in knowing they can revise their plan as the world around them changes"
>
> Ontario Ministry of Education, 2013a.

To help answer the questions, students explore

- experiences that create a "spark" for them,
- how features of programs and opportunities fit with who they are,
- what and where programming opportunities are in the broader community, and

FIGURE 5.3

Experiential Learning Journey

Experiential Learning Journey

What kind of learner am I ?

How can I apply this new learning to my futures plans?

Student

What are the best ways for me to demonstrate my learning?

What opportunities would extend and refine my learning?

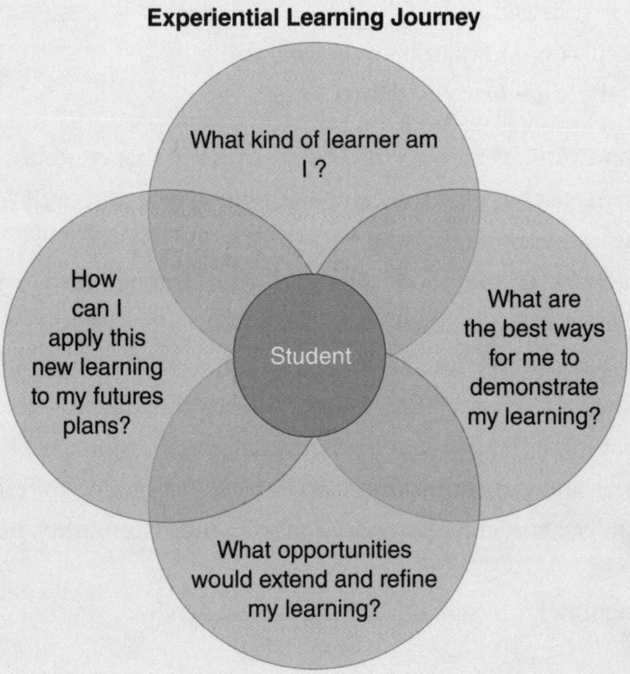

- how they review and revise their plans in light of the changes they recognize in themselves.

Clearing the *Pathway* Congestion

For informed student choice to be achieved, it is essential that there is **a robust, relevant K–12+ curriculum** with clear expectations that frame the educational program in the system/state/country outlined in Guiding Principle 2 (see Chapter 1). In a Recalculated Route, within that educational program there needs to be

- an inclusive learning culture where all destinations are valued and accessible through programming and/or course selections;
- fundamental beliefs that
  - each student can achieve given the right time and resources,
  - success comes in many forms, and
  - there are many *Pathways* to success;

- opportunities for informed choices within that educational program, so that learning can be individualized and optimized for each student;
- intentional alignment and matching among the curriculum content delivery, student skills/abilities and aptitudes, and the opportunities afforded (see Figure 1.3);
- "yield signs" and "turn-abouts," strategically placed, for choices that might lead to dead ends, traffic jams, or collisions;
- clear and ongoing communications differentiated for all stakeholders: students, parents, teachers, and community partners; and
- ongoing Professional Learning for teachers.

Robust and Relevant Curriculum Needed

Indiana, in the United States, is making career and vocational education a priority in every high school in the state. Currently, 11 Regional Work Councils made up of educators and business leaders are working to design new career and vocational curricula that are relevant to jobs in their communities. To support this curriculum development, Indiana has created the Center for Education and Career Innovation (CECI). CECI is an innovative approach to the education and workforce preparation pipeline that breaks down the silos that exist among K–12+ schools, higher education, and workforce development as the state believes that change starts with fresh thinking about where kids are headed after high school graduation.

Source: Pascopella (2013).

Clearly Articulated *Pathways* Matter!

If our goal is to ensure that students complete high school, efficiently and effectively, then clearly articulated *Pathway* opportunities need to be understood by students and parents so they can make informed choices. Students need to be able to navigate their way through the educational system with smooth transitions while making well-considered decisions derived from multiple choices that teachers present to them.

The role of the teacher is key. Each teacher must have the capacity, commitment, and accountability to weave the student Skill Development DNA Strand into the learning as well as matching the relevant, authentic Knowledge Application DNA Strand. To do this in the context of postsecondary destinations requires a broad level of knowledge by the teacher. Given that most teachers' experience is limited to university or college training, this is a huge knowledge gap that needs to be addressed as part of Recalculating the Route.

High-performing systems prioritize the Professional Learning of their teachers. They are cognizant that ignorance and misinformation can act as roadblocks to youthful ambition. Through professional networks, systems provide learning opportunities for both teachers and students that align with and support the clear and high expectations they hold.

Our survey results and experiences indicate that high-performance systems

- **invest time and resources** for teachers to attend Professional Learning sessions and industry/college/workplace and university tours, with the explicit expectation that the learning is shared among their colleagues and discussed in classrooms;
- **prioritize** *Pathways* on their system improvement plans and use the *Pathway* data to inform program planning, decision making, and resource allocations;
- **build in time** for elementary, middle, and high schools to work collaboratively (K–12+) to support the transition planning crucial to engage the *Student Pathway DNA*; and

- **reach out** to parents and community partners to develop a professional network supported by **a comprehensive communication plan** that encompasses
  - an up-to-date database of relevant *Pathway* information,
  - the diversity of the audience, addressing social and cultural perspectives, and
  - an intentional approach to reculturing.

Programs for All Matter

Every student maps out his or her own unique *Pathway* within the educational programming set out by the system, state, or country. A robust and relevant curriculum becomes the backbone to a comprehensive, inclusive educational program. It captures and reflects critical thinking expectations and the diversity of learners through programming that is broad enough to capture all of the talents of the population it serves.

Depending on how comprehensive and inclusive that educational programming is, specialized programs are often added to the mix. These programs are strategically developed either at the school, system, or government level, with the clear intent of supporting and extending the learning for targeted groups of students. Specialized programs are intended to enhance the focus and intentionality of a student *Pathway* and are aligned with the broader educational programming framed by the system, state, or country. Program examples include, but are not exclusive to, college and career readiness; language (i.e., English language learners); gifted and special education; the arts; Advanced Placement; cooperative education; apprenticeship and school-to-work; science, technology, engineering, and mathematics (STEM); prior learning assessment; and the Specialist High Skills Major (see page 100).

While every student has a *Pathway*, not every student has a specialized program as part of that *Pathway*. That is OK. What is important is that each student has equitable access to his or her postsecondary destination of choice, supported by learning opportunities to develop the requisite skills and abilities. For this to happen, schools, systems, and governments need to think carefully about the following questions:

- Are the education programs offered broad enough to meet the learning needs of all students but narrow enough to provide focus and precision?
- What elements of the educational programs require additional specialized programs?
- Who is the intended audience for these specialized programs?
- Are the programs inclusive of all postsecondary destinations?
- What are the transition points for student access to these specialized programs?
- What are the supports and resources that will be required?
- What are the strategies to support teacher and leadership learning? and
- What is the **comprehensive communication plan** in place to ensure students and parents are able to make informed choices regarding individualized student *Pathways*?

Bringing Stakeholders Together to Answer the Right Questions

Charting a new road map for Ontario, the Task Force on Competitiveness, Productivity and Economic Progress identified a number of key recommendations needed in both the private sector and the government sector to get Ontario's economy on the right track. One recommendation is that Ontario needs to ensure those entering the labor force have the right skills to become entrepreneurial and innovative economic agents. Students today need a combination of job preparation and a well-rounded skill set that will help them to succeed in the ever-changing workplace. Another recommendation is that Ontario reform its training routes for skilled trades to help increase the quantity and quality of graduates of skilled trade programs. Ontario's high youth unemployment—16.9% in 2013—and low labor productivity are prime signals that better human capital development is strongly needed to build the province's future prosperity.

Source: Thompson (2013).

Shared Learning: What's Working?

Qualitative and quantitative data, as well as other predetermined performance measures, indicate that success is possible and doable in developing programming for all. The challenge is how to bring that learning to large-scale system change. How do we go about doing this important work on a grand scale? What "up-shifts" (mind-set changes) are required to do so, and how can we learn from each other?

In our survey results gathered from systems across four countries (Australia, Canada, the United States, and the United Kingdom), respondents (comprising teachers, school administrators, and system leaders) were asked to

1. identify a high-yield program or strategy that they felt was having a significant impact on student academic success or well-being,
2. indicate how they knew that what they were doing was making a difference, and
3. prioritize the conditions they felt were essential for program success.

The survey program responses highlighted the fact that

- as an educational institution, there is a demonstrated ability to adapt and respond to the learning needs of individual students, especially those deemed "at risk" by coming up with "fixes" for the challenges as they present themselves;
- effective programs are put in place for targeted students with adjustments and changes being made over time;
- local context matters—while there are many effective programs in place for students, not everything works everywhere; and
- more programming opportunities are framed within the structure of the school building than beyond them.

Interesting to note, the focus of the majority of programs and strategies identified (Figure 5.4) was on improving outcomes for students deemed to be "at risk" (SaR). "At risk" students are categorized as exhibiting social/emotional issues, behavioral/attendance issues, low credit attainment rates, or disengagement.

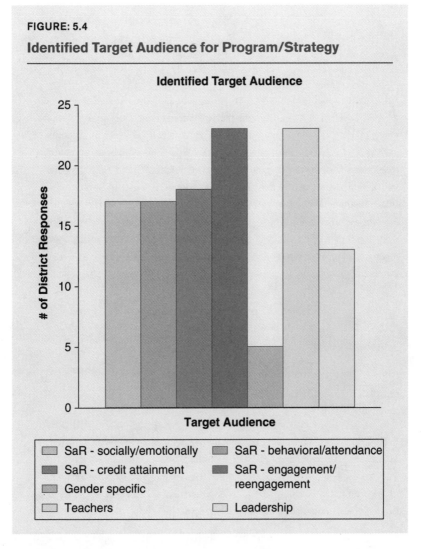

FIGURE: 5.4

Identified Target Audience for Program/Strategy

Identified Target Audience

# of District Responses

Target Audience

- SaR - socially/emotionally
- SaR - credit attainment
- Gender specific
- Teachers
- SaR - behavioral/attendance
- SaR - engagement/ reengagement
- Leadership

Less focus was on programs and strategies impacting gender-specific considerations. In almost equal measure, programs and strategies also included teachers as the target audience. There appears to be a recognition that any "up-shifts" in programming/instructional practice also require a corresponding "up-shift" in teacher mind-sets and leadership development. We believe that there is a critical need to apply *Pathway* programming to the needs of all students, not just "at risk" students—an important "up-shift" that is recognized and articulated in every Professional Learning session.

A System Story: Simcoe County District School Board

As the Student Success lead for the Simcoe County District School Board (SCDSB) in Ontario, Canada, high school principal Tracy McPhail was charged with the reengagement of SCDSB "early leavers"–that is, students leaving high school without completing their high school diploma. At that time, the Ontario Ministry of Education had provided school board–specific data indicating there were 569 early leavers as of June 30, 2010. In September 2010, this number climbed to 711 as a result of students who did not return after the summer break. These data provided clear impetus for change and evidence for the need to develop a vision and strategy for the reengagement of these early leavers. Two reengagement programs were developed as a result of the data:

1. The *Educational Outreach* program (a form of Supervised Alternative Learning, or SAL) is a prevention program for students aged 14–17 who have "tuned out" or disengaged from learning.

2. The *Pathways to Student Success (PASS)* program is an intervention program for students aged 18–20 who have left school early but have not graduated.

In the Educational Outreach program, the percentage of students engaged in academic programming in SCDSB increased from less than 5% prior to 2011 to 89% and 94% in 2012 and 2013, respectively. Since the inception of the program in February 2011, credit attainment for students engaged in Educational Outreach has also increased by 52%.

Through the focused and determined efforts of the reengagement teams and programs, in 2010–2011, the PASS program saw an additional 99 students graduate with that number increasing to 139 and 161 in 2012 and 2013, respectively. Also, the resulting increase in the number of graduates was accompanied by a dramatic decrease in the number of early leavers.

What did it take to bring about this astounding level of programming implementation? **What Mattered Most?** Principal McPhail (personal communication, December 11, 2013) understood the importance of ensuring the development of

- a system vision for the programming developed and shared with all stakeholders and decision makers;
- a framework (structures and resources) in place to support the consistency of program delivery, student identification, and the monitoring and tracking of student achievement;
- a focus on conversations with stakeholders about the desired outcome of "more high school graduates," not on the barriers and obstacles;
- a shared belief that "all students have the capacity to learn and achieve success and that educators, parents, and community members have a moral obligation to support them";
- a strategy for exploring all funding sources to support educator learning needs;
- a teacher selection process that ensured staff would have not only the skills and knowledge necessary to connect students to appropriate programming but also a proven ability to establish positive and productive relationships with the complex needs of disengaged youth;
- a community partnership agenda that emphasized student empowerment built into cooperative education, including other forms of experiential and/or out-of-school learning opportunities;
- expanded opportunities for students to extend their learning through dual-credit programs (students earning college and high school credits simultaneously) with postsecondary institutions; and
- collaborative supportive learning teams established through intentional relationship and trust building.

McPhail, as a strategic innovative leader, achieved success building on four key strategies:

1. Knowing the status and progress of every student.
2. Providing relevant student appropriate programming.
3. Investing in improving daily teaching and learning.
4. Connecting with **a broad base of community partners**.

The SCDSB story reminds us that every student who is an early leaver has a reason for being so. Each student has a unique story whether it is struggles with learning disabilities, boredom, challenges at home, mental health issues, or another challenge. In addition, many

"

> "Students with low skills are less likely to feel socially, institutionally and intellectually engaged; but students' with high skills who feel under-challenged in class are also prone to disengagement. Shifting the relationship between instructional challenge and student engagement requires a reorientation in the way we think about the qualities of effective learning and a commitment to supporting the organizational, pedagogical and curricular changes required for all students to experience intellectually engaging learning environments"
>
> Willms & Friesen, 2012, p. 1.

drop out long before they actually leave. In other words, they may be attending school and classes but not actually be gaining any knowledge. They have disengaged from the learning. Two key reports coauthored by Kate Tilleczek of University Hospital and Bruce Ferguson of the Hospital for Sick Children, *Early School Leavers* (Tilleczek et al., 2005) and *Fresh Starts and False Starts* (Tilleczek, Ferguson, & Laflamme, 2010), summarize that we all need to be

1. proactive in helping to reduce and prevent barriers to success;
2. more understanding of the lived experience of youth, especially where it deviates from that of educators; and
3. more flexible in helping students address their needs (Glaze, Mattingley, & Andrews, 2013, p. 99).

Student achievement and student retention data now let us put a **FACE** on each of these students, and we, in turn, respond with instructional strategies and specialized programs to meet their learning needs to reengage them in the learning process. Across Ontario, the Reengagement Initiative, which is part of the larger Student Success Strategy, has highlighted the importance of *student choice and voice*. Through supported follow-up conversations with a caring other (teacher mentor), it became evident that many early leavers were unclear about their programming options and choices. They could not see a future for themselves. Somehow and somewhere along their *Pathway* they had lost their resilience for school-based learning. Their *Student Pathway DNA* had not been activated.

Specialized programs for at-risk students, similar to the SCDSB story, have a history of being highly successful in terms of reengagement. Common to all are

- personalized instruction for the students,
- strong instructional practice,
- relevant learning outcomes with close connections to the community,
- a broad curriculum base from which to build, and
- students engaged in Experiential Learning of one form or another (K. Robinson, 2013).

Where we see differences in approaches, it is in how these programs are viewed and presented. Are they seen as preventative, an intervention, or a Band-Aid solution? The SCDSB journey illustrates a high-yield blended approach, a preventative strategy for the most marginalized students, and then an intervention approach for those students who have "fallen through the cracks."

In some systems, these programs are referred to as alternative, implying that students who might benefit from these programs somehow do not conform to the standard educational program that is in place. They don't quite measure up. This negative connotation is compounded by educators waiting until the students fail before offering them these programming options. This is unacceptable. We must realize our moral imperative **EARLY** and **OFTEN**.

A Recalculation is in order—capturing what works so well in these specialized programs and making it standard practice for a revised and refreshed comprehensive, inclusive educational program. Separate is not always equal and certainly not inclusive. The importance of reculturing is confirmed in Chapter 3; specifically, we need to be mindful of our language and the unintentional messages we convey to our students.

We believe these dynamic programs should be available to all students. And we really do mean ALL. Where, then, can we find examples of how the benefits of specialized programming are built into the everyday culture and norm of the broader educational program?

A System Story: York Region District School Board

In Ontario, we have previously cited the Specialist High Skills Major (SHSM) (page 100) as a specialized program that honors learning for all four destinations: apprenticeship, college, university, and workplace. Students receive a Red Seal designation on their high school diploma as an indication of SHSM program achievement. There is no differentiation of destination. For example, a student completing an SHSM to go to the workplace has the same diploma recognition as a student with an SHSM who goes to university. The student record of courses taken and achievements is personalized to the student and the destination.

In Ontario's York Region District School Board (YRDSB), there is a commitment to ensure that all students will have equitable access to the programming options developed and offered. It is apparent that the most vulnerable and marginalized students will have a larger gap to close if they are to have a chance of participating in and completing an SHSM program. So, a specialized program called Exploring Opportunities (EOP) is in place. Students are required to apply and go through a preplacement interview. Student choice and student voice are given high priority. The EOP program incorporates all the value-added instructional pieces previously identified as best practice.

Being introduced to *informed choice* gives students hope. They see EOP as a way to propel them forward on their individualized *Pathway*. The same group of students, who had repeatedly failed courses and grades and who were at risk of leaving school, become engaged in their learning. Their self-agency improves. Credit attainment and grades improve significantly, and students gain a newfound confidence in themselves and the possibilities that the future might hold.

The gap is closed and the bar raised as students rise to the occasion.

YRDSB intentionally frames EOP and SHSM as programs of choice for students. They are no longer viewed as alternatives. It is viable, doable programming that supports *Student Pathway DNA*, enabling students to achieve more than they ever imagined as illustrated by the differential in EOP credit accumulation in Appendix I.

In all cases, time and again, when the layers of these programming strategies are peeled back, we see **What Matters Most**:

- **Student Choice**—students choose or apply for the program;
- **Student Voice**—students are actively involved in constructing their learning;
- **Cross-Curricular or Interdisciplinary Approach**—multifaceted instructional approaches that add to the relevance and Collaborative Inquiry approach;
- **Real Applications** to life—timely and relevant experiences that are constructed and connected to the broader community;
- **Value-Added** for immediate use—additional training or certifications that are recognized in the workplace; and
- **Relationship Building**—teachers who are powerful motivators and expect great things for all students.

How, then, do we take this learning and apply it to building *Pathways to Career Readiness* for *The Literate Graduate*? What else needs to be considered in our program planning?

Embracing Innovation, Creative Thinking, and Collaboration Matters!

Sir Ken Robinson (2013) frames three beliefs about human nature to be considered for the human mind to flourish. Building upon these beliefs, we can start to explore how a culture of innovation, creative thinking, and collaboration might be embraced in our instructional practice to support *The Literate Graduate*.

1. **Human beings are naturally different and diverse.**

   As we Recalculate the Route to *Career Readiness*, we need to ensure that our education programming captures what is necessary but also what is beyond sufficient in the curriculum.

2. **Human beings are naturally curious.**

   We need to be mindful of ways to "light the spark" for students and teachers. Student voice is an excellent way to find the *hook* as we move away from compliance and one answer fitting all.

3. **Human beings are inherently creative.** On the assumption that we all create our own lives, education can either awaken this ideal, keep it dormant, or suppress it.

The challenge lies in how to nurture a learning culture that acknowledges these three principles that are crucial for the human mind to flourish. Our success in doing so will ultimately determine how the educational system thrives. Robinson (2013) reminds us that education is a human system, not a mechanical system—a system where people (teachers and students) either do or don't want to learn. The choice is ultimately theirs to make. How do we as educators and innovation leaders turn on the "switch"?

If our goal for *The Literate Graduate* is to develop an "innovation mind-set," in which students can apply problem-solving skills and creativity to any context, then our teachers also need to have opportunities to be innovators themselves. Systems set the stage for innovation, but it is within the culture of each individual school and classroom that innovation will either flourish or flounder.

Student voice and student choice are powerful change agents for school culture and instructional practice. Skilled teachers and innovative school leaders capitalize on this when considering programming, assessment, and instructional strategies. Student choice gives "voice" to students' own interests. "Only when children learn what they

---

A GOOD ACTIVITY FOR STAFF:

Have each staff member recall and discuss a learning experience that was powerful for him or her. Have staff members consider what activated them. What gave them a sense of agency? What enabled them? The core elements that come out of that conversation and are recorded will help direct the staff to unpack and reflect on their school learning culture that needs to be embraced to help their students find their *TrueNorth*.

❝ *"Educators who have the innovators' mind-set don't get frustrated by 'yeah, but . . . ' thinking. They find work-arounds to obstacles . . . "*

Boss, 2012, p. 34. ❞

want to learn and begin to take the responsibility for learning and living can they stay truly engaged" (Zhao, 2012, p. 171). Attending to the *Student Pathway DNA* (Figure 1.3) guides students' discovery of their passions is a critical first step, Zhao (2012) would argue, in the innovative thinking process. Student voice and choice are essential.

Innovative teachers are quick to realize that developing a student innovation mind-set requires the nurturing of a student's innate abilities, such as creativity, as well as his or her critical thinking and problem-solving skills. As one teacher put it, "I had to unlearn the idea that teaching was about my content; I had to learn it was about their thinking and their skills" (Boss, 2012, p. 39).

> "Alice laughed. 'There's no use trying,' she said. 'One can't believe impossible things.' I daresay you haven't had much practice,' said the Queen. 'When I was your age, I always did it for half-an-hour a day. Why, sometimes I've believed as many as six impossible things before breakfast"
>
> Carroll, 1871, chap. 5.

> "A recent IBM poll of fifteen hundred CEO's from sixty nations identified creativity as the top leadership competency for the future"
>
> Carr, 2010, as cited in Boss, 2012, p. 21.

Fostering Creativity

Creativity is listed as one of the top sought-after workplace competency skills along with problem solving, ability to communicate, flexibility, and adaptability to change (Partnership for 21st Century Skills, 2008). Thinking creatively is closely related to thinking critically and problem solving. When we work collaboratively with others to further develop and refine creative ideas, we are applying problem-solving and critical thinking skills, and that is what leads to useful innovations (Boss, 2012).

Creativity is more than artistic expression. It is our innate ability to see things from different angles, to connect seemingly irrelevant things (Boss, 2012). How, then, can creativity, something that is supposedly innate, be in short supply? Sir Ken Robinson (2006) suggests that, in fact, our current North American educational system "grows kids out of creativity" by failing to foster a learning environment that grows these innate abilities.

Finland, on the other hand, gives creativity a high priority in the desired outcomes for its students' learning. The country does this by adopting learning environments that tap into students' imagination, where the creativity is nurtured by learning environments that foster questioning, patience, openness to fresh ideas, high levels of trust, and learning from mistakes. In addition, the concept of a dropout rate is not part of the Finnish vocabulary. The country's broad approach to education embraces the core belief that problems are challenges to be solved and will be addressed through an innovative team approach across its educational system.

Unpacking Problem Solving

Becoming competent in any subject area means developing both the knowledge and the skills to apply that knowledge to the kinds of questions and problems experts in the field would tackle. Problem solving requires persistence. You need to care about the problem and have a commitment to see it through.

> " *"It is your attitude not your aptitude that determines your altitude"*
>
> Unknown.

For many students, their ability to self-regulate is an essential life skill that builds toward effective problem solving. Through instructional approaches such as project-based learning and Collaborative Inquiry (see Chapter 6), teachers strive to engage students by assisting them to find their personal connections to a task or lesson. The personal connections in turn keep them motivated, even when the learning becomes challenging. Where students are involved in learning that is aligned with their interests and passions, the learning experience can last a lifetime (Boss, 2012).

Innovation

The *Framework for 21st Century Skills* reminds us that creativity is about generating original ideas while innovation is more practical in nature. It is about possibilities and moving new thinking forward toward positive change (Boss, 2012).

One of the hallmarks of innovators is being comfortable with risk taking and the willingness to learn through failure (Boss, 2012). We would expect no less from our students. Questions that are critical for us to be asking include:

- How do we encourage our students to think boldly and take risks?
- What changes need to occur in our instructional and assessment practices to do so?
- What are the mind-set changes or "up-shifts" that need to occur as students move from answering multiple-choice tests to asking open-ended, higher-order questions in which the thinking process is assessed, not the memorization of facts?
- What are the new sets of skills students need help developing?
- What must the climate or culture of our classrooms, schools, and organizations look and feel like in order that innovative thinking occurs?

The opportunity for students to make choices builds engagement in and commitment to their learning. Programming decisions that support students in making informed choices, teaching them to use their voice, and dealing with the consequences of those choices will ultimately empower students to become *The Literate Graduates* of the 21st century.

From Good to Great to
INNOVATE

The following visiting teacher blog, from Koulumestari School in Espoo, Finland, provides the reader insight into the some of the strategies this school's teachers use to instill an innovator's mindset in their students.

Hands-On Learning

I started off my day in another first grade class, the room was silent and each student was working with an extreme focus on the task at hand. Students weren't reading, writing, or doing math, but doing "handicrafts." They were diligently working on finishing stitching patterns on their pieces of fabric. I was amazed by the intricate designs the students were creating and the care with which they were finishing their projects. In the handicrafts class students not only complete their projects by themselves but are responsible for designing what they are going to make. The teacher of this class told me that "handicrafts" is her pupils favorite class, and that they take a lot of pride in the things they create.

Watching this class just made me think how great it is to allow students to use different parts of their brains in school. At Koulumestari, these classes allow students, who don't connect as strongly with other aspects of learning in school, to apply themselves and feel included. This type of learning encouraged the students to be creative and be their own problem-solvers. When a student was struggling, it was not about telling them what to do but to encourage them to seek solutions for themselves. How did they think that they could fix what they were unhappy about?

Innovative and creative thinking is what this school is all about. Students are given the chance to take wood shop classes and those that focus on technological innovations. As educators I think we all strive to inspire students to be independent thinkers as an important aspect of the sometimes "unwritten" curriculum. I look forward to more opportunities to witness this "hands on" innovative learning as I visit new classes in the days to come!

posted by Beth Harild @ 11:24 AM April 2011

Innokas

I hope that this week I will be able to answer all your questions regarding innovation and the use of technology at Koulumestari school. Technology is used at Koulumestari as a tool to allow children to learn how to be innovative and creative.

Children at Koulumestari have music classes but don't formally study the other arts. That being said, they are provided with the opportunity to think creatively in other ways. I have mentioned already that students have a handicrafts class where they work with textiles etc. They are also given the option of taking a wood working shop class starting in the third grade. I visited a 6th grade class today in the shop that was working on making their own CD holders out of wood. It was amazing to watch the students work with saws and drill presses with such confidence at such an early age. The teacher pointed out that some of these students will go on to choose a profession in a skilled trade.

How fantastic is it that they are given the opportunity to begin learning important skills for their future jobs so early! Students at Koulumestari are not given a blue-print that they must follow to complete these projects. They are encouraged, if not expected, to be creative and innovative thinkers. Towards the end of the wood shop class students were given their next project—a small bag of screws and gears, and were told they were to create a car that will move. Each student will be responsible for designing their own car and making all of the parts. I wish I was going to be here to see the finished products!

Sir Ken Robinson (2013) reminds us that "no system, no school, no program is better than its teachers. They are the engine of achievement. They are the life blood—a creative profession not a delivery system." Great teachers mentor, motivate, stimulate, provoke, engage, and empower. Education is about learning, and the role of the teacher is to facilitate (and extend) the learning—to encourage students to think boldly, "to frame problems, to generate ideas, test solutions and learn from what works well and what doesn't" (Boss, 2012, p. 4) as we discuss in Chapter 6.

Reflective Pause
by Yong Zhao

It is almost ironic that a chapter has to be devoted to arguing for student voice and choice in education, not the least because in other industries, what the customers want and how they want it are a mandate, the beginning place for designing and delivering products and services. It is more because education, by definition, is about support, not indoctrinate, children's growth and fulfillment of their dreams. But I am glad to see the long list of reasons why education must provide choices to students. I am even more pleased to see examples of schools and education systems working hard to develop and provide innovative programs to give students the choice they deserve and demand.

STEPS TO STUDENTS' SUCCESS

1. Personalize the learning.
2. Capture student voice.
3. Build capacity for informed student choice.
4. Have a **comprehensive communication plan** with all stakeholders.
5. Build time for collaboration.
6. Make sure the educational program is broad enough to meet learning needs, but narrow enough to provide focus and precision.
7. Consider specialized programs, inclusive of all postsecondary destinations.
8. Match teacher and leadership development with programming and instructional practices.
9. Encourage cross-curricular, interdisciplinary approaches using Collaborative Inquiry.
10. Nurture a learning culture that acknowledges diversity, curiosity, and creativity.

Giving choice to students and respecting their voice is not something nice adults can do. It is more than acknowledging students' innate diversity, creativity, and curiosity. It is an economic necessity for nations and individuals. In the new economy that favors creativity and entrepreneurship, an education that serves our future well is one that fosters creativity, celebrates diversity, and motivates the pursuit of greatness. That can only be achieved through a personalized education experience with rich "choices."

It is, however, crucial to provide genuine choices, rather than dictated ones. Genuine choices start with students' interest, passion, and strengths, not government mandates based on guesses of adults or the convenience of operations. Thus a real choice-based education is one that is defined and designed by students, with the support and guidance of adults.

About Yong Zhao, PhD

Yong Zhao is presidential chair and a professor in the College of Education at the University of Oregon. He is an internationally known scholar, author, and speaker. His works focus on the implications of globalization and technology on education. He has designed schools that cultivate global competence, developed computer games for language learning, and founded research and development institutions to explore innovative education models. He has published over 100 articles and 20 books, including *Catching Up or Leading the Way: American Education in the Age of Globalization* and *World Class Learners: Educating Creative and Entrepreneurial Students*. Zhao is a recipient of the Early Career Award from the American Educational Research Association and in 2012 was named one of the 10 most influential people in educational technology by *Tech & Learning* magazine. He is an elected fellow of the International Academy of Education. His latest book, *World Class Learners,* has won several awards including the Society of Professors of Education Book Award (2013), the Association of Educational Publishers' Judges' Award, and the Distinguished Achievement Award in Education Leadership (2013).

SKILLED TEACHERS MATTER!

According to our survey respondents (Figure 6.1), **skilled teachers**, our foundational Guiding Principle 4 (see Chapter 1), are one of the most critical factors in educating our students—far surpassing high expectations, a whole-school approach to improvement, and access to technology as critical programming considerations. The respondents described **skilled teachers** as those who have assorted tools and strategies in their instructional toolbox to ensure that the learning needs of every student are addressed and assessed.

Skilled teachers strive to promote higher-order thinking skills with *all* of their students by developing and activating their problem-solving abilities, critical thinking and reasoning skills, and creativity. These teachers engage their students through a Collaborative Inquiry instructional practice (our Curriculum Knowledge Strand) that is student centered, authentic, and timely. It is a practice that is responsive

QUESTIONS THAT MATTER MOST

1. What high-impact instructional and assessment practices are you using to feed the seed of innovation?

2. What is the "buzz" is in your classrooms and schools?

3. How are you using Collaborative Inquiry to encourage students to think boldly, be creative, and take risks?

4. Are your assessment practices in line with such an instructional focus?

5. How are you encouraging creativity in your students, staff, and leadership?

6. Are you asking the right questions?

7. What percentage of your programs and courses offer Experiential Learning opportunities?

8. How are you matching the knowledge acquisition with the students' skills and abilities while providing relevant opportunities to practice and refine learning?

9. How are you building, across grade levels, habits of being observant, asking questions from multiple perspectives, and challenging preconceptions?

10. What strategies are you using to ensure *Pathways* are visible and accessible to students?

11. What are the workplace/essential skills you are hoping to develop in the students, and do you have a means to assess these skills?

to students' cultural and lived experiences (our Knowledge Application Strand). Teachers understand and value opportunities for personal reflection on self-knowledge and skill development for themselves and their students. Programming is focused on knowledge application and making the learning processes and critical thinking visible versus memorization of facts and recitation of curricular content (our Skill Development Strand).

Our survey results indicate that individualized instruction and the co-teaching cycle (see Appendix F) are rated highest and that differentiated instruction, inquiry-based learning, and Experiential Learning are rated almost equally as influential, high-yield instructional approaches that make a difference to all students' achievement (Figure 6.2). These practices operate synergistically when used by **skilled teachers** in classrooms, K–12+. Hattie (2009) reports that inquiry-based learning can foster critical thinking if students have the cognitive capacity to think critically. Similarly, Bangert-Drowns and

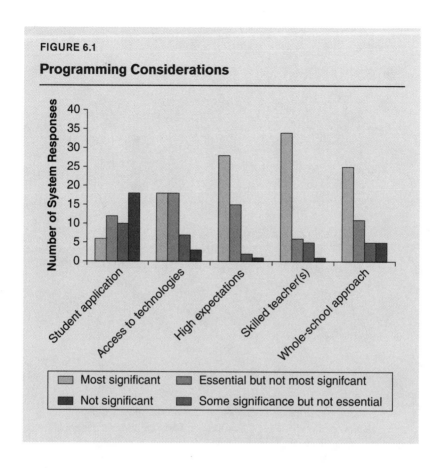

FIGURE 6.1

Programming Considerations

Bankert (1990) found that inquiry-based instruction can foster critical thinking, which is our continuing quest in this book.

Knowledge Building and Knowledge Creation

Transforming instructional practice to include knowledge building and knowledge creation as an iterative process (Literacy and Numeracy Secretariat, 2010) requires the support of the entire school community. To create that new knowledge, students, teachers, parents, leaders, and community partners must engage, together, in the Collaborative Inquiry process to align structures for deep thinking and problem solving throughout a system.

Our survey results in Figure 6.1 indicate that a whole-school approach is seen as one of the essential conditions for programming

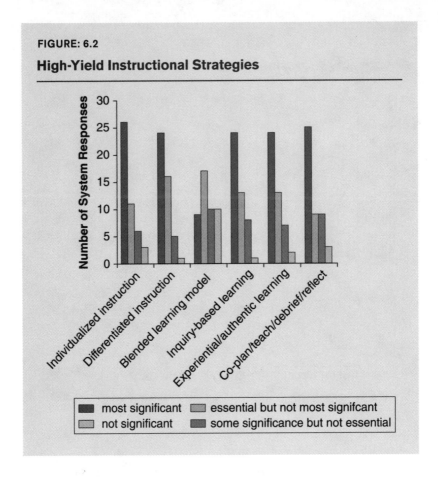

FIGURE: 6.2

High-Yield Instructional Strategies

Number of System Responses

Legend:
- most significant
- essential but not most signifcant
- not significant
- some significance but not essential

Categories: Individualized instruction, Differentiated instruction, Blended learning model, Inquiry-based learning, Experiential/authentic learning, Co-plan/teach/debrief/reflect

consideration, after ensuring that **skilled teachers** are in place and that they all hold high expectations. Engaging the whole-school community in Collaborative Inquiry involves a common commitment from all stakeholders in the education system as partners in student learning and success. Within our concept of **a broad base of community partners** (Guiding Principle 3), many resources will be involved and committed to activate the *Student Pathway DNA* from businesses and industries, health care institutions, social work agencies, municipal infrastructures and services, community associations, religious groups, and especially families all working together. Teachers, supported by these resources, will continue to create curious, learning-focused students, capable of changing their world to be a better place.

Acknowledging the need for learning experiences that encourage innovation and creativity among students demands that **skilled teachers** understand what is different and essential for teaching 21st-century learners—our *Literate Graduates*. Together, teachers foster a shared vision of global learning and leading that includes an understanding of the skills and characteristics of the learning competencies such as the Six Cs (Grose, 2014), introduced in Chapter 2:

1. Character Education
2. Citizenship
3. Communication
4. Critical Thinking and Problem Solving
5. Collaboration
6. Creativity and Imagination

Skilled teachers work together to increase understanding of how critical thinking and reasoning underlie the Collaborative Inquiry process. They connect the character traits of being a proficient thinker with the development of learning and leading in a global world (Greenan & Fornasier-Reilly, 2013).

Learning Spaces

Skilled teachers know that getting the right design of the learning space "to develop independent and rigorous thought" is "both an art and a science to design (as opposed to decorate)" (Student Achievement Division, 2012, p. 2). As Heard and McDonough (2009) say, "We need to think about creating classroom environments that give children the opportunity for wonder, mystery and discovery" (cited in Student Achievement Division, 2012, p. 2). To develop students who are capable of learning and leading in a global world, teachers need to be adept at and passionate about

1. ongoing learning and frequently searching for more enriching and enticing ways of teaching and learning;
2. creating programs that feature open-ended, rich performance tasks that demand use of the higher end of Bloom's

taxonomy (Johnson & Lamb, 2011)—the critical thinking skills;

3. questioning to heighten students' curiosity, wonder, and inquiry;
4. learning with students—knowing when to give input, when to be guides of self-assessment, and when to learn from students;
5. inspiring to promote self-regulatory, resilient learners;
6. knowing and using a rich array of digital tools at "just the right time"; and
7. building on community resources and partnering with communities to build on and strengthen our students' interests, skills, and dispositions.

Boss (2012, p. 64) recommends that to design thinking in an innovative learning culture teachers need to

1. defer judgment,
2. encourage volume,
3. be visual [use graphics],
4. be succinct [summarize ideas],
5. listen to others,
6. build on others' ideas, and
7. encourage wild thinking.

Boss (2012) feels it is important for teachers to feel principals have their backs—to let them run with "out of the box" ideas in creating that culture of innovation. Melanie Greenan (personal communication, November 23, 2013) says if teachers can let go of control, have trust in their students, and learn to get the right design for the curricular content through student-led inquiry and knowledge building, then Collaborative Inquiry will create huge learning gains for all students.

Like our leaders who need to trust and be trusted, teachers will need from principals

- trust to try things,
- resources to try new ideas, and

- time for *a structured, collaboratively planned approach* with emphasis on learning together (see Appendix F).

Critical: Planned, Ongoing Professional Learning

To accomplish the above knowledge building, **skilled teachers** require access to ongoing Professional Learning in achieving each of the following:

1. **Accomplishing a balance** between
   - students' discovering and explicit teaching, a balance of all three strands of the *Student Pathway DNA* (see Chapter 1);
   - student-chosen and teacher-chosen performance tasks (see Chapter 5);
   - student-led and teacher-directed work;
   - whole-group, small-group, and individualized teaching; and
   - in-school, out-of-school, and virtual experiences.

     To us, the art and science of teaching is not one or the other, but the harmony that constitutes what is best to engage students in the learning needed (adapted from Giasson, 2003).

2. **Letting students do more** by
   - orchestrating a learning-centered classroom where student voices are at the heart of the learning.

3. **Thinking outside the box** by
   - solving real-world problems with students; and
   - going to extremes to create artificial pressures as a strategy to force new ways of looking at problems (Boss, 2012).

4. **Being smart problem solvers** by
   - creating spaces for students to solve problems; and
   - finding soul mates to learn from and collaborate with in learning networks focused on increasing all students' achievement and empowerment.

5. **Co-constructing learning** by
   o setting clear expectations through deconstructed Learning Goals/Intentions and co-constructed Success Criteria so that students know how to be successful;
   o communicating curriculum expectations clearly and visually;
   o listening carefully to students, who will reveal what they need to learn more about. The **skilled teacher** is an observer, a questioner, and an articulate summarizer. She or he hears what students say and asks questions at just the right moment to find out clues to unlock students' interests, dreams, and desires; and
   o pausing often and frequently to allow think time for all students—a very simple but sophisticated teaching tool. Time to puzzle out the insights and engage in accountable talk with others are critical to supporting 21st-century learners.

6. **Being collaborative and entrepreneurial** by
   o accessing community partners to open the world to students.

7. **Creating a culture of innovation** by
   o finding new solutions to new problems;
   o experiencing trial and error to scaffold the learning; and
   o giving permission to change the mind-set that there is only one way—one solution.

8. **Learning from students** by
   o listening to and reaching out for help from students to engage their expertise. For example, the "learning teacher" uses student voice and expertise wisely to understand more deeply the powerful digital tools available to use in lessons to expand students' thinking and engagement.

9. **Crafting inquiry-based practice** by
   o reflecting students' interests and needs based on school and system data.

10. **Using assessment of inquiry** by
   o constructing Success Criteria with students.

11. **Creating thinking spaces** by
    - planning 20% of teacher instructional time for open-ended, student work when students are engaged in open, creative thinking (Boss, 2012); and
    - using the organizational frame of co-planning, co-teaching, co-debriefing, and co-reflecting (see Appendix F) with teachers who want to learn to use Collaborative Inquiry together and reflect on their classroom practices.

Our Innovation Leadership Prism (Principal Lens) in Figure 6.3 highlights how the school principal, teachers, and community partners work collaboratively to determine what opportunities and resources they can provide to support the practice and programs established. The practice and programs, in response to the targets set by the system or state, are personalized to meet the learning needs of the community, based upon the **FACES** of the students and the resources that can be accessed.

The principal–teacher–community partner lens taken out of our Innovation Leadership Prism (Figure 2.3, page 65) reinforces how critical it is that not only principals but also **skilled teachers** and business/community partners have the skills to

- think outside the box,
- be open-minded,
- take risks,
- be politically aware and astute,
- live with ambiguity,
- read voraciously and challenge others to think through new concepts,
- have cognitive insights and make emotional connections with learners,
- find creative solutions with partners,
- balance the need for protocol (rules) with the need for form (structure) to follow function (student need),
- have a high percentage of successes to failures but learn that failures serve as a critical catalyst to further focus the work, and
- have a social conscience.

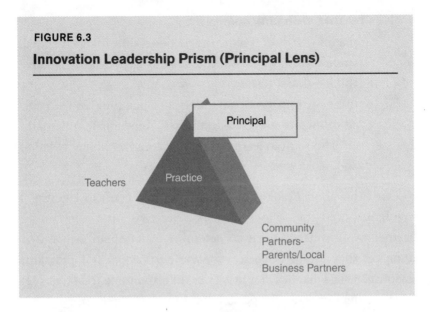

FIGURE 6.3

Innovation Leadership Prism (Principal Lens)

Principal

Teachers

Practice

Community
Partners-
Parents/Local
Business Partners

Skilled teachers, with the aforementioned skills and continuous Professional Learning that explicitly supports these skills, are ready to engage in the two high-impact instructional strategies identified in Figure 6.2 that go hand in hand with **a broad base of community partners**. These are

1. Collaborative Inquiry, and
2. Experiential Learning.

They are discussed here.

Collaborative Inquiry as Knowledge Mobilization

> *"Inquiry-based learning describes a range of philosophical approaches to teaching. Its core premises include the requirement that learning should be based around students' questions."*
>
> —Harvey & Daniels (2009, p. 56)

Building on and adding to this definition of teacher and student inquiry-based learning, we include system and leader inquiry because we believe that Collaborative Inquiry is based on data and questions at every level of education to develop critical thinking skills and interdependent learners—who know how to learn from each other. Only when inquiry is more about the complexity of the issues than about coming up with simple solutions to complex problems does building and applying new knowledge replace regurgitation of boring facts and often little-understood memory work (Harte, 2001). Stoll (2010) described Collaborative Inquiry as a means in which learning communities "deconstruct knowledge through joint reflection and analysis, re-constructing it through collaborative action, and co-constructing it through collective learning from their experiences" (p. 247).

Clearly our work is learning. As Hattie says, "learning is hard work" (Hattie & Yates, 2013, p. 76). It can be defined through Collaborative Inquiry as the ability to create and apply new knowledge in different and relevant ways in any situation. Addressing student learning needs depends no longer on individual teachers but on the collective wisdom brought by a team of educators with diverse experiences and expertise (Donohoo, 2013). For us, Collaborative Inquiry is an effective reflective process at all levels: states, systems, schools, and classrooms.

Over 50% of our respondents viewed Collaborative Inquiry as most significant with an additional 25%-plus viewing it as essential (Figure 6.4). In summary, approximately 80% of survey participants viewed inquiry, essential or above, as a high-yield, structured instructional approach. This leads us to seriously discuss how Collaborative Inquiry brings together critical thinking at every level.

System, leadership, teacher, and student inquiries are not separate entities. Each of these interrelated levels of inquiry supports increased student learning and achievement—our core business.

System inquiry supports problem solving by providing resources and creating infrastructure capable of building and mobilizing knowledge across the system. *Leadership inquiry* focuses on how to support teachers and build professional capacity in the interest of increasing student achievement within individual schools and across systems. *Teacher inquiry* focuses on supporting every student by

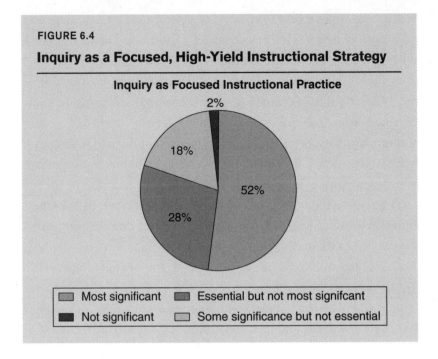

FIGURE 6.4

Inquiry as a Focused, High-Yield Instructional Strategy

Inquiry as Focused Instructional Practice

2%

18%

52%

28%

- Most significant
- Essential but not most signifcant
- Not significant
- Some significance but not essential

- having courageous conversations,
- making cognitive demands,
- planning environments to learn from and with other students,
- making time for the Co-Teaching Cycle (see Appendix F),
- hiring and working alongside Knowledgeable Others (Sharratt, Ostinelli, Cattaneo, 2010);
- orchestrating collaborative marking of student work (Sharratt, 2013b); and
- implementing the Collaborative Inquiry practices (Figure 6.4) to activate deep thinking.

Most importantly, student inquiry focuses on engaging students intellectually with the curriculum, developing collaborative dispositions by putting **FACES** on the data through *Student Pathway DNA*, and achieving *The Literate Graduate* skills.

We agree with Greenan (2012) that **skilled teachers** consider their lesson design as having three dimensions:

1. Types of Thinking—thinking typologies contained in the curriculum (summarizing, recognizing perspective, personal opinion, critical stance, etc.);
2. The Gradual Release/Acceptance of Responsibility Model (Vygotsky, 1978)—containing modeled, shared/collaborative, guided, and in[ter]dependent practice; and
3. The Collaborative Inquiry Cycle (illustrated in Figure 6.5)—involving developing collaborative dispositions.

These three axes form the framework for all curriculum, unit, and lesson designs. This ensures that student inquiry is firmly supported through explicit instruction and an understanding and identification of the thinking that is required to complete each task. The complete framework contains opportunities for assessment for, as, and of learning as well as student reflection and metacognition.

In *Putting FACES on the Data* (Sharratt & Fullan, 2012), we discussed the foundational practices intrinsic to a comprehensive literacy program that ensures students are explicitly taught through the Gradual Release/Acceptance of Responsibility Model (Vygotsky, 1978). For **skilled teachers** to move forward with student-led inquiry and for students to be able to fully participate in the inquiry process, foundational instructional skills must be present, including

- an asset-based learning stance (Dweck, 1999);
- assessment (for and as learning) that informs instruction (Sharratt & Fullan, 2012);
- Learning Goals/Intentions, Big Ideas, co-constructed Success Criteria, Descriptive Feedback, and Individual Learning Goals that are all linked (see Chapter 4);
- oral language—accountable talk and listening;
- balanced, comprehensive literacy—modeled, shared, guided, and independent reading and writing;
- precise instructional strategies;
- whole-group, small-group, and individual guided practice; and

- independent and collaborative work with continuous peer and self-assessment woven into the work.

Teachers ensure that these skills are developed in unison with an inquiry habit of mind (M. Greenan, personal communication, November 23, 2013).

Sustainable Student-Centered Instruction

"Smart Flipping" is the phrase that Greenan and colleagues (Lexicon Newsletter, 2013) use to describe the pedagogical practices of Collaborative Inquiry that allow for students to act independently as their own teachers and assessors and to partner with teachers in the production and sharing of knowledge.

In Smart Flipping, teachers become engaged in self-generative and sustainable change by becoming intrinsically motivated through the thinking and actions of their students, and thus teachers become students of student learning. Smart Flipping leverages the learners' recreational and directed use of technology as a way for them to access information and content in pursuit of the curriculum expectations; to build and share knowledge through social networks, online democratic spaces, and community partnerships; and to partake in local and global activism and leadership through the power of the Internet and global connectivity (Lexicon Newsletter, 2013).

Educators need the time to think through the concepts related to global learning and leading themselves. They need time to engage in Collaborative Inquiry together, as leaders and teachers, before they can implement this integrated type of pedagogy in systems, schools, and classrooms. As well, educators need to self-assess to ensure that they are engaging students in rich tasks that are relevant, authentic, and realistic.

As Thomas Edison recognized, "Inventions rarely come in a single flash of inspiration. You set a goal, measure progress using data, see what's working—and what isn't working—adjust your plan, and try again. This process can be very frustrating because it means running into a lot of dead ends. But each dead end tells you something useful" (DeGraaf, 2013, Foreword).

This causes us to consider that important cycle of experimentation and reflection in harnessing inquiring minds—as Edison knew, *the innovator is planned, persistent, and resilient*—three characteristics that we believe can be taught as demonstrated in our Collaborative Inquiry Cycle (Figure 6.5).

> " *"I have not failed 10,000 times. I've successfully found 10,000 ways that will not work"*
>
> Bill Gates, quoted in DeGraaf, 2013, Foreword. "

The Collaborative Inquiry Cycle (Figure 6.5) and Detailed Matrix (Table 6.1) work as a self-assessment framework for how system

FIGURE 6.5

Integrative Thinking Through the Collaborative Inquiry Cycle

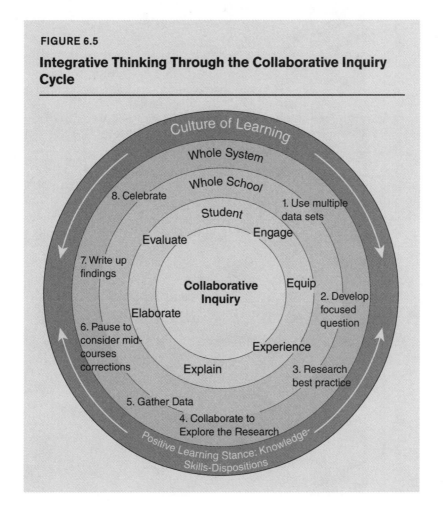

TABLE 6.1

A Detailed Matrix for Implementing a Collaborative Inquiry Cycle for Students, Teachers, and Leaders

Big Ideas	Student-Teacher-Leader Collaborative Inquiry Cycle	Questions	Actions
Engage	1. Multiple data sets	• What do I/we wonder about? • What is the issue identified by data? • What do we already know? • What does the environmental scan say? • What question do we want to know more about?	• Set curriculum/system expectations • Identify the Big Idea • Plan with others: teachers and community partners • Conduct a prior learning assessment—determine what we already know • Consider interests—voice • Consider choice—to spark passion • Make personal connections to issue/data • Develop a draft question that best highlights the Big Idea and questions from the data
	2. Focused question		
Equip	3. Research/information that might answer question	• What's out there about our question? • What tools will we need? • What support can we tap? • Can we design a new tool/practice?	• Source resources in system and broader community • Identify digital needs • Consider which community partners can add to our information • Consider how we going are to proceed

		Questions	Actions
Experience	4. Collaborate to explore the research	• How will we move forward? • What do we think will happen? • How will we move to collect the data, research, or information? • How will we reach consensus?	• Collate the research/information • Note what has been learned to date • Share and collaborate on the artifacts • Discuss if predictions are coming true • Learn to agree and disagree agreeably
Explain	5. Gather relevant data	• How do we analyze the data? • What can we interpret? • What is reasonable?	• Teach each other new ideas • Integrate new ideas that emerge • Delete what we all agree doesn't fit • Compare and contrast evidence • Get feedback from other peers
	6. Pause to consider midcourse corrections	• What will we cull? • Does the question need fine-tuning?	
Elaborate	7. Write up findings	• What is new that has been found? • Can new understandings be applied to other situations? • Are there any incongruencies?	• Identify the learning and supporting evidence • Apply to a new situation what has been investigated and found to be robust • Write up the findings in a draft • Determine what artifacts represent the learning • Prepare to present to a "real" audience
Evaluate	8. Celebrate the learning	• How do we mobilize the knowledge in a sharing forum and record so others will learn? • Where will learning be posted? • How will we answer questions for others' learning?	• Determine what artifacts represent the learning • Discuss what worked, what didn't, and what we will do differently • Next steps: incorporate listening and learning from others • Publish!

leaders, principals, teachers, and students can assess how they are leading inquiry together. It is cyclical and has multidirectional arrows as learners go back and forth among the layers and between the signposts in each layer because inquiry is not linear but is intentional. **Skilled teachers** guide the back-and-forth learning. Therefore, this is not a lockstep journey but a framework for moving the inquiry forward.

EXAMPLE OF COLLABORATIVE INQUIRY AT THE SYSTEM, SCHOOL, AND CLASSROOM LEVELS

In the 2013–2014 school year, the Brampton North East Family of Schools (a part of Canada's Dufferin-Peel Catholic District School Board, which has over 85,000 students and 7,500 teachers and leaders) refined the overall design of its Professional Learning model to better support the work of its teachers and administrators. In previous years, Professional Learning had taken a variety of forms, including formal principals' meetings, network meetings, in-services, and various other structures. We felt that it was necessary to reevaluate the framework through which Professional Learning was provided. Our leadership team sought to create a structure that honored the commitment of all participants and reduced the inefficiency that is often evident in complex institutional cultures.

Given the multiple requirements of accountability and monitoring placed on schools and managed by system office staff, the team put forward a model whereby an array of processes would be folded into one cohesive and continuous Collaborative Inquiry framework. All schools were surveyed with the intent of identifying common areas of need to provide a basis for professional discussions and related learning. Survey data results informed the establishment of clusters of schools that we came to refer to as "pods," which, in turn, meet six to eight times throughout the school year to explore their common areas of need, with each pod creating a Collaborative Inquiry focus. Each school is hosting a minimum of two meetings in which discussion of student data is beginning to be organic and cofacilitated.

The superintendent, present at all meetings, contributes to discussions alongside administrators and teachers. In short, the pods are both efficient and effective, allowing participants to learn with and from one another in small and safe settings in which they celebrate sharing, questioning one another, risk taking, and authentic learning. The Collaborative Inquiry verbs *experience*, *explain*, *elaborate*, and *evaluate* are in motion throughout this process. An important role of the superintendent is to ensure alignment of the Collaborative Inquiry focus, based on data, at the system, school, and classroom levels.

Because of the smaller groupings, there are ample opportunities for principals and teachers to de-privatize persistent problems of practice: Not only are these shared without fear of being misunderstood or judged, but the development of relationships within the smaller groups ensures that people get to know one another's settings well enough to provide meaningful suggestions that might lead to avenues for sustainable solutions.

Smaller groupings also enable conversations that are increasingly close to the experiences of students. Data such as student work, in the form of written assignments, videos, presentations, classroom visits, and so on, are brought to the table to illustrate learning "moments" in answer to the Collaborative Inquiry question. For all participants, but in particular the superintendent, the pods' structure also ensures significantly enhanced accountability: Participants come to meetings prepared and ready to share, confident that they will be heard and supported, but also aware that a meeting could be easily hampered by the diminished participation of even one member of the team. This thoughtful small-group approach actively negates the worry of "social loafing" and "groupthink" to which Ken Leithwood alluded in his Reflective Pause in Chapter 2.

The above Collaborative Inquiry process, at both the leader and teacher level, models how we can meet the needs of students, teachers, and administrators through focused dialogue and data, collected in a variety of ways, while being nimble enough to value individual contributions.

Source: Max Vecchiarino, Superintendent of Education, and Dan Compagnon, Principal, St. Thomas Aquinas Secondary School, Dufferin-Peel Catholic District School Board, Toronto, Canada (personal communication, January 9, 2014).

> *"When teachers and students truly engage with one another as a means of examining and changing their own understanding of how the world works (students) or understanding of what makes the biggest impact in their professional practice (teachers) which is the cause, the effect becomes enhanced inquiry and more profound conceptual understandings for students and teachers alike—learning for all"*
>
> Kim Newlove, personal communication, January 2, 2014.

When considering any instructional task for the student in using a Collaborative Inquiry approach, systems, leaders, and **skilled teachers** consider the correct starting points in the curriculum, the **FACE** of each student, and each student's *Pathway DNA*. When considering Experiential Learning tasks, we consider the **FACE** of each student, the opportunities our community partners can provide, and the correct starting points in the curriculum. In both cases, teachers are clear about Learning Goals/Intentions, and students are clear about how to be successful by co-creating the Success Criteria.

Through Collaborative Inquiry, global issues can be acted upon locally, with community partnerships, which brings us to investigate the second high-yield approach that our respondents identified, Experiential Learning.

Experiential Learning Is for Everyone!

ex·pe·ri·en·tial learning: The process of making meaning from direct experience; learning through reflection on doing.

Source: http://en.wikipedia.org/wiki/Experiential_learning

Experiential Learning is a process, personal to each learner, during which the participant makes meaning from direct experience and learns by reflecting on the doing. In everyday life, there are numerous "day to day" opportunities to apply this process—we "try" new things, and we "explore" new challenges. We do not automatically apply this learning process to every experience we have in life. We can each think of experiences, or tasks undertaken, where someone has shown us how to do something—we tried it; we did it—but the next time we faced that same task we were back to "square one," requiring

> " *"Tell me and I forget. Teach me and I remember. Involve me and I learn"*
>
> Benjamin Franklin [Brainy Quote, 2014a]. "

someone to show us once again how to do it. What we missed in the learning process was the guided reflection on what we did and what happened when we did it. We may not have summarized the reflection: How and why did we do that? How does this new learning relate to what we learned previously? What strategies do we need to remember that we were just shown so we can replicate them later?

Experiential Learning also referred to as autodidactic learning—a process that any learner can bring to an experience. The intentionality of the process is what sets it apart. In education, teachers apply this process in a more structured way, with instructional intentionality—a process within a process—that is sometimes referred to as experiential education. Technically, Experiential Learning and experiential education can be happening simultaneously. Educators do this by

1. designing and facilitating activities that require students to learn through engaging directly with their subject matter—the **What**; and

2. building time into the instructional tasks for structured reflection

   o throughout the activity—the **So What**?—and
   o at the completion of the activity—the **Now What**?

This instructional process of students' deep reflection on their learning is captured in Figure 6.6 (adapted from Kolb, 1984). David Kolb, an educational theorist, identifies certain abilities that are required for an individual to gain knowledge from an experience. According to Kolb (1984), the learner must

- be willing to be actively involved in the experience,
- be able to reflect on the experience,

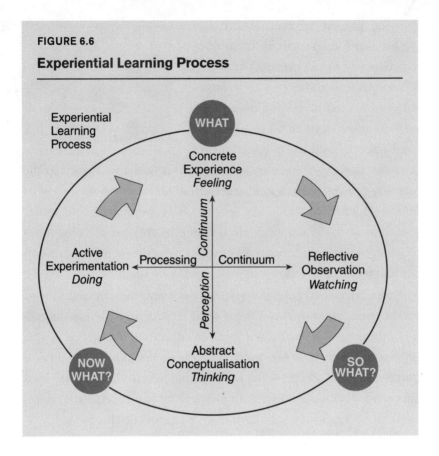

FIGURE 6.6

Experiential Learning Process

- possess and use analytical skills to conceptualize the experience, and
- possess decision-making and problem-solving skills to use the new ideas gained from the experience (p. 41).

The *Student Pathway DNA* strands (Figure 1.3, page 18), capture the interdependence and interconnections of the

- Experiential Learning Journey that frames the Knowledge Application Strand;
- Collaborative Inquiry Learning Journey that frames the Curriculum Knowledge Strand; and
- Self-Knowledge Learning Journey that frames the Skill Development Strand.

The **skilled teacher** considers all three strands when incorporating Experiential Learning into the development of his or her course or program content.

Experiential Learning occurs when carefully chosen authentic experiences are supported by reflection (Self-Knowledge Learning Journey), critical analysis (Collaborative Inquiry Learning Journey), and synthesis. Through active engagement, students are required to take initiative, problem solve, make decisions, and be accountable for their actions and results. The students construct meaning from the experience as they explore and examine their own values and consider how this impacts the future they envision for themselves. They experience how relationships are developed, progressive, and nurtured: learner to self, learner to others, and learner to the world at large.

The teacher's primary roles, in incorporating Experiential Learning as an instructional strategy, include setting suitable experiences, posing problems, setting boundaries, supporting learners, ensuring physical and emotional safety, and facilitating the learning process. Orchestrating Experiential Learning and reflection is challenging, but "a **skilled teacher**, asking the right questions and guiding reflective conversations before, during, and after an experience, can help open a gateway to powerful new thinking and learning" (Jacobson & Ruddy, 2004, p. 2).

The Experiential Learning Journey (Figure 1.6, page 25) is supported by our Guiding Principle 3—**a broad base of community partners**. It takes students out of school or into virtual workspaces by connecting to

- workplaces (locally and globally),
- community agencies, and
- postsecondary institutions.

It also brings local business and professional people into schools. Experiential Learning is a powerful instructional approach as it has the potential of breaking down the walls of the school and connecting schooling to "real" life.

Our survey results, captured in Figure 6.7, indicate that 43% of responders viewed Experiential Learning as a "most significant" high-yield instructional strategy, while 41% rated it as "essential." Only 4% indicated it was not a consideration in their successful programming strategies. Clearly, Experiential Learning strategies are making a difference for the responding schools and systems in increasing student outcomes.

Two reports, *For the Love of Learning* (Royal Commission on Learning, 1994) and *Education to Employment* (Mourshed, Farrell, & Barton, 2012), found that high school students were most successful and preferred to learn when they had opportunities to apply their learning in a workplace setting. In fact, Experiential Learning is given such credence in Ontario schools that the Specialist High Skills Major (SHSM) program has embedded multiple forms of Experiential Learning (job shadowing/job twinning, work experience, and cooperative educations credit) as mandatory components of obtaining a high school graduation diploma.

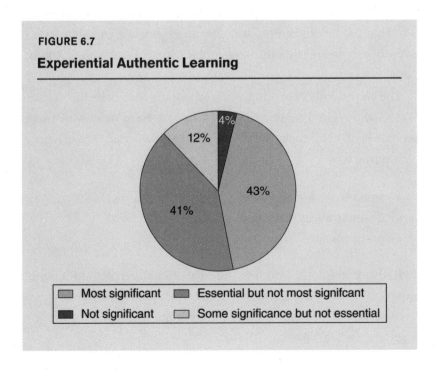

FIGURE 6.7

Experiential Authentic Learning

12%

4%

43%

41%

- Most significant
- Essential but not most signifcant
- Not significant
- Some significance but not essential

In the United States, we see the expansion of Career Academies, many of which involve paid or unpaid work experiences/internships, community service assignments, or attendance at college classes as part of the Experiential Learning model. In the Swiss model, in the canton of Bern, career counseling and lessons are mandatory for all students between ages 12 and 15. They learn about various occupations as well as vocational and academic training paths. They visit companies and prepare interviews, which can lead to internships (Mourshed et al., 2012).

To ensure that the benefits of Experiential Learning opportunities are maximized, key considerations require "intentionality" in the ways in which teachers, schools, and systems construct Experiential Learning.

Intentionality is required in

1. the instructional decisions that support the development of the *Student Pathway DNA*;
2. the application of Experiential Learning, either as part of programming use or as day-to-day instructional practices;
3. the operational/cost considerations that need to be planned for; and
4. the connections established through **a broad base of community partners**.

Instructional Decisions Supporting the Development of *Student Pathway DNA*

We know that *Student Pathway DNA*, as illustrated in Figure 1.6 (p. 25), is incomplete without

- the Knowledge Application Strand, and
- opportunity for ongoing reflection.

Experiential Learning is integral to the Knowledge Application Strand given the nature of its "hands-on" or "authentic" way of learning. It is through the process of "trying" new experiences that one learns more about oneself as a learner. The "ladder rungs" support the Experiential Learning Journey of the student. They are represented by

- project-based learning,
- work experience/internships, and
- cooperative education programs.

Each of these rungs represents a form of Experiential Learning, each has its assets, and each has its considerations for application.

A **skilled teacher**, using Experiential Learning as part of his or her instructional strategy,

- considers and activates the best form of Experiential Learning for students to practice and refine, through Knowledge Application, the learning from the Curriculum Knowledge Strand;
- uses a Collaborative Inquiry process, guiding students through the intentional learning, taking newly gained knowledge and applying a "next steps" or "goals for growth" approach to enhance their educational experiences; and
- builds on the learning opportunity by incorporating reflection as a consistent and expected part of students' Skill Development Strand.

As represented in Figure 1.4 (p. 21), **skilled teachers** match the Knowledge Application Strand with each student's skills, interests, and abilities (Skill Development Strand) and the curriculum content (Curriculum Knowledge Strand), thus enabling each student to not only develop a better sense of him- or herself as a learner but also reinforce his or her sense of relevance of the course of study.

The power of Experiential Learning in this context is that it lends itself to reinforcing ultimate life skills: highly relevant skills, inclusive values, and positive dispositions. As students grow through the experience, **skilled teachers** take time for students to explore and reflect on the importance of these life skills. Out of this reflection, students can set a personal growth plan or, as they do in Ontario, Canada, an Individual Pathways Plan (IPP) (see Chapter 5).

Regardless of the reflection tool used, the outcome is the same. By enabling students to gain a better understanding of where they are on the skill development continuum, they are more able to self-assess the learning or development they need to become more competent *Literate Graduates*. It is not enough to provide an isolated experience or singular opportunity. To bring about this level of awareness, the planned experiences must be constructed and connected with sound assessment and instructional practices in mind to ensure all students can self-assess to learn and adopt the new strategies.

Ontario is one of the few jurisdictions with a large-scale high school Cooperative Education (co-op) program that has rigor and accountability built into its structure. In 2011–2012, the province reported over 83,000 students taking at least one co-op course (A. Sasman, personal communication, July 11, 2013).

In the Ontario model, high school students, regardless of their post-secondary destination, are eligible to earn co-op credits. These credits count toward their diploma requirements and are part of their daily school schedule. The co-op out-of-school, or work placement, portion of the credit is linked to a related curriculum course. For example, a student working at a veterinary placement might have biology or science as the related linking course while another student in the same co-op class who is working at a construction placement might have construction technology or mathematics as the related course.

The intent of the co-op program, made up of (1) an in-school pre-placement component and (2) a placement component, is to provide an opportunity for the student to practice and refine the knowledge acquired in the related course. The co-op placement serves as the Knowledge Application Strand while the related curriculum course serves as the Curriculum Knowledge Strand. The teacher sets up the knowledge application through the development and assessment of a Personalized Placement Learning Plan (PPLP) where students are expected to self-reflect and self-assess on the total experience.

Appendix J shows that the PPLP is developed in conjunction with the co-op monitoring teacher, the related subject teacher, the placement supervisor (in the workplace), and the student. Demonstrations of learning at the workplace are aligned with the curriculum-related course expectations. In addition, the work placement supervisor is required to identify workplace expectations and demonstrations of learning. Success Criteria are established among the teacher, student, and work placement supervisor. The student receives Descriptive Feedback throughout the placement with opportunities to provide input, establish and revise goals, and measure his or her performance against the Success Criteria. The teacher uses the PPLP as a "living," working document to track and assess student progress and achievement. Through a process of assessment for, as, and of learning, the teacher then determines a grade or mark representing the student's achievement for report card purposes.

By using this common framework to guide the instructional practice and assessment, alignment, rigor, and accountability are purposefully built into the program. Community partners, supporting the program, see a common approach across all high schools in the 72 districts across Ontario. The standardization provides credibility to the program, as a value-added Experiential Learning opportunity for all students. It is possible to Recalculate the Route on a large scale to increase all students' achievement!

Cooperative Education programming is but one form of Experiential Learning. There are other forms to be considered and instructional decisions to be made.

Parent Quote:

"The Ontario Youth Apprenticeship/co-op program has helped my son become more confident and mature and has raised his self-esteem through hands-on (real-life) training. Our conversations are now positive, and we get pleasure from seeing and hearing the excitement in his discovery that learning and schooling can be fun and rewarding."

–Lorraine Hood, Parent, Newmarket,
Ontario (personal communication, May 29, 2013)

Applying Experiential Learning in Instructional Practice

Building successful *Pathways to Career Readiness* requires a systematic K–12+ application of the *Pathway* lens. As represented by the Innovation Leadership Prism (Figure 2.3, p. 65), it is a lens requiring a community-based approach. It embraces structured Collaborative Inquiry, blended with Experiential Learning, as an essential component of the delivery of the core curriculum from the primary grades to the completion of high school.

As shown in the *Pathways to Career Readiness Frame: Finding True-North* (Figure 1.1, p. 12), the developmental lens is mindful of *Career Readiness*. It starts with self- and community awareness in the early years and expands to focused experiential programming and training opportunities throughout high school. It recognizes the importance of how Experiential Learning can help students, from a very young age, to

- appreciate and value human diversity,
- understand that they can learn from everyone they meet, and
- have a sense of the role that education and training plays in the lives of adults in their community.

Every field trip, guest speaker, or "book read" presents an opportunity for students to learn from and about the people represented: Who does what? What skills are involved? How did they acquire the skills? What do they need to know?

Each teacher has a range of Experiential Learning formats to consider, based on the

- learning outcomes the teacher and students are hoping to achieve,
- grade level,
- program readiness, and
- resources available.

Figure 6.8 illustrates the K–12+ Experiential Learning Continuum that can be built across classes, grades, and divisions.

As students move along the K–12+ Experiential Learning Continuum (Figure 6.8), the walls of the school fall away as opportunities to extend the connections into the community and workplace broaden. Student voice and choice can be leveraged to engage students in the learning they are passionate about.

> "*Every zoo trip is an opportunity to learn from and about the people who work there: Who feeds the animals, and how did zoo keepers train for their jobs? Who decides what plants to put in the enclosures, and what do they have to know in order to do that?*"
>
> Royal Commission on Learning, 1994, p. 147.

Some would argue that students should pursue Experiential Learning opportunities on their own time and at their own expense. While many high school students have part-time jobs, for the most part these jobs are one-dimensional and are carried out alongside their peers with no reflection on skills acquired. Planned work experiences,

FIGURE 6.8

K–12+ Experiential Learning Continuum

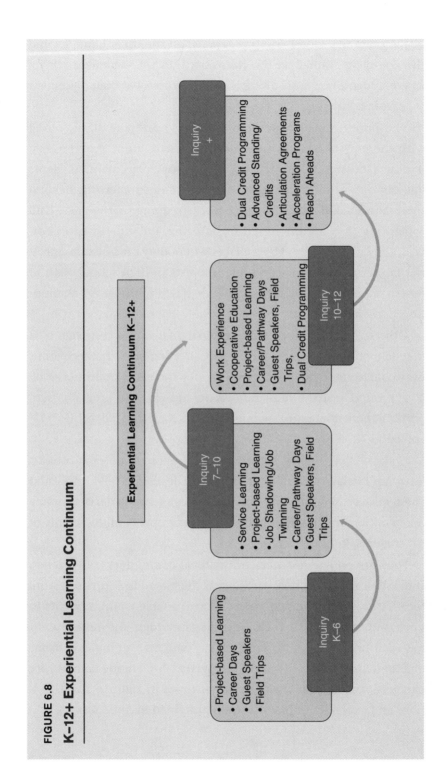

Experiential Learning Continuum K–12+

Inquiry K–6
- Project-based Learning
- Career Days
- Guest Speakers
- Field Trips

Inquiry 7–10
- Service Learning
- Project-based Learning
- Job Shadowing/Job Twinning
- Career/Pathway Days
- Guest Speakers, Field Trips

Inquiry 10–12
- Work Experience
- Cooperative Education
- Project-based Learning
- Career/Pathway Days
- Guest Speakers, Field Trips,
- Dual Credit Programming

Inquiry +
- Dual Credit Programming
- Advanced Standing/ Credits
- Articulation Agreements
- Acceleration Programs
- Reach Aheads

internships, and robust co-op programs, on the other hand, extend the knowledge gained in the classroom into the workplace setting where students now work alongside adults who act as their placement supervisors.

The opportunity to develop workplace and life skills, along with the practice and refinement of the curriculum expectations, is now a possibility. By "trying on" a work placement, students have an opportunity to explore a new *Pathway*, something beyond their current skill and knowledge level. In doing so, they may find something they are interested in pursuing, but equally as important, they may find out those places where they are not suited. Is it not far better to explore multiple interests in high school than to invest years of specific postsecondary training under an assumption of preference?

Others would argue that Experiential Learning is restricted to a high school strategy. Given the current direction of the new economy, we would argue that this is certainly not the case. Mourshed et al. (2012) found that the most innovative and effective programs supported Experiential Learning opportunities for their students **EARLY** and **OFTEN**.

Collaborative Inquiry, interdisciplinary approaches, project-based learning, character communities, service learning, field trips, and guest speakers are just some of the strategies the **skilled teacher** draws on to construct Experiential Learning opportunities for his or her students, K–12+.

Drawing on the resources of the local community, the teacher, students, and community partners, as illustrated in Figure 6.9, work together to define the rich tasks that will enable young students to learn and reflect upon their interests, aptitudes, and responsibilities within a community framework. Common "high yield" forms of Experiential Learning, using the partnership among community partners, students, and teachers, are mapped in Figure 6.10. Definitions and examples of practice are highlighted in Appendix K.

FIGURE 6.9

Innovation Leadership Prism (Teacher Lens)

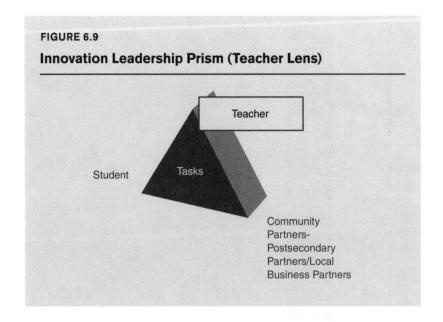

This is not to say that every instructional decision needs to be experiential in nature. **Skilled teachers** know that Experiential Learning is a powerful engagement strategy when framed through a Collaborative Inquiry approach. They know how and when to utilize it. Optimizing this instructional approach requires that systems, leaders, school administrators, and teachers consider a scaffold approach. Building and layering Experiential Learning across grades and subjects ensures that all students complete their high school education with the self-knowledge, requisite skills, and dispositions to move through their next transition.

For some students, their *Pathway* may involve service learning and global education opportunities. Others, moving directly into the workforce, might require a more comprehensive *Pathway* with multiple job shadowing and twinning opportunities, work experiences, and internships, followed by a Cooperative Education program. Regardless of destination, students, in a Recalculated Route, need to have multiple

FIGURE 6.10

The Experiential Learning Journey—Model of Gradual Release of Responsibility

The Experiential Learning Journey—Gradual Release of Responsibility to Independence

Knowledge Application Strand	Project-Based Learning (Shared Learning)	Work Experience/Internships (Guided Learning)	Cooperative Education Programs (Independent/ Self-Directed Learning)
Field Trips/Guest Speakers			
Job Shadowing		↑	
Job Twinning		↑	
Service Learning		↑	
Global Education			↑
Virtual/ Online			↑
Career Focused Programs			↑
School-Work Transition Programs			↑
Apprenticeship Training			↑

Experiential Learning Journey Continuum K–12+

seamless opportunities to connect their learning to the real world. Teachers need to have not only the resources to allow students to do so, but also the requisite skills to provide Experiential Learning through a Collaborative Inquiry approach.

Operational Considerations

For such a value-added instructional strategy, Mourshed et al. (2012) noted that while "58% of youth reported that practical hands-on learning was the most effective in terms of learning, less than half of this percentage were involved in that type of programming" (p. 37). Where and what are the roadblocks? What can be done to remove them? Who needs to be involved?

In a Recalculated Route, our leadership structure recognizes that teachers, regardless of the grade level, benefit from **a broad base of community partners**. As general practitioners/diagnosticians, they know

- who can provide assistance,
- when it is needed, and
- how to access the resource.

We recognize that it is an *unrealistic expectation* for teachers and other school staff members *to be solely responsible* in meeting individual student need for exposure to a variety of learning experiences and opportunities. To do this, however, they need to have the resources on hand and readily accessible. Community partners (Chapter 3) need to be engaged and challenged to participate in this responsibility.

In a Recalculated Route, there needs to be support at the school and system level to coordinate such Experiential Learning opportunities. Whether that is positions filled by system integrators, as recommended by Mourshed et al. (2012), or some other structure, a new role needs to be in place to help education providers and employers develop skill to *The Literate Graduate* profile.

In the United States, Career Academies have a team of dedicated teachers working with partners from the selected career field. In Ontario, a designated SHSM coordinator serves as a facilitator for his or her school team, working collaboratively in planning all the elements of the diploma requirements.

While it is clear that there is recognition that such a role is required, there is a less defined recognition of the time and dollars to be committed, and by whom. This incongruity of identified need and actual implementation often results in teacher burnout and ultimately program "gatekeeping" by staff and administration. If we are indeed going to successfully leverage the educational system to meet the learning needs of the masses for the 21st century, then all stakeholders, as discussed in Chapter 3, have a role to play in ensuring funding is available that will provide equitable access.

Without a doubt, Experiential Learning opportunities can be expensive components to the educational experience, especially where the programming takes the students out of the school building. Transportation, training and equipment, liability and workplace insurance, and staffing allocations, to name a few, are costs incurred in high school Experiential Learning programs. However, *the societal cost of not providing these learning opportunities will be even greater when one considers a future workforce that is unskilled and untrained for the jobs at hand.*

One viable solution may lie in scaling up distance or e-learning as a cost-effective way to provide more Experiential Learning opportunities. Virtual work experience and co-op programs allow students to engage with their placements and employers in a digital world. Online collaboration tools such as Google Docs have dramatically changed not only the way we do work but the spaces in which we work.

In addition to direct costs, Experiential Learning opportunities have a significant risk management component for systems, schools, teachers, students, and parents. Student exposure to workplace hazards requires vigilance on the part of the students, teachers, and school administrators to ensure that safe and supportive learning environments are provided at all times. These programming considerations are not insurmountable. Through *a structured, collaboratively planned approach*, early adopters are using their creativity and problem-solving approaches to break down the barriers and find solutions. It is called **innovation**.

Given the complexities of Experiential Learning programming and opportunities, teachers need to become skilled practitioners. They require numerous examples of community and workplace visits, preparatory and follow-up activities, and the use of high-impact assessment and instructional practices to develop the ability to support age-appropriate Experiential Learning opportunities. This requires a commitment by states and systems to specific, ongoing professional learning for teachers, administrators, and system leaders.

Supporting a Broad Base of Community Partners

Community partners are fundamental to a Recalculated Route. We need to "invite them in" to be partners in our shared beliefs and understandings (see Chapter 3). It is important for educators to be mindful of the perspectives of our

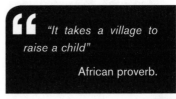

"It takes a village to raise a child"

African proverb.

community partners. Many will provide Experiential Learning opportunities from which, in all likelihood, they will not reap any immediate benefits or profits. This in itself is counterintuitive for businesses that operate from a bottom-line perspective. For many students, learning from the opportunities they are afforded may take years to solidify. In the end, it is often other organizations that benefit from the opportunity someone else provided—justified as our collective "Moral Purpose."

While we know co-op and other forms of Experiential Learning to be effective strategies, enabling students to "try on" a career, to develop networks in the community, and to focus their learning, there is a growing desire by postsecondary community partners and employers to see standardization in the credentials coming out of such specialized programs and opportunities.

Tracking and assessment tools, such as the Ontario Skills Passport (Ontario Ministry of Education, 2014) and the WorkKeys assessment system (ACT, 2014), have been developed to help students measure the extent to which they have the foundational and advanced skills required for success in the workplace. They also provide a frame of reference for teachers, as to the evolving skill sets of *The Literate Graduate*.

In Ontario, students completing the SHSM receive a Red Seal on their high school diploma serving as a credential to their skill and training. Scaling up *Pathway* programming, such as the SHSM, has contributed to the impressive increase in Ontario high school graduation rates from 68% to 82%. This is a testimony to the Student Success initiative and *Pathways* programming that are Recalculating the Route for students across Ontario (Levin, 2012).

In the United States, the National Career Readiness Certificate (NCRC) guarantees employers a certain level of students' readiness. According to Mourshed et al. (2012), to date 40 states recognize NCRC accreditation. Third-party assessment tools offer some comfort to community partners and educators—that we are "getting it right" in terms of *The Literate Graduate*—but until we see universal acceptance within our communities, there will be continued confusion around program value and standards.

In a Recalculated Route, we need to "up-shift" our thinking and views about who provides what and when. While "the pot can certainly be sweetened" with tax incentives for participating partners, ultimately, on a societal level, we need to see this as our shared social responsibility—our common moral purpose. ***A structured, collaboratively planned approach*** requires no less. We all have a role to play in providing our youth with the best advantages.

Reflective Pause by Suzie Boss

In this chapter, the authors stake out the high ground when they describe the purpose of education. I was struck by their assertion that teachers, if adequately supported, will "create curious, learning-focused students, capable of changing their world to be a better place." That's an audacious goal—but one that's not impossible to imagine, if schools and communities can come together around a shared vision of students as society's future change agents.

FROM GOOD TO GREAT TO INNOVATE

If we are going to build successful *Pathways to Career Readiness*, then we need a "road system infrastructure" that will deliver students there.

A great road system is one that has many routes to get to the same destination, on- and off-ramps that are easy to access and navigate, excellent signage, clear directions, express lanes, collector lanes, connecting bridges, and some circling-back routes for wrong turns inadvertently taken and subsequently corrected.

A great road system is where one can see the interrelationship and interdependence of all structures—how everything is interconnected and linked, and how one structure complements another. In other words, while there might be many things going on in a system, there needs to be cohesion and coherence. That is, the road system must be permanent and, thus, constantly under repair; its architects, engineers, and maintenance crews must stay the course, committing to make strong and lasting connections.

An innovative road system incorporates all of the above but also embraces the reality that if one thing is certain, it is that change is inevitable. Structures need to be changed, signage adjusted, and new routes explored.

In the same way, we must commit to making strong and lasting connections for students so they can drive into the future, confidently. It is no different in Recalculating the Route for all students. We must move from Good to Great to Innovate—now.

Andy Hargreaves and Dennis Shirley concur in *The Global Fourth Way* (2012) by asking, "without continual innovation from within, what chances do schools have not only to survive but also to prosper in a world where students' lives and everyday experiences and interactions are undergoing profound . . . transformations"? (p. 26).

STEPS TO STUDENTS' SUCCESS

1. Strive to promote critical thinking in every activity.

2. Have the skills to use a multiplicity of resources.

3. Promote an inquiry habit of mind.

4. Know and apply 21st-century skills.

5. Use curriculum expectations combined with students' interests and experiences to craft structured Collaborative Inquiry approaches co-led with students.

6. Make cognitive demands on students that extend thinking through interesting and relevant problem solving.

7. Manage and sustain student-centered assessment that improves instruction.

8. Learn about all students by giving and getting feedback from them on Experiential Learning opportunities within and beyond school walls.

9. Support Experiential Learning by identifying and using *a broad base of community partners.*

10. Align learning expectations with community partner needs.

11. Remove barriers to valuing human diversity.

12. Step into one another's world.

13. Work collaboratively with students **EARLY** and **OFTEN**.

14. *Never* give up on one student!

How might we create an educational system that prepares students to become innovative thinkers and capable problem solvers? This is a rich question for inquiry, and the authors wisely suggest that teachers, school leaders, community members, and students need to work together to respond with practical action steps. This chapter offers several useful tools for advancing this agenda. For example, the process of Collaborative Inquiry (outlined in Figure 6.5) includes roles for students, teachers, leaders, and community partners. The end goal of this process is student-driven learning, but that doesn't happen automatically. The authors are wise to point out that students will need support—and thoughtfully designed learning experiences—to get proficient at the inquiry process. Similarly, educators need ongoing opportunities to engage in Collaborative Inquiry with their colleagues and with members of the broader community. This means investing in time and resources for educators; the authors point out the opportunity cost if we fail to act.

In their extensive discussion of Experiential Learning, the authors help us envision what a new road map for education might look like as students make their way from K to 12+. I can imagine that project-based learning, introduced in the primary years, will become more student driven, individualized, and ambitious as students gain in experience and maturity. Similarly, community connections are likely to be mediated by teachers when students first begin to take their inquiry beyond the classroom. Gradually, however, students will likely show more agency when it comes to connecting with mentors and learning in real-world contexts. Taking this a step further, it's not hard to imagine community members turning to students when they have problems in need of innovative solutions. When that starts to happen, we'll have compelling evidence that the new road map for education is indeed taking us where we want to go.

About Suzie Boss

Suzie Boss is an education writer and consultant who focuses on project-based learning and innovation to improve lives and transform communities. Her most recent books are *Bringing Innovation to School: Empowering Students to Thrive in a Changing World* (Solution Tree, 2012) and *Thinking Through Project-Based Learning* (Corwin, 2013), coauthored with Jane Krauss. She is a regular contributor to *Edutopia* and the *Stanford Social Innovation Review* and has written for a wide range of other publications, including *The New York Times, Educational Leadership,* and *Principal Leadership.* She is on the national faculty of the Buck Institute for Education and has worked with educators internationally to bring project-based learning and innovation strategies to both traditional classrooms and informal learning settings. Suzie resides in Portland, Oregon.

EPILOGUE

S
o here we are—the final chapter; the last words; the epilogue to an epic work. Jim Collins's well-known and widely used book *Good to Great* (2001) shows just what it takes in terms of extraordinary effort and exceptional imagination to move from being a merely good organization to becoming a truly great one. And in *Great by Choice* (2011), Collins and his colleague Morten Hansen go on to show how achieving greatness not only requires the introduction of something unusual or novel (the Latin origin of *innovation*) but also entails the relentless application of discipline—hard work, trial and error, and readiness to rebound from countless setbacks to achieve brilliance and success.

This has been the spirit and the substance of this exceptional and cleverly titled book by Lyn Sharratt and Gale Harild: on *Good to Great to Innovate*. The book's core argument has been that innovation is not just about introducing a new thought or idea but also about applying it in practice. Dazzling creativity comes to nothing without the grit and determination of industry and toil. Innovations are like babies. It's one thing to bring them into the world; it's another thing altogether to bring them up in it.

Sharratt and Harild know this from decades of their own practice working as teachers, leaders, and change agents around the world, but especially in the internationally renowned and highly regarded educational system of Ontario, Canada. They have, for years, played an integral and instrumental part in transforming the province's strategies and results in literacy through widespread implementation of evidence-informed practices of effective instruction. They have used data systems to guide good pedagogy and trigger just-in-time interventions whenever students have been at risk of falling behind in their learning. They have insisted on maintaining a relentless focus on equity and achievement, and they have played leading roles in training principals to be the instructional leaders who enable their teachers to become more effective and innovative in their practices and to have an increasingly positive impact on achievement and results.

The systemic and systematic work of the authors as change leaders has made a major contribution to Ontario's record of steady and sustainable success that has become the envy of the world and one of the province's greatest knowledge exports all across the globe. Sharratt and Harild have seen students' success and achievement rise and witnessed how a number of inequities have begun to recede to a degree that has never happened before. They have made a major contribution to substantial and sustained educational improvement, and they have done this in a province with a population that exceeds 13 million and that is also one of the most diverse societies on the planet.

But like many high-performing organizations and their leaders, now they know that they, the province, and the world have to do more. They grasp that we do not get better by staying where we are, and that the practices that bring success do not extend it further. It is just when organizations have significantly improved that they then need to innovate. Nokia passed up on finger-swiping technology because it wanted to stick with the all-thumbs platform that had brought about its stellar mobile phone success. It remained no fingers and all thumbs, and a crisis that threatened its very existence rapidly ensued.

In today's world, if you try not to change, your environment will anyway. So either you will be forced into change by default, or you will lead the way by design. Sharratt and Harild list some of the changes that are already transforming the world of education: the changing nature of work, the exponential impact of digital technologies, the compression of time and space that accompanies accelerating globalization, and—amid all this fast and furious change—the looming crises of core purpose and mental health that affect and afflict more and more of our teenagers in an age of escalating anxiety. These authors give us somber and salutary warnings about the impending risks of decline at time when society seems to be struggling to find its *TrueNorth*.

We have to innovate, then. But we cannot do this at the expense of improvement—at the cost of the crucial gains that have already been made. In industry, Dyson refined the design of its vacuum cleaner through more than 5,000 prototypes before it finally went to market. When the innovations we introduce involve children's lives, they must be even more disciplined in their implementation. We somehow have to innovate and improve at once, and bring together the alternative and opposing mind-sets that underpin these two orientations to change as we do so. Michael Fullan's famous implementation dip should be treated as an avoidable average, not an existential necessity.

In our new book, *Uplifting Leadership* (2014), my coauthors Alan Boyle and Alma Harris and I describe how we must work with a world where opposites attract if we are to uplift people's spirits, performance, and opportunities. We argue that in unusually high-performing businesses, sports teams, and educational systems, people dream big about better futures, but they also pursue their dreams with relentless determination. High-performing organizations are prepared to go against the grain of accepted tradition and past practice not as a quirky eccentricity but through courageous tenacity that can overcome ridicule and doubt. People in high-performing organizations know how to collaborate with competitors, how to pull people into change and not just push them through it, and how to join up the dots between short-term results and long-term success. They get the yin and the yang of change rather than swinging from one side of their brains to the other.

Sharratt and Harild call for an "up-shift" in mind-sets that is required to achieve what we call uplift in opportunities and outcomes. This "up-shift" also brings together opposites that attract. It unites change elements and change strategies that others too readily set apart. The authors provide many examples of this both/and thinking. They do not pit instructional leadership against transformational leadership or vice versa (as competing sects of leadership researchers are overly inclined to do) but understand that the two can and should work together. They believe in engaging with digital technologies but also warn that we must offset their most distracting and harmful effects. And while they advocate for recalculated creative *Pathways* (**a structured, collaboratively planned approach**) through which students can effectively map their way toward *Career Readiness*, they also insist on the disciplined use of data-driven tracking and monitoring of every student's progress so that no one will get lost along the way.

Sharratt and Harild have shown us that they are conversant with the bold and imaginative futures thinking that is helping us to figure out how to engage with and anticipate the trajectory of our rapidly changing world. They have shared with us their extensive research knowledge of high-yield instruction, high-impact leadership, and the science of effective implementation. But, in this comprehensive text, they have also given us something else that the blue-sky dreamers, the number-crunching researchers, and the system-level policy wonks have not: ideas, evidence, and examples of exactly how to do all that they advise, in the everyday detail of practice.

The writers of this book have opened doors to a new educational world without taking us too far from the existing one with which we are already familiar. They have been the Lev Vygotskys of educational change: taking us into and through our proximal zones of cognitive and emotional development so that we feel able to engage with and embrace changes that we might have otherwise thought were beyond us. Changes in education today should feel neither too familiar nor too strange. Sharratt and Harild have shown us just how to navigate past the siren calls of these seductive extremes.

—Andy Hargreaves
Thomas More Brennan Chair in Education
Boston College

About Andy Hargreaves, PhD

Andy Hargreaves is the Thomas More Brennan Chair in the Lynch School of Education at Boston College. Before that, he was the cofounder and codirector of the International Centre for Educational Change at the Ontario Institute for Studies in Education in Canada.

Andy has authored or edited around 30 books. Several of these have achieved outstanding writing awards from the American Educational Research Association, the American Library Association, the International Leadership Association, the National Staff

Development Council, and the American Association of Colleges for Teacher Education and are translated into many languages. His most recent books are *Uplifting Leadership* (with Alan Boyle and Alma Harris—Jossey-Bass Business, 2014), *Professional Capital: Transforming Teaching in Every School* (with Michael Fullan—Teachers College Press, 2012), and *The Global Fourth Way* (with Dennis Shirley—Corwin, 2012). Andy has received many awards including an honorary doctorate from Scandinavia's oldest university (Uppsala).

APPENDICES

Appendix A Recalculating the Route—Striking a New Leadership Balance

Traditional Leadership Attributes	Innovation Leadership Attributes
Narrowly Defined	Broadly Based
Teacher Centered	Learner Centered
Knowledge Acquisition	Knowledge Mobilization
Content	Process
Theory	Theory Into Practice
Time Slotted	On Demand
One Size Fits All	Personalized
School	Multiple Stakeholders
Classroom	Global Community
Learning for School	Learning for Life
Problem Solving	Innovative Approaches
Competitive	Collaborative
Summative	Formative
Mechanical	Organic
Conformity	Diversity

As Appendix A illustrates, moving from traditional leadership attributes on the left to innovation leadership characteristics on the right will create leadership styles that enable innovation to occur within the classroom and outside school walls.

To create a shift, how do we move more of our thinking and actions to the right-hand side of our chart to create innovation? By the very definition, we

- foster a learning institution that recognizes that taking something and making it better is a process;

- take time to establish equitable inclusive processes that support opportunities for dialogue;
- build trust and accountability to the expected outcomes;
- embrace a culture of learning where exploring new work, in new ways, is welcomed and expected;
- assume there might be missteps but anticipate the safety nets that need to be put in place;
- strengthen the learning culture through collaborative peer-based accountability; and
- remove structures that foster isolation in the classroom and throughout the learning process.

Source: Adapted from Trilling & Fadel (2009).

Appendix B A Detailed Explanation of How Individual Lenses of the Innovation Leadership Prism Are Relational

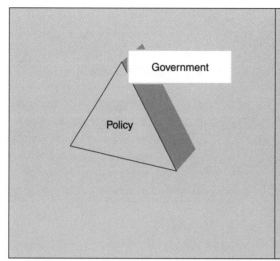

In a Recalculated Route, there needs to be "pressure and support" for all of the stakeholders to come to the policy planning table. Education policy must be aligned with economic (social welfare and business) policies for systems, schools, and teachers to have the tools and resources to do the work they are challenged to undertake supporting the learning of all students.

System leaders, principals with their school leadership teams, and community partners need to be responsive to the policy mandates and set achievable, measurable targets and goals supported by high-yield strategies and inclusive resources.

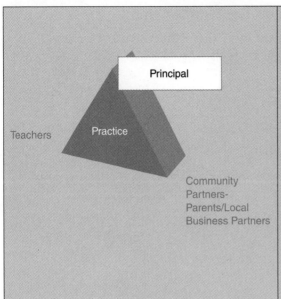

Schools need to become part of their communities, and communities need to become part of their schools. Principals and their teachers work with their community partners, including parents, local business and industry, and postsecondary destination representatives, to explore and plan for the programming and practice that will support the targets set by the system as they pertain to the learning needs of particular school communities.

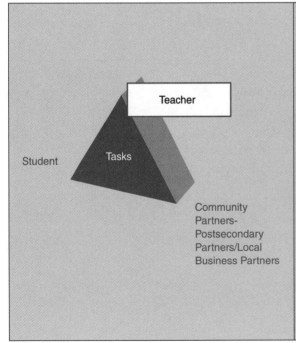

Teachers work with their students to establish rich performance tasks, Learning Goals/Is and Success Criteria and give and get Descriptive Feedback that will move learning. They collaborate and consult, and move forward as needed, with the community partners to ensure that opportunities and experiences are accessed that will enhance the rich performance tasks or program offerings. These actions will inform the individual learning goals that students and teachers establish together.

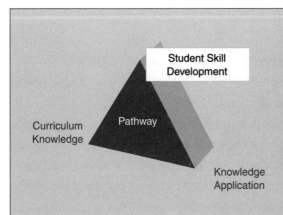

When rich performance tasks are provided in such a way that the curriculum knowledge becomes the vehicle by which students apply that knowledge in an authentic, timely application with multiple opportunities for self-reflection and skill development, then the *Student Pathway DNA* is being developed.

Appendix C Tips for Parents

- Help your teen understand who he or she is.
- Encourage dialogue that reflects what your teen might like to "try" rather than what he or she wants to "be."
- Encourage participation in a variety of extracurricular activities.
- Become familiar with the graduation diploma requirements and the expected educational outcomes of postsecondary training.
- Take an active role in your teen's annual planning process to ensure his or her options and course selections are realistic.
- Talk about results in your teen's courses.
- Talk about a variety of career options and encourage your teen to explore Experiential Learning opportunities.
- Help your teen develop good work habits.
- Help your teen build a personal portfolio.
- Provide advice on money management.
- Help your teen to see that every meeting with an individual is an opportunity to learn from someone else. Introduce your teen to your friends and colleagues to broaden his or her network and sphere of influence.
- Recognize the importance of setting directions for the future by encouraging your teen to
  - consider long-range planning options,
  - research job opportunities, and
  - set aside time for reflection and discussion.
- Honor your teen's decisions.
- Remember it is not the destination that matters, but rather the learning that takes place on your teen's educational journey that will ultimately get him or her there.

Source: York Region District School Board (2004c).

Appendix D A System, School, Classroom *Pathways* Self-Reflection Tool

Teacher Questions

A. Opportunities for Students

1. I provided career information to students that addressed

   a. the university *Pathway* destination related to my subject area.

   b. the college *Pathway* destination related to my subject area.

   c. the apprenticeship *Pathway* destination related to my subject area.

   d. the workplace *Pathway* destination related to my subject area.

   Scale: 1 = Extensive, 2 = Moderate, 3 = Minimal, 4 = Never

2. In my department, there are impediments to providing programming opportunities across all *Pathways* (workplace, college, university, apprenticeship).

   Yes No (Circle one.)

3. The biggest impediments are

   a. school timetabling decisions.

   b. student/parent course selection.

   c. facility/space restrictions.

   d. staffing decisions.

B. Strategies for Teachers

1. My department promotes the alignment of individual student strengths and well-being to *Pathway* options (i.e., understanding personal skills, learning styles, and multiple intelligences).

   Scale: 1 = Very often, 2 = Often, 3 = Sometimes, 4 = Never, 5 = Not applicable

2. How often do you use the following to help students learn about their personal interests, skills, and career options?

Please select all that apply.

a. Ontario Skills Passport (OSP)

b. Career Cruising

c. Career Fairs

d. Guest Speakers

e. Experiential Learning (job shadowing, job twinning, work experience)

f. Reach Ahead Opportunities (visit workplace)

g. Contextualized Learning Activities

h. Field Trips

Scale: 1 = Very often, 2 = Often, 3 = Sometimes, 4 = Never, 5 = Not applicable

C. Training/Teacher Knowledge

1. I can confidently discuss all *Pathway* and program options with my students.

   Scale: 1 = Strongly agree, 2 = Agree, 3 = Disagree, 4 = Strongly disagree, 5 = Don't know

2. I could use more information about the following programs (please select all that apply):

   a. Ontario Youth Apprenticeship Program (OYAP)

   b. Cooperative Education Programs

   c. Community Living

   d. Dual Credits

   e. Specialist High Skills Major (SHSM)

   f. Personalized Alternative Education

   g. International Baccalaureate (IB)

   h. French Immersion

3. I make connections for my students with community partners.

   Scale: 1 = Extensive, 2 = Moderate, 3 = Minimal, 4 = Never

4. I can confidently discuss all *Pathway* and program options with parents.

   Scale: 1 = Strongly agree, 2 = Agree, 3 = Disagree, 4 = Strongly disagree, 5 = Don't know

School Administration Questions

1. Which *Pathway* destinations would you like to see expanded through your school course offerings?

   Please select all that apply.
   a. Academic
   b. Applied
   c. Locally Developed
   d. Workplace
   e. Open
   f. College
   g. College/University
   h. University

2. To what extent do the following factors impact ability to provide appropriate programming for your students?
   a. Bus transportation
   b. Timetabling
   c. Staffing
   d. School-day start and finish times
   e. School-year calendar
   f. Budget
   g. Course selection decisions
   h. Access to regional programming (i.e., virtual learning, summer school, continuing education)
   i. Private school courses

   Scale: 1 = Positive impact, 2 = Negative impact, 3 = No impact

3. My current staffing allocations are sufficient to meet my school's current programming needs.

   Scale: 1 = Strongly agree, 2 = Agree, 3 = Disagree, 4 = Strongly disagree

4. My current staffing allocations are sufficient to meet my school's new programming needs.

   Scale: 1 = Strongly agree, 2 = Agree, 3 = Disagree, 4 = Strongly disagree

5. My school would benefit from additional support in developing the following programs:
   Please select all that apply.

   a. Specialist High Skills Major (SHSM)
   b. Ontario Youth Apprenticeship Program (OYAP)
   c. Dual Credits
   d. Exploring Opportunities Programs (EOP)

6. I have enough knowledge about *Pathways* to inform the development of programs within my school.

   Scale: 1 = Strongly agree, 2 = Agree, 3 = Disagree, 4 = Strongly disagree, 5 = Don't know

Sample Student *Pathway* Questions					
19.How is your school preparing you for what you want to do or try after high school?					
	Strongly Agree	**Agree**	**Disagree**	**Strongly Disagree**	**Not Sure**
This school is helping me learn about myself and what I want to do/try after high school.	❑	❑	❑	❑	❑
This school provides enough information about the workplace.	❑	❑	❑	❑	❑
This school provides enough information about apprenticeships.	❑	❑	❑	❑	❑
This school provides enough information about university.	❑	❑	❑	❑	❑
This school provides enough information about college.	❑	❑	❑	❑	❑
This school provides enough information about living on my own.	❑	❑	❑	❑	❑
Teachers at this school help me to understand the wide variety of career/*Pathway* options available to me.	❑	❑	❑	❑	❑

(Continued)

(Continued)

	Strongly Agree	Agree	Disagree	Strongly Disagree	Not Sure
This school provides enough courses to prepare me for what I want to do/try after high school.	❑	❑	❑	❑	❑
This school provides a variety of ways for me to learn and ways in which to demonstrate that learning.	❑	❑	❑	❑	❑
This school provides programming that is engaging and relevant to me.	❑	❑	❑	❑	❑

2. Do you plan to graduate from high school?

❑ Yes ❑ No ❑ I'm not sure

3. What do you plan to do <u>immediately after</u> high school?

(Choose ALL that are true for you.)

❑ Apprenticeship ❑ Other ❑ College ❑ University ❑ Work ❑ I'm not sure

Sample Parent *Pathway* Questions					
1. How is your school preparing your son or daughter for what he or she wants to do or try after high school?					
	Strongly Agree	**Agree**	**Disagree**	**Strongly Disagree**	**Not Sure**
This school is helping my son/daughter learn about him-/herself and what he/she wants to do/try after high school.	❑	❑	❑	❑	❑
This school provides enough information about the workplace.	❑	❑	❑	❑	❑
This school provides enough information about apprenticeships.	❑	❑	❑	❑	❑
This school provides enough information about university.	❑	❑	❑	❑	❑
This school provides enough information about college.	❑	❑	❑	❑	❑
This school provides enough information about living on your own.	❑	❑	❑	❑	❑
Teachers at this school help me to understand the wide variety of career/*Pathway* options available to my son/daughter.	❑	❑	❑	❑	❑

(Continued)

(Continued)

	Strongly Agree	Agree	Disagree	Strongly Disagree	Not Sure
This school provides enough courses to prepare students for what they want to do/try after high school.	❑	❑	❑	❑	❑
This school provides a variety of ways for students to learn and ways in which to demonstrate that learning.	❑	❑	❑	❑	❑
This school provides programming that is engaging and relevant to students.	❑	❑	❑	❑	❑
This school provides a safe caring learning environment for all students.	❑	❑	❑	❑	❑

2. Do you have sufficient information to assist your son or daughter in making informed decisions regarding postsecondary planning?

❑ Yes	❑ No	❑ I'm not sure

3. What does your son or daughter plan to do <u>immediately after</u> high school? (Choose ALL that are true for you.)

❑ Apprenticeship	❑ Other	❑ College	❑ University	❑ Work	❑ I'm not sure

Source: York Region District School Board (2012).

Appendix E Career Tree Charts

Career Pathways in Agriculture

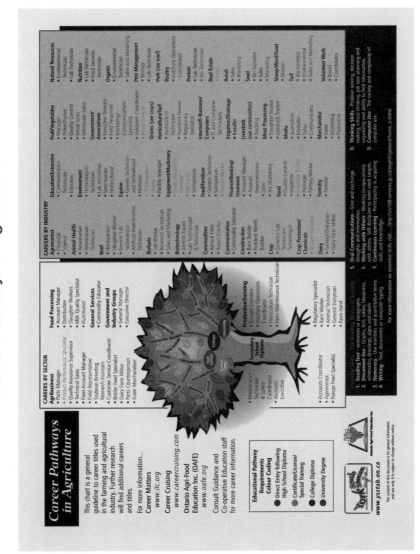

Source: Workforce Planning Board of York Region and Bradford West Gwillimbury, Ontario.

Career *Pathways* for Health Care Settings in York Region

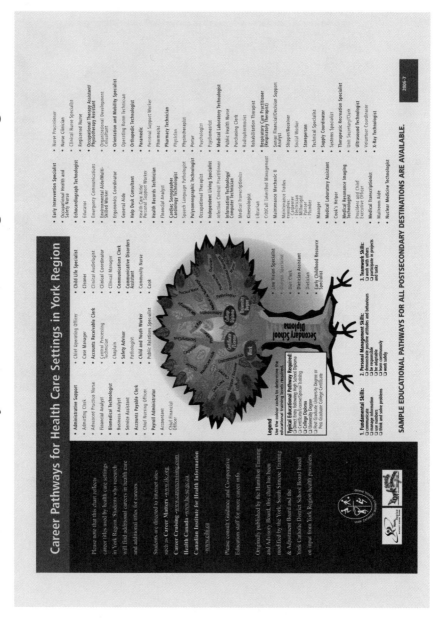

Source: Workforce Planning Board of York Region and Bradford West Gwillimbury, Ontario.

Appendix F Co-Teaching Cycle

1. Co-Planning
- Find time to plan, teach with video, debrief and reflect with trusted colleague
- Discuss what you each want to improve about your practice to give each other Descriptive Feedback during the process.
- Begin with curriculum expectations, Learning Goal, draft Success Criteria to co-construct
- Plan before during and after lesson; think about timing, flow and pace
- Use research-based, high-yield instructional strategies differentiated based on student need
- Discuss Collaborative Inquiry focus for the teaching based on assessment for learning data

2. Co-Teaching
- Work side-by-side in classroom
- Co-Facilitate classroom discussion
- Focus on students' thinking
- Monitor students' engagement
- Change pace and flow if needed
- Ask "How do you know all students" are achieving?"

THE CO-TEACHING CYCLE

4. Co-Reflecting
- Engage with co-teaching partner in candid, open, honest dialogue about their teaching and learning
- Identify and understand changes needed in practice and beliefs to become consciously skilled
- Plan next steps for student and teacher learning based on formative assessment – working from where ALL students are in their learning

3. Co-Debriefing
- Examine video clips to look/listen for student voice, questions/responses and higher-order thinking
- Examine teaching questions and prompts used
- Consider if taught, learned and assessed curriculum were aligned
- Discuss joint teaching, thinking about what worked, didn't work, what to do differently
- Evaluate Collaborative Inquiry focus for improved practice

Source: Adapted from Sharratt & Fullan (2012, p. 119).

Appendix G Sample *Pathway* Tracking

Sample: Primary Division Programs/*Pathways* Indicators	Examples of programs that exist within your division that support these sources of evidence	Examples of instructional strategies teachers use to support these sources of evidence	Examples of additional activities/resources (internally or externally) that support these sources of evidence	Gaps
At the school: • Programs and *Pathways* address all destinations; • Teaching and learning opportunities are provided for all *Pathways* and support career planning; • A variety of diverse programs are accessible to meet the needs of learners; • Students are supported in education and career planning; and • Structures and processes are in place to support students in all transitions (e.g., grade, school, postsecondary).	Reading Recovery French Immersion Building Blocks for Kindergarten Students Early Learning Programs	Scaffolded Learning Gradual Release/Acceptance of Responsibility Modeled Shared Guided Independent Differentiated Instruction Small-Group Lessons Special Education Modules New Arts Curriculum	Getting Started ASD Resource: Effective Instructional Strategies for Students With an Autism Spectrum Disorder (ASD) What Did You Do in School Today? Gifted Education for All Social and Emotional and Academic Learning (SEAL) Screening Transition Meetings With Support Staff	

In the classroom / Students	Book Studies	Early Intervention Services
In the classroom:		
• Instruction supports students to make informed and appropriate choices to support their successful transitions;	Assistive Technologies	Special Education Modules
	Getting Started	Inclusive Environments
• Opportunities are provided for students to learn about their personal interests, strengths, and career options; and	Learning for All	Guides to Effective Instruction
		Differentiated Instruction (DI)
		Kits
• Respect for all destinations is evident in instruction.		Math Volumes
		Individualized Education Program (IEP)
Students:		Education Quality and Accountability Office (EQAO)
• Know, understand, and respect all programs and *Pathways*;		Developmental Reading Assessment (DRA)
		PM Benchmarks
• Explore and evaluate education and career opportunities;		Field Trips
		Guest Speakers
• Make appropriate choices from among those opportunities and set goals; and		
• Create and evaluate plans for the future.		

Source: York Region District School Board (2012).

Appendix H Student "Innovation Mind-Set" Self-Assessment Sheet

Student "Innovation Mind-Set" Self-Assessment Sheet

Student's Name: _____

Teacher: _____   Room #: _____

Learning Skill	Date (DD/ MM)	Evidence	Goals for Growth	Plan to Reach My Goals	Initial		Monitoring/ Conferencing/ Feedback	Date (DD/ MM)	Initial	
					S	T			S	T
Oral Communication • gives and gets feedback; • articulates options based on information shared; • listens actively; • expresses ideas and thoughts; • articulates how to improve measured against success criteria.										

(Continued)

Reading

- accesses and makes meaning from rich and diverse texts;
- summarizes and makes connections;
- identifies important ideas, visualizing, predicting, evaluating, questioning, and inferring (reading between the lines);
- applies information read to other disciplines and situations.

Writing

- understands the ongoing, recursive nature of the writing process;
- expresses him-/herself clearly and in a variety of genres and formats;
- self-assesses against a developmental writing continuum;

(Continued)

Learning Skill	Date (DD/MM)	Evidence	Goals for Growth	Plan to Reach My Goals	Initial		Monitoring/ Conferencing/ Feedback	Date (DD/MM)	Initial	
					S	T			S	T
Problem Solving • tries new strategies; • thinks through alternative solutions; • exhibits persistence.										
Critical Thinking • revises and reflects on his/her thinking; • evaluates and distinguishes sources of information for bias, points of view, deception, or social justice issues; • applies previous knowledge to a new context; • determines what information might be needed or required; • accesses and interprets information from multiple media and digital sources and text forms.										

Creativity
- improvises;
- asks questions;
- sees things from different angles and points of view.

Curiosity
- searches for "sparks" of interest;
- uses his/her "voice" and "choice" to pursue the sparks;
- is open to learning through mistakes.

Collaborative Approaches
- works with others to refine and explore new ideas;
- gives and gets feedback;
- is patient and respectful of others;
- compromises when needed.

Initiative
- uses constructive feedback to move forward confidently;
- evaluates his/her own thinking and sets goals to improve;

(Continued)

(Continued)

Learning Skill	Date (DD/MM)	Evidence	Goals for Growth	Plan to Reach My Goals	Initial		Monitoring/ Conferencing/ Feedback	Date (DD/MM)	Initial	
					S	T			S	T
Self-Regulation • resolves differences in respectful ways; • identifies where to go for help beyond the teacher; • reflectively considers implications of actions; • perseveres with a task.										
Decision Making • defends choices; • is flexible; • measures risk taking.										
Innovative Thinking • applies problem solving and creativity to any situation; • takes new thinking and applies it with improvement; • embraces multiple "tries" to get the results; • exhibits continuous learning.										

Peer's Anecdotal Comments:

Teacher's Anecdotal Comments:

Appendix I Exploring Opportunities Program (EOP) Credit Accumulation

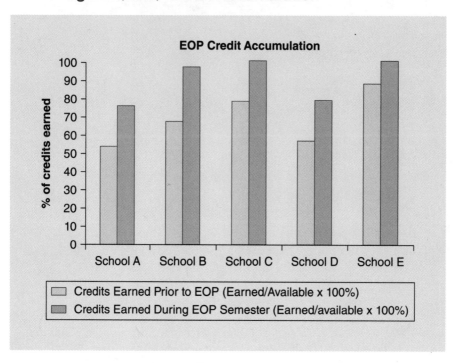

Source: York Region District School Board (2012).

COOPERATIVE
EDUCATION PROGRAM
(Sample)
PERSONALIZED PLACEMENT
LEARNING PLAN

COOPERATIVE EDUCATION PROGRAM (Sample)
PERSONALIZED PLACEMENT LEARNING PLAN

SCHOOL YEAR:	❏ Semester 1	❏ Semester 2	❏ Full Year

STUDENT INFORMATION

Student Name	Grade	Home Phone
		E-mail
Course Code	Related Course	Type of Course
Credit Value	Curriculum Guideline	

PLACEMENT INFORMATION

Placement	Job Title	Placement Supervisor
Address	E-mail	Telephone
		Fax:

SCHOOL INFORMATION

Cooperative Education Teacher	School	Telephone
	E-mail	Fax:

ONTARIO YOUTH APPRENTICESHIP PROGRAM

Trade Area	Placement Start Date
Apprenticeship Trade Training Standard Reference	❏ Training Standards Part of PPLP
Registration/Starting Date	MTCU Telephone
❏ Summer Employment	❏ Offered Full Time Employment After Graduation

ACCOMMODATIONS: ❏ IEP   ❏ ESL   ❏ IPRC

_____

_____

_____

Parent Signature:

COPIES TO:	
❏ Student	❏ Placement Supervisor
❏ Special Education	❏ Parents, if student under 18 years
❏ OYAP Coordinator	❏ Related Courses

Key Learning Areas			Demonstration of Learning	Achievement Categories			
Classroom Component				K/U	T/I	C	A
Preplacement	1.	Job Readiness	• Applies for co-op placement (résumé, cover letter, completed application form, completed interview with employer)				
	2.	Health & Safety	• Completes a short report or quiz on workplace health and safety issues • Demonstrates understanding of safety in the workplace				
	3.	Rights and Responsibilities	• Demonstrates an understanding of employee rights and responsibilities • Demonstrates importance of confidentiality at placement • Contributes to harassment-free workplace				
Integration	4.	Reflective Learning	• Develops and maintains logs and a reflective journal • Collects evidence of this learning to support Co-op Portfolio				
	5.	Workplace Opportunities and Challenges	• Develops an exit résumé that includes the skills, knowledge, and experiences gained through this co-op course • Researches and presents information related to the co-op placement				
Placement Component (key learning areas—related course)							
Employer Expectations							

K/U = Knowledge/Understanding; **T/I** = Thinking/Inquiry;
C = Communication; **A** = Application

FORMATIVE ASSESSMENT KEY:

4 = Outstanding Achievement   3 = High Achievement
2 = Moderate Achievement   1 = Minimal achievement
R = Remediation Required

EMPLOYER - FORMATIVE ASSESSMENT - PERFORMANCE REVIEW

The purpose of this assessment is to ascertain the student's strengths and weaknesses observed by the supervisor at the co-op placement. The personal information pertaining to the student may be subject to the Municipal Freedom of Information and Protection of Privacy Act.

Please assess the student's performance as expected <u>for an individual with the experience to date</u>, according to the following scale:

4 (80%–100%) = Consistently demonstrates superior employability skills
3 (70%–79%) = Consistently demonstrates very good employability skills
              (a student at this level meets the Cooperative Education expected
              standard of performance)
2 (60%–69%) = Demonstrates some evidence of adequate employability skills
1 (50%–59%) = Demonstrates limited evidence of developing employability skills
R (below 50%) = Rarely demonstrates beginning level of employability skills.

ACHIEVEMENT CATEGORIES	EMPLOYABILITY SKILLS	Review Dates		
Knowledge/ Understanding	POLICY COMPLIANCE ❏ Consistent attendance and punctuality ❏ Follows company procedures ❏ Follows safety procedures ❏ Respects confidentiality			
Thinking/Inquiry	ATTITUDE / BEHAVIOR ❏ Appropriate dress, appearance, and grooming ❏ Demonstrates initiative ❏ Flexible, adjusts to change ❏ Shows interest, desire to learn ❏ Accepts constructive suggestions INTERPERSONAL/TEAMWORK SKILLS ❏ Demonstrates ethics and integrity ❏ Works cooperatively and positively with others ❏ Respects thoughts and opinions of others			
Communication	COMMUNICATION ❏ Speaks appropriately and effectively ❏ Listens to understand, asks questions ❏ Follows instructions ❏ Understands written material ❏ Writes effectively			
Application	WORK HABITS ❏ Works carefully with minimal supervision ❏ Solves problems independently ❏ Dependable, productive			

COMMENTS (To be completed by supervisor in collaboration with student)

REVIEW DATE: _____

Successes to Date: _____

_____

_____

_____

Short-Term Goals: _____

_____

_____

_____

Student's Signature: Supervisor's Signature:

REVIEW DATE:

Successes to Date: _____

_____

_____

_____

Short-Term Goals: _____

_____

_____

_____

Student's Signature: Supervisor's Signature:

REVIEW DATE:

Successes to Date: _____

_____

_____

_____

Short-Term Goals: _____

_____

_____

_____

Student's Signature: Supervisor's Signature:

Appendix K Forms of Experiential Learning

Forms of Experiential Learning	Definition Applied	Examples of Practice
Field Trips/ Guest Speakers	• Partial or one-day trips to explore opportunities, raise community awareness, and so on. • Can take place in school or out in the community.	Elementary students participate in a field trip to the local library. While getting instructions on how to use the library and access resources, they also get a tour around the facility and seek out information, through guided questions co-constructed with the teacher, about the various jobs within the library and the skills and training required. They then bring that learning back to the classroom for further inquiry.
Project-Based Learning	• Process of inquiry in response to a complex question, problem, or challenge. • Rigorous projects incorporating student voice and choice are carefully planned, managed, and assessed to help students learn key academic content, practice 21st-century skills (such as collaboration, communication, and critical thinking), and create high-quality, authentic products and presentations.	Students in a business Specialist High Skills Major (SHSM) program teamed up with marketing students at a local university. The university students, working in partnership with a local corporation, were charged with the task of doing market research, analysis, and development of a marketing approach for that company. The university and college students worked collaboratively to plan and implement the project. Connecting both, in person and virtually, students were able to demonstrate their respective course expectations while networking across institutions.
Service Learning	• Opportunity to provide community service in nonpaid, volunteer positions.	

	• Relevance of academic learning is enhanced by giving opportunities to apply the curriculum knowledge and learning skills while making contributions to the local community. • May or may not include academic credit, and may or may not take place within the walls of the school.	Mindfully preparing students for a transition toward instructional independence in the form of a co-op program, the teacher has the students job shadow with a volunteer out in the community. They then apply that experience to a short-term work experience where they provide either direct or indirect volunteer services in the local community. The life skills they develop are reinforced to demonstrate program readiness for cooperative education programming.
Work Experience/ Internships	• A planned learning opportunity, within any credit course, that provides students with relatively short-term subject-related work experiences. • Forms an integral part of a specific credit course.	The "Exploring Opportunities Program" offered at Richmond Green Secondary School in Richmond Hill, Ontario, is designed to ensure equitable access to apprenticeship for students who, previously, have not demonstrated work habits and life skills that support their learning. Students, in collaboration with Habitat for Humanity, engage in short-term work experiences, as part of their construction course to build on their interests and reinforce the life skills that will carry them forward in *Career Readiness*.
Job Shadowing	• One-on-one *observation* of a worker at a place of employment. • Involves the pairing of a student with a worker in a specific occupation. • May be integrated with a credit course. • May be part of a student's school-to-work transition program.	Take Our Kids to Work (TOKW) is a Canada initiative where students accompany their parents/guardians to their place of work for the day. Schools use the experience to bring the learning back to the classroom as students reflect upon their observations.

(Continued)

(Continued)

Forms of Experiential Learning	Definition Applied	Examples of Practice
Job Twinning	• One-on-one observation of a cooperative education student at his or her placement. • May be integrated with a credit course. • May be part of a student's school-to-work transition program.	Grade 8 students at a local elementary school accompany the co-op high school student from their neighboring school to learn more about the high school program and the workplace. The teachers, from both panels, co-construct the learning and follow up with the students.
School-to-Work Transition Programs	• A combination of school- and work-based education and training involving a variety of learning opportunities. • Oriented toward students who will be entering the workforce directly after high school. • Partnership used to enhance the opportunities afforded and the identification of relevant curriculum. • May involve the earning of cooperative education credits in addition to the work experience. • Usually involves multiple modes of Experiential Learning occurring across grades.	Students in a class for those with developmental delays have life skills reinforced and practiced through multiple forms of Experiential Learning opportunities. Each opportunity builds upon the previous. Students start with job twinning and job shadowing opportunities, move on to supported work experiences and then, for those who are able to handle a greater degree of independence, move into a cooperative education program that will provide a transition into the workplace.

Cooperative Education	• A planned, credit-earning learning experience that forms an integral part of a specific course and program. • Integrates classroom theory and learning experiences at a workplace to enable students to apply and refine the knowledge and skills acquired in a related curriculum course.	Students practice and refine the related course expectations while working at their co-op placement. They may be doing a 1-credit, 2-credit (half-day), 3-credit, or 4-credit (full-day) program. Employers serve as placement supervisors to the student, and the classroom teacher conducts regular monitoring visits as well as providing the in-school instruction.
Apprenticeship Training	• Opportunity for a student to meet diploma requirements while participating in an apprenticeship occupation. • May involve the student's registration in an apprenticeship. • Requires documentation by the student and trainer regarding trade-specific competencies acquired. • May involve work experience and/or the earning of cooperative education credits.	A student in Ontario, interested in pursuing a trade, participates in the Ontario Youth Apprenticeship Program (OYAP) through his/her school's cooperative education programming. Working in the trade, the student is completing the work hours and competencies of the trade at the same time he/she is earning high school credits. The student has an opportunity to accelerate his/her learning by completing Level 1.
Global Education	• Opportunities for students to extend their learning in a global setting. • May include work experience, internships, co-op credits, or service learning in another country.	Students in York Region District School Board have an opportunity to earn co-op credits while working through a nongovernmental organization (NGO) in Costa Rica with community partners in local villages. As part of their summer school program, they do preplacement curriculum prior to departure and then, accompanied by their teacher, fulfill the course expectations as they complete their work assignments on the ground in Costa Rica.

(Continued)

(Continued)

Forms of Experiential Learning	Definition Applied	Examples of Practice
Virtual	• Opportunities, either for credit or as part of a project-based learning model, where students engage virtually with and complete tasks for an outside organization or business/industry. • A simulated work experience, within any credit course, that allows students to take advantage of a greater variety of experiences than those available in the local economy. • Involves a short-term, subject-related work placement through the use of computer software and the Internet.	A school business partner meets with a student who is interested in doing a co-op placement with the company. Due to the location of the company and the nature of the work, the placement lends itself nicely to a virtual arrangement. Exhibiting a high degree of independence and responsibility, the student works independently on the work assigned while engaging virtually with the placement supervisor. Ongoing monitoring by the co-op teacher supports the learning and goal setting.

REFERENCES

ACT. (2014). *ACT WorkKeys.* Retrieved from http://www.act.org/products/workforce-act-workkeys/

Albert Einstein Site Online. (2012, January 8). "Albert Einstein quotes." Retrieved from http://www.alberteinsteinsite.com/quotes/einsteinquotes.html

Anxiety and Depression Association of America. (2014). *Facts and statistics.* Retrieved from http://www.adaa.org/about-adaa/press-room/facts-statistics

Assessment and Teaching of 21st Century Skills. (2014). *A worldwide, multistakeholder partnership can make a sustainable difference.* Retrieved from http://atc21s.org/

Averbuch, M. (2013). The other way to learn. *Yale Daily News*, October 13. Retrieved from http://yaledailynews.com/weekend/2013/10/18/the-other-way-to-learn

Bangert-Drowns, R. L., & Bankert, E. (1990). *Meta-analysis of effects of explicit instruction for critical thinking.* Paper presented at the Annual Meeting of the American Educational Research Association, Boston, MA.

Battelle for Kids. (2012). Six drivers of student success: A look inside five of the world's highest performing school systems. Presented at Global Education Summit, Columbus, Ohio, November.

Boran, S., & Comber, B. (Eds.). (2001) *Critiquing whole language and classroom inquiry.* Reston, VA: National Council of Teachers.

Boss, S. (2012). *Bringing innovation to school: Empowering students to thrive in a changing world.* Bloomington, IN: Solution Tree.

Brainy Quote. (2014a). *Benjamin Franklin quotes.* Retrieved from http://www.brainyquote.com/quotes/quotes/b/benjaminfr383997.html

Brainy Quote. (2014b). *Michelangelo quotes.* Retrieved from http://www.brainyquote.com/quotes/authors/m/michelangelo.html

Brainy Quote. (2014c). *Nelson Mandela quotes.* Retrieved from http://www.brainyquote.com/quotes/authors/n/nelson_mandela.html

Campbell, C., & Fullan, M. (2006). Unlocking potential for learning: Effective district-wide strategies to raise student achievement in literacy and numeracy—project report. In C. Campbell, M. Fullan, & A. Glaze (series editors) *Unlocking potential for learning: Effective District-wide strategies to raise student achievement in literacy and numeracy.* Toronto, Canada: Queens Printer for Ontario: Ontario Ministry of Education.

Canadian Mental Health Association. (2014). *Fast facts about mental illness.* Retrieved from http://www.cmha.ca/media/fast-facts-about-mental-illness/

Carroll, L. (1871). *Quotes.* Retrieved from http://www.shmoop.com/lewis-carroll/quotes.html

CBC Television. (2013, August 21). *Generation jobless* [Documentary, Season 2012–2013, Episode 17]. Retrieved from http://www.cbc.ca/player/Shows/ID/2330990900/

College and Career Academy Support Network. (n.d.). *College and Career Academies: An Overview.* Berkeley: University of California. Retrieved from http://casn.berkeley.edu/resources.php?r=250

Collins, J. (2001). *Good to great.* New York, NY: HarperCollins.

Collins, J., & Hansen, M. (2011). *Great by choice.* New York, NY: HarperCollins.

Conference Board of Canada. (n.d.). *Employability Skills 2000+.* Retrieved from http://www.conferenceboard.ca/Libraries/EDUC_PUBLIC/esp2000.sflb

Conger, C. (n.d.). "How to find true north." *HowStuffWorks.* Retrieved from http://adventure.howstuffworks.com/survival/wilderness/true-north.htm

DeGraaf, L. (2013). *Edison and the rise of innovation.* New York, NY: Sterling Publishing.

Dobelli, R. (2013). *The art of thinking clearly* (N. Griffin, trans.). New York, NY: HarperCollins.

Donohoo, J. (2013). *Collaborative inquiry for educators: A facilitator's guide to school improvement.* Thousand Oaks, CA: Corwin.

Dweck, C. (1999). *Self-theories: Their motivation, personality and development.* Philadelphia, PA: Psychology Press.

Earl, L., & Katz, S. (2006). *Leading schools in a data-rich world.* Thousand Oaks, CA: Corwin.

Employment and Social Development Canada. (2013a). *Essential skills profiles.* Retrieved from http://www.hrsdc.gc.ca/eng/jobs/les/profiles/index.shtml

Employment and Social Development Canada. (2013b). *Labour market information.* Retrieved from http://www.hrsdc.gc.ca/eng/jobs/lmi/index.shtml

Flavelle, D. (2013). CEO group issues call to action on skills gap. *Toronto STAR,* November 28. Retrieved from http://www.thestar.com/business/2013/11/28/ceo_group_issues_call_to_action_on_skills_gap.html

Freedman, B., & Di Cecco, R. (2013). *Collaborative school reviews: How to shape schools from the inside out.* Thousand Oaks, CA: Corwin.

Fullan, M. (2013a). Great to excellent: Launching the next stage of Ontario's education agenda. Toronto, ON: Ministry of Education.

Fullan, M. (2013b). *Motion leadership in action: More skinny on becoming change savvy.* Thousand Oaks, CA: Corwin.

Fullan, M. (2014). *The principal: Three keys to maximizing impact.* San Francisco, CA: Jossey-Bass.

Fullan, M., & Barber, M. (2010). *Building blocks for reform.* Toronto, ON: Summit.

Giasson, J. (2003). *La lecture: De la théorie à la pratique* (2nd ed.). Montreal, QC: Cheneliére Education.

Glaze, A., Mattingley, R., & Andrews, R. (2013). *High school graduation: K–12 strategies that work.* Thousand Oaks, CA: Corwin.

Glaze, A., Mattingley, R., & Levin, B. (2012). *Breaking barriers: Excellence and equity for all.* Toronto, ON: Pearson.

Gliddon, D. G. (2006). *Forecasting a competency model for innovation leaders using a modified Delphi technique.* Unpublished dissertation, Penn State University.

Goodreads. (2014). *Alvin Toffler quotes.* Retrieved from http://www.goodreads.com/author/quotes/3030.Alvin_Toffler

Greenan, M. (2012). *Mapping the right drivers for third order educational change.* Catholic Principals' Council of Ontario.

Greenan, M., & Fornasier-Reilly, A. (2013). Better together. *Principal Connections, 17*(1), 38–41. Toronto, ON: Catholic Principals' Council of Ontario.

Grose, K. (2014). *From 21st-century learning to learning in the 21st century: Influences on transforming teacher knowledge of constructivist practices in technology-rich environments.* Unpublished dissertation, University of Toronto, Canada.

Grose, K., & Freedman, B. (in press). *21st century leaders and learners.* Toronto: Ontario Principals' Council.

Haberman, M. (2013, July 19). *Fixing the school-business breakdown.* Retrieved from http://www.huffingtonpost.com/Michael-Haberman/fixing-the-school business_b_3613156.html

Hannon, V., Gillinson, S., & Shanks, L. (2013). *Learning a living—Radical innovation in education for work.* Doha: Bloomsbury Qatar Foundation Publishing.

Hargreaves, A., Boyle, A., & Harris, A. (2014). *Uplifting leadership: How organizations, teams, and communities raise performance.* San Francisco, CA: Jossey-Bass Business.

Hargreaves, A., & Fullan, M. (2012). *Professional capital.* New York, NY: Teachers College Press.

Hargreaves, A., & Shirley, D. (2012). *The global fourth way—The quest for educational excellence.* Thousand Oaks, CA: Corwin.

Harte, J. (2001). What education is and isn't. In S. Boran & B. Comber (Eds.), *Critiquing whole language and classroom inquiry* (pp. 1–17). Urbana, IL: National Council for Teachers of English.

Harvey, S., & Daniels, H. (2009). *Comprehension and collaboration: Inquiry circles in action.* Portsmouth, NH: Heinemann.

Hattie, J. (2009). *Visible learning: A synthesis of over 800 meta-analyses relating to achievement.* Thousand Oaks, CA: Corwin.

Hattie, J. (2012). *Visible learning for teachers: Maximizing impact on learning.* Thousand Oaks, CA: Corwin.

Hattie, J., & Yates, G. (2013). *Visible learning and the science of how we learn.* Thousand Oaks, CA: Corwin.

Hayter, S. (2013). Face the financial facts of education. *Maclean's*, August 30. Retrieved from http://www.macleans.ca/economy/business/its-time-students-faced-the-financial-facts-of-education

Hill, P. W., & Crévola, C. A. **(1999).** Key features of a whole-school, design approach to literacy teaching in schools. *Australian Journal of Learning Disabilities, 4*(3), 5–11.

Hoff, B. (1983). *The Tao of Pooh*. New York, NY: Penguin Books.

Jacobson, M., & Ruddy, M. (2004). *Open to outcome*. Oklahoma City, OK: Wood 'N' Barnes.

Johnson, L., & Lamb, A. (2011). *Critical and creative thinking: Bloom's taxonomy*. Teacher Tap. Retrieved from http://eduscapes.com/tap/topic69.htm

Keniston, K. (n.d.). *Teaching by example*. Retrieved from http://www.values.com/inspirational-quotes?search=keniston&commit=Search

King, A. J. C., Warren, W. K., King, M. A., Brook, J. E., & Kocher, P. R. (2009). *Who doesn't go to post-secondary education?* Final Report of *Findings for Colleges Ontario Collaborative Research Project* Social Program Evaluation Group, Faculty of Education, Queen's University, October 20.

Knight, J. (2013). *High-impact instruction*. Thousand Oaks, CA: Corwin.

Kolb, D. (1984). *Experiential learning: Experience as the source of learning and development*. Englewood Cliffs, NJ: Prentice Hall. Retrieved from http://www.success.uwo.ca/experience/faculty/experiential_learning_theory.html

Krauss, J., & Boss, S. (2013) *Thinking through project-based learning: Guiding deeper inquiry*. Thousand Oaks, CA: Corwin.

Leithwood, K. (2013). *Strong districts and their leadership*. A paper commissioned by the Council of Ontario Directors of Education and the Institute for Educational Leadership, June.

Levin, B. (2012). *More high school graduates: Helping more students succeed in secondary schools*. Thousand Oaks, CA: Corwin.

Lexicon Newsletter. (2013). Creating and assessing global learners and leaders: Transformation from me to we to local to global. Literacy and Numeracy Secretariat. Toronto: Government of Ontario.

Literacy and Numeracy Secretariat. (2010). Collaborative teacher inquiry. *Capacity Building Series,* Secretariat Special Edition #16. Retrieved from http://www.edu.gov.on.ca/eng/literacynumeracy/inspire/research/CBS_Collaborative_Teacher_Inquiry.pdf

Loveless, T. (2012). Attention OECD-PISA: Your silence on China is wrong. *Education Next* (December).

Metropolitan Regional Career and Technical Center. (2014). *Big Picture Learning*. Retrieved from http://metcenter.org/

Miner, R. (2010). *People without jobs—Jobs without people: Ontario's labour market future*. Toronto, ON: Miner Management Consultants. Retrieved from http://www.collegesontario.org/policy-positions/MinerReport.pdf

Mourshed, M., Farrell, D., & Barton, D. (2012). *Education to employment: Designing a system that works*. McKinsey Center for Government. Retrieved from http://mckinseyonsociety.com/education-to-employment/report/

Obama, B. (2013). *State of the Union 2013 speech* [Full text, video]. Retrieved from http://www.politico.com/story/2013/02/state-of-the-union-2013-president-barack-obamas-speech-transcript-text-87550_Page5.html#ixzz2Q5JNVuMS

Ontario Ministry of Education. (2011). *Secondary: Student Success*. Retrieved from http://www.edu.gov.on.ca/studentsuccess/

Ontario Ministry of Education. (2013a). *Creating Pathways to Success*. Retrieved from http://www.edu.gov.on.ca/eng/document/policy/cps/CreatingPathwaysSuccess.pdf

Ontario Ministry of Education. (2013b). *Secondary: Specialist High Skills Major (SHSM)*. Retrieved from http://www.edu.gov.on.ca/morestudentsuccess/SHSM.asp

Ontario Ministry of Education. (2014). *Ontario Skills Passport*. Retrieved from http://www.skills.edu.gov.on.ca/OSP2Web/EDU/Welcome.xhtml

Ontario Ministry of Education and Training. (1999). *Choices into action: Guidance and career education policy for Ontario elementary and secondary schools*. Retrieved from http://www.edu.gov.on.ca/eng/document/curricul/secondary/choices/choicee.pdf

Ontario Ministry of Health and Long-Term Care. (2011). *Open minds, healthy minds*. Retrieved from http://www.health.gov.on.ca/en/common/ministry/publications/reports/mental_health2011/mentalhealth.aspx

Organisation for Economic Co-operation and Development. (2010). *Skills*. Retrieved from http://skills.oecd.org/

Organisation for Economic Co-operation and Development. (2012). *OECD Employment Outlook 2012*. Retrieved from http://www.oecd.org/els/emp/EMO2012%20Eng_Chapter%201.pdf

Partnership for 21st Century Skills. (2008). *21st century skills, education and competitiveness: A resource and policy guide*. Retrieved from http://www.p21.org/storage/documents/21st_century_skills_education_and_competitiveness_guide.pdf

Partnership for 21st Century Skills. (2009). *The MILE guide: Milestones for improving learning and education*. Retrieved from http://www.p21.org/storage/documents/MILE_Guide_091101.pdf

Pascopella, A. (2013). Indiana Governor Mike Pence: Education is a shared responsibility. *District Administrator Daily Newsletter*, November 18.

Rifkin, J. (2012). *3rd revolution*. The Milan Airports Magazine Terminal 24, Periodico della Sea Spa realizzato da "il Sole 24 Ore Radiocor" Anno 3, Numero 12, Maggio 2013.

Robinson, K. (2006). *How schools kill creativity.* TED Talks. Retrieved from http://www.ted.com/talks/ken_robinson_says_schools_kill_creativity

Robinson, K. (2013). *How to escape education's death valley.* TED Talks Education. Retrieved from https://www.youtube.com/watch?v=wX78iKhInsc

Robinson, V. (2006). Putting education back into education leadership. *Journal of Leading & Managing, 12*(1), 62–75.

Robinson, V., Hohepa, M., & Lloyd, C. (2009). *School leadership and student outcomes: Identifying what works and why: Best evidence synthesis.* Wellington, New Zealand: Ministry of Education.

Robinson, V., Hohepa, M., & Lloyd, C. (2011). *Student centered leadership.* San Francisco, CA: Jossey Bass.

Royal Commission on Learning. (1994). *For the love of learning.* Retrieved from http://www.edu.gov.on.ca/eng/general/abcs/rcom/full/royalcommission.pdf

Saskatchewan School Library Association. (2014). Retrieved from http://ssla.ca/Saskatchewan

Sharma, A. (2014). 21st century school leaders. *SlideShare*, May 2. Retrieved from http://www.slideshare.net/AditiSharma28/21st-century-school-leaders

Sharratt, L. (2013a). *Learning Walks and Talks* [Training materials]. Australia and Ontario, Canada.

Sharratt, L. (2013b). Scaffolded literacy assessment and a model for teachers' professional development. In S. Elliott-Johns & D. Jarvis (Eds.), *Perspectives on transitions in schooling and instructional practice* (pp. 138–153). Toronto, ON: University of Toronto Press.

Sharratt, L., Coutts, J., Hogarth, W., & Fullan, M. (2013). Reading recovery: A high return on investment for cost-conscious and student-achievement oriented education systems. *Journal of Reading Recovery, 13*(1).

Sharratt, L., & Fullan, M. (2009). *Realization: The change imperative for deepening district-wide reform.* Thousand Oaks, CA: Corwin.

Sharratt, L., & Fullan, M. (2012). *Putting FACES on the data: What great leaders do.* Thousand Oaks, CA: Corwin.

Sharratt, L., Hine, E., & Maika, D. (in press). *Pedagogically focused leadership—Creating reciprocal and respectful relationships.* Toronto: Ontario Principals' Council

Sharratt, L., Ostinelli, G., & Cattaneo, A. (2010). The role of the "knowledgeable other" in improving student achievement, school culture and teacher efficacy: Two case studies from Canadian and Swiss perspectives and experiences. Paper presented at the International Congress for School Effectiveness and Improvement, Kuala Lumpur, Malaysia.

Stern, D., Saroyan, P., & Hester, C. H. (2013). *Longitudinal description of* students in California Partnership Academies. Berkeley, CA: College and

Career Academy Support Network. Retrieved from http://casn.berkeley
.edu/resources.php?r=400

Stoll, L. (2010). Connecting learning communities: Capacity building for sys-
temic change. In A. Hargreaves, A. Lieberman, M. Fullan, & D. Hopkins
(Eds.), *Second international handbook of educational change*. Netherlands:
Springer.

Student Achievement Division. (2012). The third teacher. *Capacity Building
Series*, Special Edition #27. Retrieved from http://www.edu.gov.on.ca/eng/
literacynumeracy/inspire/research/CBS_ThirdTeacher.pdf

Sturgis, C., & Patrick, S. (2010). *When success is the only option: Designing com-
petency-based pathways for next generation learning*. Vienna, VA: iNAVOL.

The Thiel Foundation. (2014). *Thiel fellowship*. Retrieved from http://www
.thielfellowship.org/

Thompson, J. (2013). Course correction: Charting a new road map for Ontario.
Annual Report 12, November 30. Toronto, ON: Institute for Competitiveness and Prosperity. Retrieved from www.competeprosper.ca/work/
annual_reports/annual_report_course_correction

Tilleczek, K., Ferguson, B., Boydell, K., Rummens, J. A., Cote, D., & Roth-Edney.
(2005). *Early school leavers: Understanding the lived reality of student disengagement from secondary school*. Toronto: Ontario Ministry of Education.

Tilleczek, K., Ferguson, B., & Laflamme, S. (2010). *Fresh starts and false starts:
Young people in transition from elementary to secondary school*. Toronto:
Ontario Ministry of Education.

Trilling, B., & Fadel, C. (2009). *21st century skills—Learning for life in our times*.
San Francisco, CA: Jossey-Bass.

Tucker, M. (2011). *Surpassing Shanghai: An agenda for American education built on
the world's leading systems*. Cambridge, MA: Harvard Education Press.

University of Regina. (2014). *UR Guarantee*. Retrieved from http://www.uregina
.ca/urguarantee/

Vygotsky, L. S. (1978). *Mind in society: The development of higher psychological
processes* (14th ed.). Cambridge, MA: Harvard University Press.

Wagner, T. (2008). *The global achievement gap*. New York, NY: Basic Books.

Willms, D., & Friesen, S. (2012). *What did you do in school today?* Retrieved from
http://www.cea-ace.ca/sites/cea-ace.ca/files/cea-2012-wdydist-report-2
.pdf

Willms, D., Friesen, S., & Milton, P. (2009). *What did you do in school today?* Retrieved
from http://www.ccl-cca.ca/pdfs/otherreports/WDYDIST_National_Report_
EN.pdf

Willms, J. D. (2003). *Student engagement at school: A sense of belonging and participation: Results from PISA 2000*. Organisation for Economic Co-operation
and Development, Programme for International Student Assessment.

York Region District School Board. (2002–2007). *Assessment guidelines*. Aurora, ON: Author.

York Region District School Board. (2004a). *The Literate Graduate*. Aurora, ON: Author.

York Region District School Board. (2004b). *The power of language*. Aurora, ON: Author.

York Region District School Board. (2004c). *Talking opportunities* [webcast]. Aurora, ON: Author.

York Region District School Board. (2012). *Pathways resources*. Aurora, ON: Author.

Zegarac, G. (2012). 21st century leadership: Looking forward: An interview with Michael Fullan and Ken Leithwood. *In Conversation, IV*(1). Retrieved from http://www.edu.gov.on.ca/eng/policyfunding/leadership/fall2012 .pdf

Zhao, Y. (2012). *World class learners*. Thousand Oaks, CA: Corwin.

INDEX

Corwin is committed to improving education for all learners by publishing books and other professional development resources for those serving the field of PreK–12 education. By providing practical, hands-on materials, Corwin continues to carry out the promise of its motto: **"Helping Educators Do Their Work Better."**

Advancing professional learning for student success

Learning Forward (formerly National Staff Development Council) is an international association of learning educators committed to one purpose in K–12 education: Every educator engages in effective professional learning every day so every student achieves.

The Ontario Principals' Council (OPC) is a voluntary association for principals and vice-principals in Ontario's public school system. We believe that exemplary leadership results in outstanding schools and improved student achievement. To this end, we foster quality leadership through world-class professional services and supports. As an ISO 9001 registered organization, we are committed to **"quality leadership—our principal product."**